PRAISE FOR THE LISTENING LEADER

"This luminous book guides school leaders in developing a school culture of trust, empowerment, and excellence. With compassion and clarity, Safir coaches the hard work of leading and sustaining change—while keeping our focus squarely on equity for every learner."

—Kathleen Cushman
co-author of Belonging and Becoming: The Power of Social and Emotional Learning in High Schools

"If only I had read this fifty years ago. It took me time to learn that listening is teaching; and then, that being a leader is being a teacher! Shane's wise and practical book is what I didn't have then, and it's fantastic that we all have it now."

—Deborah Meier
senior scholar at New York University's Steinhardt School of Education, author of The Power of Their Ideas, Lessons to America from a Small School in Harlem, and In Schools We Trust.

"As a leader in a diverse urban school, this book fills a void that I didn't realize was there. I'm sure these practical ideas on how to be a better listening leader will improve my practice immensely!"

—Audrey Amos
principal, John Muir Elementary School

"Shane Safir has written a brilliant book. As engaging as it is informative and as revelatory as it is relevant. It is a must-read for school leaders and those who aspire to lead."

—Chris Emdin
associate professor of science education, Teachers College, Columbia University

"This book is a 'must have' for any leader trying to move the needle on equity. Drawing from her lived experience as a principal and leadership coach, Safir offers stories that give insight and practical strategies that get results. It's one you'll keep coming back to."

—Zaretta Hammond
author of Culturally Responsive Teaching and the Brain

"In *The Listening Leader*, Shane Safir eloquently describes a powerful approach to school transformation that starts with listening to the school community—including teachers, students, and families—and highlights the importance of cultivating leadership at every level. I encourage anyone interested in understanding how to improve our schools to read her book."

—Shael Polakow-Suransky
president, Bank Street College of Education

"Shane's book is a must-read for new leaders as it underscores the often overlooked and under-practiced power of listening in leadership. This interactive book offers an alternative and empowering path to creating humanizing spaces in schools and immediately changed the way I interacted with students, teachers, families and community members."

—Tamara Friedman
assistant principal, Berkeley High School

"Shane Safir's *The Listening Leader* is a godsend to a field of thinkers, doers, and reactors. From the very first sentence, Safir draws us into her personal story of leadership as well her wisdom on how listening can be a powerful act of transformation for individuals, schools, and communities.

Reading this book illustrates how infrequently listening actually happens in our schools and school systems. Thankfully, Safir invites in a way that allows us to learn how to listen and use what we hear to take action on behalf of our students. Whether you are a teacher, coach, school or central office leader, this book will provide you with a fresh perspective and the necessary tools for moving forward as a listening leader."

—Max Silverman
associate director, University of Washington Center for Educational Leadership

"*The Listening Leader*, based on solid theoretical foundations and chock-full of stories, offers a rich and extensive exploration of this vital skill. After reading this book, you'll have no doubt about the powerful role that listening plays in leadership and you'll have many tools to refine your listening."

—Elena Aguilar
author of The Art of Coaching and The Art of Coaching Teams

"The need for action to be informed by reflection is not an idea that is foreign to social justice educators. What is often missing, however, is how one's reflective process is shaped by their ability to listen to their community. From a space of vulnerability and introspection, Safir demonstrates a commitment to praxis and the powerful role that listening plays in our work."

—Darrick Smith
assistant professor of educational leadership, University of San Francisco

"Shane Safir recognizes that in order to build equity and excellence in our schools that we have to lead with our ears and not our mouths. She provides excellent practical suggestions on how to do just that in *The Listening Leader*."

—Larry Ferlazzo
educator, teacher advice columnist, and author

"At a time when leaders are in search of different approaches to transform schools, we have a new approach. Safir offers a compelling framework on how to engage in listening as an innovative approach to leadership. Through listening in caring, empathetic, and relational ways, the ingredients for equity can become a reality. An excellent read for school leaders. Read, listen, and learn!"

—Tyrone C. Howard
professor and associate dean, University of California Los Angeles

"For today's educational leader, *The Listening Leader* gives us the most precious gift—the opportunity to pause and reflect. We must take seriously Safir's call to slow down, tune into ourselves and others, and lead with the kind of integrity that is born out of a sense of collective purpose; this is the path towards meaningful school improvement."

—Young Whan Choi
manager of performance assessments, Oakland Unified School District

"Equitable school transformation is what is most needed in today's schools, and *The Listening Leader* provides the guidance and practical tools for educators to achieve it. Shane Safir pulls on her deep knowledge of academic and professional learning communities in order to provide educators with a special resource that we can all readily use. This book is a must-have for anyone seeking to positively transform their learning community."

—Raquel Topete
instructional coach, East Side Union High School District

THE LISTENING LEADER

THE LISTENING LEADER

Creating the Conditions for Equitable School Transformation

Shane Safir

Foreword by Michael Fullan

JB JOSSEY-BASS™
A Wiley Brand

Published by Jossey-Bass
A Wiley Brand
One Montgomery Street, Suite 1000, San Francisco, CA 94104-4594—www.josseybass.com

Jossey-Bass books and products are available through most bookstores. To contact Jossey-Bass directly call our Customer Care Department within the U.S. at 800-956-7739, outside the U.S. at 317-572-3986, or fax 317-572-4002.

Wiley publishes in a variety of print and electronic formats and by print-on-demand. Some material included with standard print versions of this book may not be included in e-books or in print-on-demand. If this book refers to media such as a CD or DVD that is not included in the version you purchased, you may download this material at http://booksupport.wiley.com. For more information about Wiley products, visit www.wiley.com.

Library of Congress Cataloging-in-Publication Data

Names: Safir, Shane, 1972- author.
Title: The listening leader : creating the conditions for equitable school
  transformation / Shane Safir.
Description: San Francisco, CA : Jossey-Bass, 2017. | Includes
  bibliographical references and index.
Identifiers: LCCN 2016044749 (print) | LCCN 2016054906 (ebook) | ISBN
  9781119186342 (pbk.) | ISBN 9781119186724 (pdf) | ISBN 9781119186359 (epub)
Subjects: LCSH: Educational leadership. | Listening.
Classification: LCC LB2806 .S323 2017 (print) | LCC LB2806 (ebook) | DDC
  371.2—dc23
LC record available at https://lccn.loc.gov/2016044749

Cover design: Wiley
Cover image: © Tetra Images/Getty Images, Inc.

Printed in the United States of America

FIRST EDITION

V10010200_052019

This book is dedicated to two beloved students, Alondra and Javon, and to my own babies, Mona and Maximo.

May we build schools that celebrate the light in every child.

I have never encountered any children in any group who are not geniuses. There is no mystery on how to teach them.
The first thing you do is treat them like human beings
and the second thing you do is love them.
—Dr. Asa Hilliard

CONTENTS

PART ONE: AWARENESS

*What do I need to know and understand to become a
Listening Leader?*

PART TWO: RELATIONAL CAPITAL

*How do I build the interpersonal currency needed to support
and develop adult learners?*

PART THREE: COMPLEX CHANGE

How do I diagnose and navigate the challenges I face as a leader?

LIST OF FIGURES, TABLES, AND EXHIBITS

Figures

Tables

Exhibits

FOREWORD

There are countless books on leadership, but none like Shane Safir's *The Listening Leader*. When all is said and done, it deals with the forest and the trees. It unpacks both understanding and action. Overall, this book pays equal and integrative attention to "listening" and to "driving." It will cause you to reconsider leadership in ways that you have not thought about.

The nature of leadership in school systems these days is badly outdated, as evidenced by the long-standing failure to make improvements. We need leadership that connects with the lives and the futures of students, parents, and teachers. We need new forms of leadership that lift students from seemingly inevitable inertia to lives of action and success. *The Listening Leader* lays out how to mobilize countless numbers on the ground to forge a path forward. Old leadership discourages; Listening Leaders will unleash unrealized energy. Here's the test: Apply some of the ideas of this book to whatever you thought was an intractable situation. Then leverage the new impetus.

Every chapter has gems of insight. Each begins with "This chapter is designed to help you . . .," and lists the four or five big ideas that you will learn. Then, after delving into the topics, the chapter ends with Key Takeaways and Listening Leader Inquiry. This format alone gives the reader ready access to the ideas in the book as a whole.

Chapter 1 gets the reader immediately into courage of purpose and pathways of solution. We get to understand local accountability, formative versus punitive feedback, experiential use of data, and timeliness. In Chapter 2, we find the core tenets of the Listening Leader, which includes both rational and emotional elements.

Chapters have deeply insightful charts and frameworks. Here are a few:

Chapter 5 identifies a list of principles and pitfalls, which includes mistakenly leading from a self-proclaimed sense of urgency; viewing emotion as unprofessional; and failing to interpret nonverbal cues, including one's own. We learn how to understand and navigate complex change by engaging the Six Stances of a Listening Leader, and what to expect when leading complex change. In Chapter 9, there is a wonderful chart comparing how one would lead a technical versus a complex change. Simple rules are provided for complex change, such as "Make your first year of implementation all about learning, not performing"; and develop and learn from "skinny plans." In discussing complex change, the author shows what she and others did to guide the change and learn from it. For example, the goal of developing "expert teachers who continually refine their craft" is coupled with allocating significant time for collaboration and professional learning. Achieving "real accountability" is linked with coleadership and consensus decision making, and so on.

In another chapter, we learn how to design a game-changing meeting around listening routines. The related appendix contains quick design tips, sample team agreements, and 10 great TED Talks for better meetings. There is also a powerful chapter on listening to students, something dear to my own recent work, where we are finding that students are "radical change agents" with respect to pedagogy, learning environments, and society.[1] This chapter, written by Matt Alexander of June Jordan School for Equity, makes the case powerfully and shows the way, including five routines to build a culture of listening to students. There is an equally powerful chapter on listening to and connecting with parents for greater equity of learning.

All of Shane Safir's chapters are based on her own work and that of colleagues and coaching clients. The book reveals mistakes made by various leaders, what was learned, and how to do it better the next time. *The Listening Leader* connects us to other practical and deep work. This is a book that amplifies listening to a deep comprehensive art. What makes this book so timely is that educations systems are stuck now, mired in the status quo. Shane Safir offers a way out and forward.

Read it, act on it, and reap the benefits for all.

Michael Fullan
Professor Emeritus,
OISE/University of Toronto

NOTE

1. Fullan, M. (2016). *Indelible leadership: Always leave them learning.* Thousand Oaks, CA: Corwin Press.

PREFACE

Any citizen of this country who figures himself as responsible—and particularly those of you who deal with the minds and hearts of young people—must be prepared to "go for broke." Or to put it another way, you must understand that in the attempt to correct so many generations of bad faith and cruelty, when it is operating not only in the class-room but in society, you will meet the most fantastic, the most brutal, and the most determined resistance.

—JAMES BALDWIN, "A Talk to Teachers" (delivered October 16, 1963)

I became familiar with the stark shape of injustice while interning for civil rights attorney Jennifer Wood inside the Rhode Island youth prison system—euphemistically called a "training school." Wood was representing incarcerated youth in a class action lawsuit designed to improve conditions of confinement, such as access to education, quality food, and better facilities.

Each week, she and I followed armed guards through a half-dozen clanging security doors to meet with elected youth leaders. Sitting in a circle, we listened to young men and women share their stories and griev-ances. While taking notes on technicalities, we also witnessed much heart-break—the profound frustration of being locked up in your prime, particularly in a system that's overwhelmingly stacked against people of color. I recall Ramón, an aspiring artist who shared his vivid and haunting drawings with me. I remember Shawna, a buoyant young woman whose cousins lived down the hall from her in the female dormitory.

These youth had bright futures, but because of the institutional racism shaping so much of their lives, they lacked the second chances many White teenagers have.

Through this experience, a painful truth became clear to me: The prison system had siphoned off huge numbers of young people of color—

mostly Black, Latino, and southeast Asian—who were growing up in poverty. I was learning what many people of color know by necessity. I grew up in a majority White, middle-class suburb where many teenagers committed the same infractions that landed the youth I met in Rhode Island in prison. Yet I can't name a single kid I knew who did time for his or her behavior. This inequity branded itself on my heart and mind and fueled my later pursuit of a career in public education.

When I became an urban schoolteacher a few years later, I realized I had to "go for broke," as writer James Baldwin had instructed teachers to do 30 years prior. Like so many educators, I faced both incredible opportunities and daunting challenges. How would I humanize my classroom inside an essentially dehumanizing institution? How would I support the most marginalized students to participate in a rich intellectual world? How would I develop a learning community in the face of radically different social, emotional, and academic needs? And as a White teacher working with students of color, how would I earn trust and credibility?

There were many ways to get this wrong, not the least of which is what author and Columbia University professor Christopher Emdin calls "a pervasive narrative in urban education: a savior complex that gives mostly white teachers in minority and communities a false sense of saving kids."[1] I wish I could say I got it right from the get-go, but the truth is that going for broke is an ongoing process. Educators of all backgrounds step into an inequitable system, replete with distractions and obstacles that pull us off the path to transformation. How can one stay humble, courageous, and grounded in the face of such challenges?

Today, there are countless hawkers of solutions and programs to turn around our schools. Although these reformers are well intentioned and have at times produced some good results, I believe that the best solutions lie in the brilliance of our teachers, our students, and their families. We can't "intervene" our way to equitable outcomes without listening to the people we aspire to serve.

As I'll share in this book, I eventually left the classroom to help found and lead a new high school in San Francisco. Many years later, I spent a sabbatical year teaching Jordanian and Palestinian students in Amman, Jordan, where I learned new ways to listen. Rather than following a predetermined set of pedagogical steps, I had to study subtle cultural cues, make sense of Arabic turns of phrase with no English parallel, and create room for my students' stories. I recall one assignment for which two young women from Gaza wrote harrowing narratives about surviving a recent Israeli military assault; one minute they were sitting outside chatting, and the next, the sky exploded with bombs. This experience reminded me that to empower young people, we must welcome their untold stories and constantly adapt to the shifting nature of culture and context. Listening and "going for broke" are lifelong propositions.

I start from the premise that we already know what it takes to educate young people. So what gets in the way? We struggle with low expectations—of ourselves as leaders, of our schools, and of so many of our students. We struggle to uncouple the blunt assessments doled out by high-stakes tests from the complex and deeply human enterprise of learning. And we struggle to convince teachers to design intellectually rich environments when so often our *adult* learning environments are devoid of depth and humanity. We can address these issues, and I hope this book will begin to chart a course.

I bring two different, but related, perspectives to this project. First, I carry my own hard-won experience as a teacher and school leader who learned, through early missteps and various successes, to navigate working across difference. Second, as a school and district transformation coach for over 10 years, I have supported a diverse cross section of leaders; this work has deepened my belief in the importance of listening and of growing a culture of transformation rather than relying on charismatic leadership to save the day. I know that the strategies in this book are effective for any leader who wants to create the conditions for change.

None of this will be easy. Interrupting decades—centuries, really—of inequitable schooling seems a Sisyphean task. But it is possible. I hope this book will help you find the courage to listen—to yourself, to your community, and to what's possible when you decide to go for broke.

NOTES

1. Downs, K. (2016, March 28). What "white folks who teach in the hood" get wrong about education. *PBS Newshour.* Retrieved from http://www.pbs.org/newshour/updates/what-white-folks-who-teach-in-the-hood-get-wrong-about-education/

INTRODUCTION

I learned to listen in the row houses, apartments, and projects of southeast San Francisco. I had been teaching at a neighborhood high school, which served roughly a third Latino, a third African American, and a third Filipino students. In my second year, I had the opportunity to create a program called the Law Academy in partnership with an extraordinary English teacher named Rex de Guia. I taught pre-law and US history, managed student internships, and coordinated a group of attorneys who served as mentors. Our students conducted mock trials and debates, read legal cases alongside authors like Kozol, Baldwin, and Freire, and defended their ideas in college-level essays.

It was an invigorating experience, but also heartbreaking. Every year, we lost at least one student to homelessness, the dropout epidemic, juvenile hall, or violence. Our program constituted just three of a student's six class periods, and although the school at large was functional, it was also demoralizing and dehumanizing. To enter the building, students had to pass through a tall, guarded, wrought-iron fence. Using the restroom required a security escort. When a teacher quit midyear, as was far too common, I would walk past classrooms and see an endless stream of B movies running. Far too many young people either checked out emotionally or dropped out.

Several years later, I joined a group of colleagues who wanted to start a new school. We had heard of groundbreaking public schools in New York City that had flipped the script for students like ours, sending over 90% of their graduates to university. With a small planning grant, we visited New York and witnessed the magic of Urban Academy, the International High School at LaGuardia Community College, and Vanguard High School.

In these institutions, *everyone* appeared happy—adults and children alike. Instead of pockets of excellence, we found schools bursting with excellence! Students presented and defended their best work to "committees": small groups of teachers, students, and family members trained to listen and pose critical questions. Teachers were in constant dialogue, pushing each other's thinking and practice to new levels. Leaders listened to their school communities, valued student and staff feedback, and fended off external mandates that didn't serve their students.

Our team returned home and formed a partnership with the community-based San Francisco Organizing Project (SFOP; http://www.sfop.org/), a member of the PICO National Network,[1] to rally parent and community support for our vision of a new small high school serving the district's most underserved students. We began by conducting "one-on-one" meetings in the homes of parents, and discovered the power of story to connect people in an intimate social fabric. Throughout these meetings, we subscribed to PICO's **90/10 principle**—90% of each meeting would focus on listening and only 10% on talking. I took a year off from teaching, and listened to over 200 parents in the community.

I remember sitting in the living room of a father, and learning of his tremendous sacrifices emigrating from El Salvador so that his children could have a better life. Only now, they were attending schools with low standards and poor safety records. "I want them to be safe," he implored. "I want them to learn and to graduate. Is this too much to ask?" Listening to stories like this, I grew accustomed to giving my undivided attention to the speaker, paying attention to nonverbal cues, and asking questions to connect the speaker's hopes and dreams with the potential of a new school.

From these one-on-ones, a powerful network of parent, student, and teacher leaders emerged. At first, 10 or 15 people attended our community meetings. In short order, the rooms brimmed with 30 to 40 people. By the time we brought people together to ask the board of education to support our effort, nearly 300 people turned out. The crowd spilled out of the cafeteria doors as several students, teachers, and a diverse group of parent leaders spoke passionately. Together we secured a public pledge from board members that they would help us open a new small, in-district high school. Afterwards, the organizing team stood in a circle to debrief. One parent, whose daughter was fast approaching high school, spoke words I will never forget: "I feel like I'm part of the new civil rights movement."

We weren't just building relationships; we were building what I call relational capital—the interpersonal currency that fuels social change. We were building power. And we were building a movement. Only later did I realize the critical skill nested at the heart of this work: listening. By relying on a basic human capacity, we laid an unshakable foundation for what became June Jordan School for Equity.

EQUITABLE SCHOOL TRANSFORMATION IS POSSIBLE

This book is about creating the conditions for equitable school transformation through listening. By focusing your attention on people, and the daily stream of data they bring you, you'll learn to listen and build capacity in others. There is also a larger purpose woven into these pages: to transform our schools by transforming our school *cultures* into equitable places and spaces for every student.

Listening Leadership extends well beyond the act of listening; it is also an orientation toward collegiality, shared leadership, professional growth, and equity.

Listening is a vital and overlooked tool, and the cornerstone of leading across differences in race, gender, culture, socioeconomic status, language, and age, among other factors. Listening Leaders use their ears and eyes to understand where people are coming from. They lead with questions more than answers, and they demonstrate care, curiosity, and regard for every person who crosses their path. But Listening Leadership extends well beyond the act of listening; it is also an orientation toward collegiality, shared leadership, professional growth, and equity. It's a mindset and a way of being. Exhibit I.1 contrasts a listening mindset with a "telling" mindset.

Equity is the through line of this project. In its simplest form, **equity** means providing every student with the resources he or she needs to learn and thrive. This requires a willingness to redistribute resources in order to close entrenched opportunity gaps. In my local district of Oakland, California, gentrification and income inequality are pushing many working families and families of color out of their communities. Currently, if 100 students start high school together, 67 will graduate, 46 will start college,

---

EXHIBIT I.1   WHAT IS A LISTENING MINDSET?

The concept of mindsets has gained popularity in recent years, spearheaded by the work of Stanford University psychologist Carol Dweck. In her 2006 book *Mindset*, Dweck contrasts a *growth mindset*, the belief that ability is fluid and that effort pays off, with a *fixed mindset*, the belief that one's abilities, talents, and intelligence are static.[a] Listening Leadership offers a framework for holding a growth mindset as a leader.

Consider the difference between a listening and a telling mindset.

A Listening Mindset Reminds Us To . . .	A Telling Mindset Instructs Us To . . .
• Slow down.	• Move fast; be efficient.
• Use a thoughtful process to get to an outcome.	• Drive toward outcome; ignore process.
• Listen before making decisions.	• Use authority to make decisions.
• Harness the wisdom of the group.	• Be the expert in the room.
• Distribute leadership to others.	• Hold on to positional power.

I expect that many of you already possess a listening mindset and skills, which this book will help you sharpen.

[a]Dweck, C. (2006). *Mindset: The new psychology of success.* New York, NY: Ballantine Books.

---

and only 10 will graduate college within 10 years. As a school coach in this district and the mother of two children in Oakland schools, I am committed to building an integrated, equitable system. Each time I enter a school building, I ask myself, *Would I send my own children here?* If the answer is no, there is work to be done.

In its simplest form, equity means providing every student with the resources he or she needs to learn and thrive.

Is equitable school transformation possible? Absolutely. In 2003, I became the founding coprincipal of June Jordan School for Equity (JJSE), a social justice school preparing a working-class, predominantly Latino and African American student body for college and to become agents of positive change in the world. Now in its 14th year, and led by two incredible leaders whom you'll meet in Chapter 10 (one of whom wrote Chapter 8), JJSE continues to serve some of the most marginalized students in San

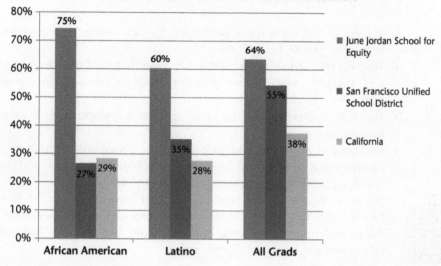

Percentage of High School Graduates
That Are 4-Year College Eligibile (meet A-G Requirments) by Race

FOUR YEAR AVERAGE - GRADUATING CLASSES OF 2010 THROUGH 2013

Graphic created by JJSE staff

Francisco, with outstanding results. From 2010 to 2013, an average of 60% of JJSE's Latino graduates were eligible for a 4-year university, as opposed to 28% in California and 35% in the San Francisco Unified School District. In that same period, 75% of JJSE's African American graduates were eligible for a 4-year university, versus 29% in California and 27% in the district.

Equitable schools like JJSE can exist for every child if Listening Leaders like you create the right set of conditions. When planting a garden, it is crucial to analyze your growing environment: sun, shade, rich soil, a seasonable climate, and moisture. No plant, no matter how tenacious, will survive without this confluence of factors to support it. Lacking an essential ingredient, it will suffer, wilt, or die. To nurture healthy students, Listening Leaders cultivate fertile conditions in their schools: a relentless focus on equity; a climate of trust that supports deep adult learning; and a commitment to student and parent voice, distributed leadership, and collaborative inquiry. Creating such a space begins with listening.

WHAT DOES A TRANSFORMED SCHOOL LOOK LIKE?

- Student performance is not predictable by race, socioeconomic status, language, gender, or zip code.
- Teachers choose to stay for many years, invest in the school community, and steadily improve their practice; veteran teachers apprentice new ones.
- The staff is diverse, and the adult culture is collaborative, student focused, and dynamic.
- Families feel respected and welcomed into a supportive community. Parents come to school to celebrate their children's learning, and the staff finds creative ways to connect with every family.
- Students engage in meaningful intellectual work that stretches their hearts and minds as they develop critical consciousness and resilience.
- Adults and students are joyful and productive, and the lines between school and the "real world" are blurred.

LEADER-FUL SCHOOLS, NOT LEADER-THIN

Who is a leader? A leader is anyone willing to take responsibility for what matters to him or her in the work of school improvement.[2] The spaciousness of that definition is an invitation to every person who has tired of the status quo and wants to create change. We need schools and districts that are leader-*ful*, not leader-thin. I offer a solution: Create a pipeline of Listening Leaders.

Schools can be rigidly hierarchical places, but we need only look beyond our field to see the impact of leader-ful organizations. Corporate innovators like Google have begun to flatten their hierarchies and empower informal leaders to innovate and drive strategy. The brilliant organizers at the helm of the Black Lives Matter movement have changed the national conversation about race and racial justice by adopting a leader-ful approach.

Pitching a big leadership tent and welcoming all who wish to enter will allow you to distribute responsibility for the complex work of school transformation. As my colleague Chris Funk, superintendent of the East Side Union High School District in San Jose, California, says, "The principal and administration team alone can't make significant change on campus unless they have fearless teacher leaders beside them." I would add nonteaching staff, students, and parents to this equation. Cultivating the leadership potential of staff, students, and parents will help you transform your school or system. Chapters 5 and 6 are designed to help you build the capacity of staff, including emerging leaders, and Chapter 9 directly addresses the topic of distributed leadership.

PRIMARY AUDIENCES FOR THIS BOOK

When I became the coprincipal of JJSE, I had a vision, passion, and instructional and strategic leadership skills. I knew how to design strong curricula and engaging professional learning. I knew how to observe classrooms and give teachers meaningful feedback. I knew how to write a coherent work plan or a grant proposal. But what I needed most, I lacked: a road map for working with adults. I needed someone to point out the land mines and commonly missed turns on the path to equitable school transformation. In short, I was unprepared for the social-emotional complexity of the job.

Despite the listening skills I had gained as a community organizer, I quickly discovered the difference between building trust with parents and building trust with colleagues. I was shocked by how easily staff members felt triggered by each other and by me as a positional leader. I didn't know how to engage people in hard conversations about equity. I wasn't sure how to nurture a healthy collaborative culture.

Since leaving JJSE in 2008, I have coached educational leaders of all stripes—teachers, principals, assistant principals, coaches, and central-office executives—who struggle with the same challenge: how to listen effectively to their stakeholders. These wonderful, passionate people care deeply about the work, but often find themselves thwarted by their own role in a dysfunctional staff culture. This book is also for these leaders, many of whose stories appear in its pages.

Specifically, I am writing for three audiences:

Site leaders
I believe the job of a school administrator is one of the toughest in the nation. Although instructional coaching programs have begun to proliferate across the country, I have yet to find a district that systemically invests in its site leaders. More often than not, principals and assistant principals stumble their way through the job, finding informal mentors and activating their own networks of support. They deserve better, and I hope this book will begin to address the struggles of this critical group of change-makers.

Teacher leaders and coaches

Look around you: Visit classrooms, watch teachers collaborate, and observe instructional coaches in action. Powerful leaders abound in our schools. Yet we tend to rotate the same cast of characters through leadership positions year after year. Alternatively, we throw teachers into the murky waters of leading a team without a life jacket, or even a set of goggles! For teacher leaders and coaches, I hope the book provides a framework for action that feels clarifying, empowering, and inspiring.

Central-office leaders

Like site administrators, central-office leaders are often the last to receive quality professional development. Many districts have complex organizational charts populated by all types of leaders who receive little to no training. This troubles me for two reasons. First, district leaders are positioned to drive whole-system change; they manage resources and make decisions that can reproduce or disrupt the status quo. Second, the behaviors modeled at the top of the system set a tone that trickles down to sites.

Every district has a prevailing narrative about "those people" in the central office. In a healthy system, the narrative might describe central-office staff as "listeners," "supportive," "site-focused," and "competent." The book offers this key group a new way of being and relating to school sites and one another.

THE LISTENING LEADER MAP

In today's increasingly complex schools, the need to listen is more urgent than ever, but few leaders do it well. We march through our buildings at breakneck speed, zooming past the one element that most deserves our attention: human beings. Listening Leadership will teach you to slow down, invest in relationships, and grow a sustainable culture of improvement.

Four writing principles have shaped the book:

The Listening Leader through stories

Each chapter opens with a vignette and closes with my reflections on the same vignette. You'll find anecdotes threaded throughout the chapters to illustrate key concepts. I'll ask you to think about your own story as a leader. What are your core values, and what experiences have shaped them? Who are you as a leader, and who do you aspire to be? Gardner and Laskin argue, "Leaders achieve their effectiveness chiefly though the stories they relate.... Leaders not only communicate stories, they embody those."[3]

The Listening Leader through rigorous intellect

I will honor your intellect and professionalism by inviting you to engage with high-level concepts. Although I use accessible language, I haven't shied away from rigor because I believe in your ability to grapple with these ideas. Too often, adult learning content gets watered down. The more we challenge ourselves, the more likely we are to challenge our students.

The Listening Leader through practical tools

The book is full of tools, tips, and templates to help you turn your learning into action. The chapters include concrete strategies that you can adapt to listen to colleagues, parents, and students; to construct an annual calendar; to plan a staff retreat; or to design a great meeting.

The Listening Leader through inquiry

I don't believe in one-size-fits-all approaches to school reform. Nor do I believe in scripted curricula or quick fixes to the problems that have confounded public schools for decades. Real transformation requires a willingness to sit with hard questions and to take bold action without always knowing the outcome. To make the text more dynamic, I've ended each chapter with an element called Listening Leader Inquiry where I respond to real questions I've received from readers and colleagues. At the end of your reading journey, I hope you have as many questions as answers and a desire to continue learning.

Structurally, the book is organized into three parts, corresponding to three developmental areas that make up the acronym ARC: awareness, relational capital, and complex change. You'll see a small stack of rocks at the beginning of each chapter that signal which area we are in. Each part of the book includes anchor frameworks and tools to guide your listening (see Table I.1). Here is a brief overview of the content.

Part 1: Awareness outlines the essential bodies of knowledge behind Listening Leadership, namely neuroscience, equity, and mindfulness.

Part 2: Relational Capital helps you apply your growing awareness to navigate the choppy waters of working with adults and across difference. We unpack the Six Stances of a Listening Leader, tactical approaches to building trust and capacity in others, and we examine powerful ways to listen to families and students.

Part 3: Complex Change sheds light on the nature of the living system that you lead—be that a team, school, or organization. We study the properties of complex change, distinguish technical problems from complex challenges, and learn to *influence* change without micromanaging people. We conclude with practical chapters on how to leverage listening routines as you design meetings and professional development, and concrete ways to grow and sustain a listening culture.

At the back of the book is a glossary of key terms and several appendices, which include a Listening Leadership rubric, and hands-on tools linked to content in various chapters. On my website, shanesafir.com/resources, you'll find additional downloadable tools.

Table I.1 is a quick reference guide to key frameworks you'll find within the book.

TABLE I.1   ANCHOR FRAMEWORKS FOR LISTENING LEADERSHIP

CHAPTER	FRAMEWORK	DESCRIPTION
PART 1: AWARENESS		
2	The Core Tenets	Simple, brain-based tenets that inform all of your moves as a Listening Leader. Each tenet is coupled with a brain "mandate."
3	The Equity Channels	A listening tool that helps us to pay close attention to equity. The first two channels are based in part on the work of Professor john a. powell (who does not capitalize his name).
4	The Six Circle Model	A simplified model of a living system, developed by Tim Dalmau and Steve Zuieback based on the work of Margaret Wheatley.
PART 2: RELATIONAL CAPITAL		
5, 6	Deep Listening and Strategic Listening Stances	A practical toolkit I created to help you plan for and engage in productive conversations with colleagues and other stakeholders.
PART 3: COMPLEX CHANGE		
10	Group Dynamic Temperature Checks	Visual thermometers that allow you to diagnose and respond to positive and negative group dynamics.
10	Experiential Learning Cycle	My favorite framework for designing great adult learning experiences; based on the work of John Heron.

HOW TO READ THIS BOOK

I have a few suggestions for how to get the most out of this book:

Use the rubric.
I have included a Listening Leadership rubric in Appendix A for you to track and self-assess the competencies in the book. Feel free to use this as a prereading tool, section by section as you read, and/or as a postassessment.

Shrink the change.
This is one of my favorite phrases from the Heath brothers' book *Switch*. If you start to feel overwhelmed by the number of things that you could improve, take a deep breath. Then take 5 or 10 minutes to journal on this question: *Where will I get started? What is one leadership skill or stance that I want to work on?* Trust that a small change can have far-reaching implications.

Set a reading intention.
Ask yourself before you dive in: *What do I want to learn, and how do I want to grow as a leader? What are the challenges and dilemmas that keep me up at night? What would wild success look like for me as a leader?*

Challenge your inner self-critic.
As you read the stories in this book, you may recognize your own mis-steps from time to time. Facing our leadership gaps can be sensitive, but I encourage you to notice your discomfort and stay curious. More important, hold a growth mindset with respect to your own leadership. Your work is incredibly complex. The book is here to help you reflect and grow.

Highlight and annotate.
There is a lot of content in this book. As you move through it, high-light the pieces that stand out to you. Jot a note in the margins to remind yourself why a passage resonated or to ask a question that it surfaced. Interact with the text as if it were a quiet coach—a guide-by-your-side helping you become the leader you want to be.

Form a study group.
What other leaders do you know who are struggling with issues similar to yours? Can you create a learning network of colleagues with whom

to read and discuss the ideas in the text? This could look as informal as a happy-hour chat about a particular chapter, or as formal as an ongoing study group with peers.

Practice, practice, reflect. Rinse and repeat.
The Listening Leader is full of provocative ideas and frames that might jolt you into new ways of seeing your work. I've also baked in many practical examples and tools. Give yourself permission to try out a new move or strategy that might feel awkward at first. You might even say to your team, "I read about a strategy that I want to try out today. It might feel a little awkward, but go with me here for a minute!" As you practice, you'll form deeper and deeper grooves in your brain until suddenly, you will have mastered a new skill. Play with the ideas and make time to reflect on how your experiments go.

ANONYMITY AND PSEUDONYMS

To safeguard the privacy of leaders I have coached or collaborated with, as well as the institutions in which they work, I have altered most names and identity features. A notable exception is in Chapter 10, which pivots around a meeting at JJSE and for which I have permission to use participants' real names. Note that every story in this book is real, stemming either from my personal experience or from interviews with colleagues.

NOTES

1. PICO stands for the Pacific Institute for Community Organizing (http://www .piconetwork.org/), a national network of faith-based organizations working toward creative solutions to challenges facing urban, suburban, and rural communities.
2. Adapted from Weissglass, J. (1990). Constructivist listening for empowerment and change. *Educational Forum, 54*, 351–370.
3. Gardner, H. E., & Laskin, E. (2011). *Leading minds: An anatomy of leadership.* New York, NY: Basic Books, p. 9.

THE LISTENING LEADER

Chapter 1

The Transformative Power of Listening

Preview: Listening is the gateway to equitable school transformation. The "test-and-punish" era created a culture of compliance that made it difficult to hear parent, student, and staff voices. Listening Leadership offers a simple yet groundbreaking way of being and leading.

This chapter is designed to help you:

- Consider the impact of the testing era on educational leadership.
- Compare and contrast common leadership archetypes.
- Gain a practical tool for shifting school conversations toward equity.
- Explore critical challenges that listening addresses.

LEARNING TO LISTEN

When I arrived as a school coach in fall 2009, the Arts Academy was in disarray. A year before, the district had appointed a new principal named Lauren to tackle declining test scores and parent concerns at this racially and economically diverse middle school. During her first month on the job, Lauren had made sweeping changes, including dismantling a signature arts program, without consulting any of the staff. According to one veteran teacher, "The arts program was our whole identity as a school. It allowed struggling students to become successful through the arts, and she chopped it up into a horribly watered-down version. She didn't consult with teachers on a lot of decisions that affected us." In short, the leader had failed to listen.

Her purpose made sense: She hoped to close the school's achievement gap by increasing instructional math and English language arts instructional time for students. But her process alienated the staff and diminished the value of the arts to the school's identity. Veteran teachers felt particularly disrespected, and in the spring of Lauren's first year, they organized a vote of no confidence in her leadership. Soon after, the assistant superintendent brought me in as a coach to help her repair this contentious relationship.

In our early conversations, Lauren seemed puzzled. A first-time principal but a longtime district teacher, she had arrived with a clear vision for the school and felt she had begun to implement it. She couldn't understand why the staff had chosen to publicly humiliate her. For the next few months, I held one-on-one sessions with her, as well as what felt like educator group therapy sessions with her and a cadre of teachers we came to call the Veteran Seven. The union president, a remarkable woman, participated in these meetings as a listener and cofacilitator.

Through coaching, I asked Lauren to identify her core beliefs, to observe where her behavior had deviated from those beliefs, and to consider small shifts in approach. She articulated what she thought was missing at the Arts Academy: "People need to feel they can take risks.... In a well-functioning school, there's respect and a generative discourse." She acknowledged her miscalculations in addressing the issue: "I made a lot of individual decisions my first year. In my actions, in my persona, I have created a lack of trust." From there, we set a basic goal: to reopen dialogue in what was by now a toxic climate.

The group sessions were awkward at first, but over the course of several meetings, the dynamic began to shift. I invited the teachers to voice their concerns and encouraged Lauren to practice listening and taking responsibility for her actions when appropriate. At one emotionally charged gathering, she raised her hand. Everyone seemed to hold his or her breath as she spoke slowly and steadily: "I want to apologize. I am sorry for the ways in which I disrespected you and the history of the school. That was not my intent, and I know we can do better moving forward together."

The room heaved a collective sigh of relief. Shoulders relaxed, and contorted facial expressions loosened into something closer to acceptance. We didn't sing "Kumbaya," but I sensed that this once-demonized leader had become more human in the eyes of her teachers.

At the heart of this process lay a simple, yet transformational, skill: the leader's ability to listen. Listening allowed Lauren to discern her colleagues' unspoken messages—their deeply human need to matter, to be seen, heard, and valued. It gave her the courage to take in difficult feedback. And it helped her recognize and transform a negative group dynamic.

The principal repositioned herself as an ally, but she didn't stop there. Lauren asked the Veteran Seven to help her reimagine the school's identity: "In this moment, with our increasingly diverse student body, how do our mission and model need to evolve?" Together, she and her former foes led their colleagues through a process to address the question, What do we want our students to know and be able to do as young artists and thinkers, and how will we measure this? The ensuing conversations were rigorous and generative, and they built social capital—the collaborative power of the group.[1]

By June 2010, the Arts Academy staff had rallied around a shared vision. Polished through dialogue with families, this vision established a local definition of success that all stakeholders signed on to. How did a divided community unite within a year? It was actually very simple: The leader slowed down and learned to listen. Rather than continuing to go it alone, she harnessed the collective intelligence of her staff to fashion a new future for the school. Moving from the politics of resistance to the promise of collaboration, the Arts Academy was reborn through its leader's willingness to listen.

WHAT WE'VE INHERITED

In her initial struggle to listen, this leader was not alone. The test-and-punish era made it increasingly difficult for leaders to listen to their communities. Parent, student, and teacher voices receded amid a cacophony of well-packaged interventions and initiatives. Ask yourself and ask a colleague, *When is the last time you felt truly listened to at work? To what extent do you feel seen, heard, and valued in your organization?* Listen for the human data that surfaces.

We have all inherited the consequences of this era of mandates, accountability systems, and sanctions. (Figure 1.1 humorously depicts the competing messages leaders have to contend with.) A 2013 Metropolitan Life Insurance Company survey revealed that 75% of principals feel that their job is too complex, and half feel under stress most of the week.[2] Central-office administrators, teacher leaders, and coaches endure similar levels of stress in a domino effect that intensifies across the system. In this compromising situation, even the best-intentioned leader can become overwhelmed and begin to miss critical signals coming from stakeholders.

FIGURE 1.1   SHEEPISH THOUGHTS

Anthony Taber/The New Yorker Collection/The Cartoon Bank

Two leadership paradigms became prominent in the accountability climate: the Manager and the Driver. The **Manager** gets things done within the parameters of the status quo. He or she is widely viewed as competent and reliable, and follows the system's playbook to keep his or her school running smoothly. With a focus on compliance over cultivating relationships, however, this leader can become tone deaf—unable to perceive and respond to subtle messages.

The **Driver**, by contrast, is a change agent. Propelled by a sense of urgency, this leader is decisive and authoritative, moving quickly to promote a results-driven agenda. Although people tend to respect this leader as a visionary, the Driver often creates a fraught adult culture, as he or she tends to view the concerns of teachers and staff as a distraction from student needs.

A third, less common paradigm is the **Peacekeeper**—the leader who places a high value on relationships but lacks a strong change agenda.

In the Peacekeeper's context, people tend to *feel* good and enjoy their work, but little improves with respect to student learning.

This book proposes a powerful alternative, Listening Leadership, which draws on the strengths of the other three approaches while mitigating their weaknesses. The Listening Leader cares about getting things done; he or she is a skilled manager or effectively delegates managerial tasks. Like the Driver, the Listening Leader has a deep and abiding commitment to equity and is a change agent at heart. And like the Peacekeeper, the Listening Leader has a people-first orientation. But his or her methodology stands apart.

First, the Listening Leader understands that school transformation, if it is to be sustainable, requires a long-term investment: There are no quick fixes, "turnarounds," or shortcuts.

First, the Listening Leader understands that school transformation, if it is to be sustainable, requires a long-term investment: There are no quick fixes, "turnarounds," or shortcuts. Second, this leader uses *listening* to foster a healthy culture of improvement and to build the skills and capacity of the staff. Third, instead of proclaiming a vision, the Listening Leader *constructs* a vision through a collaborative process in which dialogue and dissenting perspectives are welcome. Finally, this leader embraces an expansive view of data, including human experience as a vital source of evidence.

Think of Figure 1.2 as like a Twister board—that childhood game where you spin a wheel and then stretch your hands and feet to reach different circles. As a leader, you want to have a limb (or at least a pinky!) in each quadrant, but you need to be firmly rooted in the Listening Leader domain.

A FEW CORE BELIEFS

This book will encourage you to slow down and tune in to the range of voices in your community, particularly the quietest ones and those that are most often silenced. This includes strong dissenting voices and those of historically marginalized stakeholders, such as immigrant and monolingual families, students and staff of color, and paraprofessionals. Through

FIGURE 1.2   LEADERSHIP ARCHETYPES

listening, you'll discover the missing ingredient in most school reform efforts: a deeply felt, *collective* sense of purpose.

Listening Leadership is not a recipe or a curriculum but an adaptive framework anchored in a few core beliefs:

• Communities have the ability to solve their own problems.
• Although we can learn from other schools and districts, the best solutions are homegrown.

- Every community must shape its own path to excellence.
- Through listening, leaders can create the conditions for equitable school transformation.

These beliefs represent an unwavering faith in people and democracy that runs counter to the educational policies of the early 21st century, when policymakers increasingly tried to control and "teacher-proof" schools with pacing guides, rigid curricula, and centralized assessments. Well, enough is enough. It's time to entrust leaders, educators, and communities to chart their own course. We begin by exploring the critical challenges that listening can help correct.

KEY CHALLENGE 1: THE PERSISTENCE OF INEQUITY

Not everything that is faced can be changed, but nothing can be changed until it is faced.

—JAMES BALDWIN[3]

Listening Leadership will help you make progress on the fundamental issue facing American public schools: inequity. Far too many children continue to attend substandard schools and receive a low-quality education. In a groundbreaking article, authors Eugene Eubanks, Ralph Parish, and Dianne Smith explain how the dominant language of school improvement serves to maintain the status quo and perpetuate inequitable outcomes. They call this Discourse I and furnish familiar examples:[4]

- Children "need more structure" because they are "from disadvantaged conditions" or "from single parent families" or "working families" or are "more dangerous."
- Teachers participate in "staff development," "in-service," and "school improvement," which have evolved to mean that "people in schools can go through a process that appears to be change oriented but, in fact, has not resulted in any substantial improvement of student learning."
- Staff may say, "We're a school in transition. Things have changed; students just aren't what they used to be. You just can't teach as much as you used to."

To be clear, as coauthor Smith reminded me in an interview, discourse isn't just the words educators speak. It includes our beliefs; our values; our perceptions of children from urban communities; and our perceptions of race, racism, and gender equality in schools. Recent research at Johns Hopkins University confirms the power of perception in a study demonstrating that White teachers tend to have lower expectations of African American students. For example, White teachers were 30% less likely than their Black colleagues to believe that the same African American student would graduate from a 4-year college and 40% less likely to believe that the student would graduate from high school.[5]

Listening Leaders tune in to the power of perception and language and model a shift toward Discourse II, in which uncomfortable truths are laid squarely on the table for discussion.

As leaders, we have the power to transform this reality by first listening to the ways in which our schools and districts talk about, think about, and organize the work of improvement. Listening Leaders tune in to the power of perception and language and model a shift toward Discourse II, in which uncomfortable truths are laid squarely on the table for discussion. (Table 1.1 summarizes the differences between Discourse I and II.) They reject a quick-fix mentality, taking time to ask hard questions and examine root

TABLE 1.1   DISCOURSE I VS. DISCOURSE II

Discourse I	Discourse II
Language typically used to talk about, question, and design the work of school improvement. Discourse I maintains the status quo while appearing to respond to demands for change.	Language that names uncomfortable, unequal, ineffective, prejudicial conditions and relationships in schools. Discourse II explores the root causes of inequity and models an inquiry approach to improvement.
Attributes • Singular truths • Answers and technical fixes • Symptoms • Improving what exists • Externalization/"looking out the window" • Limited time and ability • Reproduction of inequity	**Attributes** • Multiple stories • Inquiry, adaptive challenges, and root causes • Causes • Changing something significant • Internal reflection/"looking in the mirror" • Getting started anyway • Transformation

Adapted with permission from "The Nature of Discourse in Education," by the Bay Area Coalition for Equitable Schools, now the National Equity Project, 2004.

causes. And they ensure that colleagues of color and those from other historically marginalized groups feel safe enough to share their perspectives and experiences. Table 1.2 provides examples of shifting the discourse, and Exhibit 1.1 models how a white ally can practice Discourse II.

For students to attend humanizing schools, adults must *work in* humanizing schools. Every grown-up who enters your building—whether he or she is a custodian, parent, paraprofessional, or teacher—should feel seen, heard, and valued. This begins with listening—not to external demands, but to your own community and to what you believe is right.

TABLE 1.2 EXAMPLES OF SHIFTING THE DISCOURSE

Area	Discourse I	Shifting to Discourse II
Academic data and equity	The achievement gap	The opportunity gap or the "education debt" to historically disenfranchised students.[a]
Time and change	"We don't have time for all this talking and processing about equity. We have students to teach!"	"Changing the status quo takes courage and time. We need to make a long-term investment and still get started somewhere."
Student behavior	"We can't let *those* students interrupt others' learning."	"It seems like there's a cultural disconnect between some of our staff and students. As a result, Black and Latino boys are frequently getting kicked out of class. How do we consciously name and address this pattern?"
Student expectations	"Not all our students are college material. Some of them would just do better in the trades or remedial classes."	"We have to ensure that all of our students have choices, just as we did as young people. How do we guarantee that every student is college-*ready* so she is empowered to make a decision about her future?"
Universalism vs. targeted support	"We want *all* students to succeed. We make decisions to serve *all* students' needs."	"According to our data, we are struggling to meet the needs of English language learners (ELL students). How can we build our capacity as ELL instructors and culturally responsive practitioners?"
Instruction	"I teach the content. It's just that the kids are lazy and don't want to do the work."	"How will we know students have learned the content? How can we differentiate based on interests, learning modalities, and culturally responsive practices to engage every student in the learning process?"

[a] Ladson-Billings, G. (2006). From the achievement gap to the education debt: Understanding achievement in U.S. schools. *Educational Researcher, 35*(7), 3–12.

MAKE IT MINDFUL

Take a few minutes to jot down your thoughts on these questions:

- In your context, how do people think about and talk about school improvement?
- What common examples of Discourse I would you like to shift?
- What would Discourse II sounds like?

EXHIBIT 1.1   WHITE ALLIES AND DISCOURSE II

In November 2015, Black student leaders at the University of Missouri initiated a wave of protests against the university president for his mishandling of certain racist incidents. The football team, including White players and coaches, went on strike, and within 3 days the president had resigned. A backlash by White students ensued, including anonymous death threats to students of color. Should students be required to attend classes in this environment?

Here's the stance of one White professor, Bradley Harrison Smith, which I offer as an example of Discourse II practiced by a White ally. In this Facebook post (https://www.facebook.com/bradley.t.smith.587/posts/101005497030 32872), Smith directly names the unequal experience of students of color and White students and "looks in the mirror" to consider his own potential complicity in an unjust scenario.

I'm writing to tell you that I'm cancelling class tomorrow (Wednesday 11/11/15).

The truth is, despite all of the threats on social media, I would still probably feel safe on campus were we to have class. But that's because I am a white man. I would not feel safe were this not the case.

By holding class at our regular time, I would be forcing my students who do and probably should feel threatened to implicitly disobey me in order to protect their lives by not attending my class.

Which means that, were I to tell you something like, "We are going to still have class, but stay home if you don't feel safe . . ." (which is what I originally planned to say) I think I would be participating in the marginalization of minority students by tacitly supporting an educational environment in which certain students feel safe while others cannot. Attending class tomorrow, in light of the recent threats, would be a privilege not available to all my students, and I have therefore decided it will not be a privilege for any of my students.

KEY CHALLENGE 2: INTEGRITY IN THE FACE OF PRESSURE

The test-and-punish era created another serious challenge for leaders: how to maintain integrity in the face of mounting pressures. Listening supports integrity by allowing us to slow down, turn inward, and reflect on our core values. C. S. Lewis defined integrity as "doing the right thing, even when no one is watching"; researcher Brené Brown describes it as "choosing courage over comfort. Choosing what's right over what's fun, fast, or easy. And *practicing* your values, not just professing them."[6] Given the number of demands placed on leaders today, it can be easier to maintain the status quo than to practice our values. We may be so busy *doing* that we forget to do the right thing.

A study by Rick Mintrop and his colleagues at UC Berkeley found that schools with high levels of integrity are able to manage external pressures by holding strong to their values.[7] Of particular interest, they found that integrity comes directly from a school's leader and the culture he or she builds. A high-integrity faculty culture is characterized by open communication, dissent, and a learning orientation.

So just what does integrity look like in the context of schooling? It looks like Cindy Marten, superintendent of San Diego Unified School District, choosing to scale back test mandates in her system. "Students come to school to learn, not to take tests," Marten said. "Testing takes up valuable time that could be used to teach and learn."[8] Another example of integrity comes from the San Francisco Unified School District. In 2015, the state superintendent of California cancelled the summer administration of a mandatory high school exit exam, leaving thousands of students across the state in the lurch and disproportionately affecting students of color and ELL students. The San Francisco school board chose to flout the law and award diplomas to 104 students who had completed all graduation requirements but failed to pass the now-defunct exam.

Integrity can also look as small as taking time to listen deeply to a parent or a colleague in distress. It can look like committing to weekly one-on-one coaching meetings with teacher leaders to make sure they feel supported. It can look like encouraging a student leadership initiative, even if you don't entirely agree with the students' perspectives. It might even look like modeling the value of work-life balance by scheduling cell phone- and email-free times and encouraging colleagues to do the same. At whatever grain size, integrity implies listening to and acting on your internal moral compass.

Throughout this book, you'll meet high-integrity leaders at all levels of the school system. Each of these people has found ways to manage external demands with integrity. Each inspired me to share a vision of what's possible by choosing what's right over what's fun, fast, and easy. They taught me that in any political climate, you have agency. You can decide what you believe is the right thing to do for your students and your school, and you can decide how to navigate demands that run counter to your beliefs. Exhibit 1.2 offers an example of bold, integrity-driven leadership from outside the education field.

EXHIBIT 1.2   FINDING COURAGE

Brittany "Bree" Newsome removes the Confederate flag from a pole at the Statehouse in Columbia
Note. Stringer/Reuters Pictures. Used with permission.

When we hold strong to our beliefs and values, we are more likely to act courageously in service of our students and communities. Educational leaders can gain inspiration by looking outside our field to contemporary activists like Bree Newsome. On June 27, 2015, Newsome scaled the 30-foot pole in front of South Carolina's capitol building to take down the Confederate battle flag. In the wake of the Charleston church shooting, in which a White supremacist murdered nine African Americans sitting in a prayer circle, calls to remove the symbolic flag had been on the rise. Ms. Newsome was part of a collective action to construct a new symbol and foster collective consciousness of the power inherent in bold, direct action. This iconic image has become a visual touchstone of empowerment and courage across the globe, inspiring a hashtag, artistic renderings, and superhero cartoons.

Commenting on her participation in the action, Newsome said, "We removed the flag today because we can't wait any longer . . . It's time for a new chapter, where we are sincere about dismantling white supremacy and building toward true racial justice and equality."[a]

[a] Hale, J. (2015, July 15). Confederate flag controversy underscores need for educational activism (commentary). *Education Week*. Retrieved from http://www.edweek.org/ew/articles/2015/07/16/confederate-flag-controversy-underscores-need-for-educational-ac.html

? MAKE IT MINDFUL

As you cultivate integrity, think about the symbols of oppression in your context that you would like to take down or transform. What are they? What level of courage would it take for you to transform them, and where will you find that courage?

KEY CHALLENGE 3: DEALING WITH TRAUMA

Listening will also help us address a pressing challenge that confronts so many of our schools today: students who come to class having experienced trauma in their home or community. A listening approach will sharpen your **emotional intelligence**—the ability to detect others' emotions, understand your own, and use this information to guide your interactions. Daniel Goleman popularized a framework for emotional intelligence that includes self-awareness, self-management, social awareness (or empathy), and relationship management.[9] In later work, Goleman highlighted a strong link between emotional

A listening approach will sharpen your emotional intelligence—the ability to detect others' emotions, understand your own, and use this information to guide your interactions.

intelligence and leadership, noting, "Without it, a person can have the best training in the world, an incisive, analytical mind, and an endless supply of smart ideas, but he still won't make a great leader."[10]

Several studies document a correlation between school leaders' emotional intelligence and school performance.[11] Stone, Parker, and Wood looked at 464 principals and vice principals and found that those who received above-average ratings from teachers also scored higher on a survey of emotional intelligence.[12] The most effective leaders showed skill in the areas of empathy and relationship building. In another study of 48 administrators, emotional intelligence explained nearly 40% of the perceived variance in leadership abilities.[13]

Listening with emotional intelligence is crucial in school communities impacted by **trauma**, which is defined by the American Psychological Association as "an emotional response to a terrible event" such as an accident, violence, or even relentless poverty.[14] In the immediate wake of a traumatic incident, victims typically experience shock and denial—but delayed reactions include volatile emotions, flashbacks, strained relationships, and physical symptoms like headaches or nausea. If you work (or grew up in) a high-trauma environment, you know these signs well. At schools, they're often the harbinger of academic and behavioral challenges.

I remember a girl, whom I'll call Tiana, from my ninth-grade English class in East Oakland. One day she arrived to class in the foulest of moods, refused to engage in the lesson, and when pressed, spouted off the classic, "I don't have to listen to you!" At that point, I summoned deep wells of patience and asked her to step into the hall. "What's going on, Tiana?" I questioned. "This behavior is totally out of character for you." Her eyes brimmed with tears as she stammered out, "Yesterday I saw someone get shot in my neighborhood. I'm really upset and don't know what to do." Had I not checked in with her, Tiana and I would have sparred over her "defiance," and she might have landed in the office with a referral, as do so many children suffering from trauma. Instead, I dug deep to listen, she took a risk and told me what was going on, and we strengthened our relationship. More important, I gained insight that led to action: I soon reached out to my school's mental health team to arrange some support for her.

Education professor Christopher Emdin and co-researcher Napoleon Wells studied the symptoms of posttraumatic stress disorder (PTSD) among young Black males in urban public schools.[15] Wells, a PTSD specialist and psychologist, compared students' avoidance of certain topics of discussion and heightened reactions to others with the ways in which military veterans respond to sustained trauma. The overlap was so striking that Wells coined the term "post-racial tension stress disorder" to describe the experience of youth who feel powerless in a world rife with conflicting messages: They hear that race no longer matters, while at the same time they are subjected to "physical and symbolic violence (at the hands of police and schools) because of their race."[16]

Recent studies have identified the phenomenon of secondary trauma for educators working in communities impacted by poverty and violence. Secondary trauma manifests in various types of symptoms—for example:[17]

- Emotional—feeling numb or detached; feeling overwhelmed or maybe even hopeless
- Physical—having low energy or feeling fatigued
- Behavioral—changing your routine or engaging in self-destructive coping mechanisms
- Professional—experiencing low performance of job tasks and responsibilities; feeling low job morale
- Cognitive—experiencing confusion, diminished concentration, and difficulty with decision making; experiencing trauma imagery, which is seeing events over and over again
- Spiritual—questioning the meaning of life or lacking self-satisfaction
- Interpersonal—physically withdrawing or becoming emotionally unavailable to your coworkers or your family

One teacher leader I interviewed reflected on the absurdity of attending run-of-the-mill staff meetings after dealing with student trauma:

> The education context is so stressed that people often aren't at their best, especially when working with kids in trauma. You're just always frazzled. You're going from being with kids all day and all of the different stresses that go with that, and then you have your staff meeting after school with the message: "Okay, now be fresh and professional! Be your best self." Well that's just not going to happen 90% of the time.

A listening orientation will help you address trauma and secondary trauma by honing your emotional intelligence. Too often, we ask young people and adults to check their emotions at the school door, and then lament the absence of trust that inevitably results. A powerful antidote lies within reach: Learn to listen and listen to learn. Learn to treat people's experiences and feelings with compassion. This doesn't mean that we have to solve every issue that crosses our path, but it does mean standing with people in their struggles. Chapter 5 provides practical strategies for deep listening, and Chapter 10 offers adult learning routines that allow people to safely express their emotions.

KEY CHALLENGE 4: DISCONNECTED DATA

Finally, listening will help us address a troubling consequence of the test-and-punish era: overreliance on data that is far removed from student learning. Many of us have grown accustomed to setting goals in reaction to periodic bursts of data that rain down on schools. This leads to a mismatch between the problems we face and the solutions we design. Assessment expert W. James Popham argues, "America's students are not being educated as well these days as they should be. A key reason for this calamity is that we currently use the wrong tests to make our most important educational decisions."[18]

Listening Leaders recognize that much of the data we need is right before us if we choose to listen—speaking, sending emails, showing up in our offices every day.

Listening Leaders recognize that much of the data we need is right before us if we choose to listen—speaking, sending emails, showing up in our offices every day. It's in our close observations of students working on tasks and of teachers engaged in collaboration. These street-level data tell the story of school transformation. The Levels of Data framework (see Figure 1.3) allows us to consider the types of data we need in any given context. Although Level 1 "satellite" data orients us in a general direction, it fails to illuminate what's getting in the way of student (or adult) learning, or what's working best for kids. Level 2 "map" data gets us closer to pinpointing a subskill or priority area of need. But Level 3 "street" data is the key to designing supportive structures, achieving equitable outcomes, and developing high-capacity teachers.

My colleague Noelle Apostol Colin taught under a new administrator who asked her staff to regularly analyze benchmark assessment results—Level 1 data—in order to determine which skills to reteach. Apostol Colin found this process frustrating for a couple of reasons. First, her students struggled mightily on the tests, and in the absence of additional data, the results made her feel like a "bad teacher." Second, the benchmarks failed

FIGURE 1.3   LEVELS OF DATA

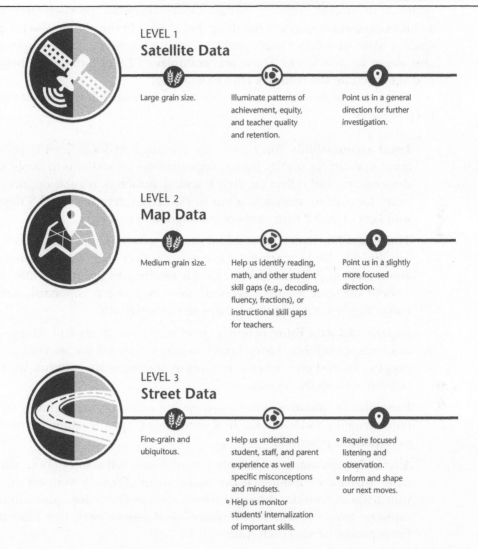

LEVEL 1
Satellite Data

Large grain size.

Illuminate patterns of achievement, equity, and teacher quality and retention.

Point us in a general direction for further investigation.

LEVEL 2
Map Data

Medium grain size.

Help us identify reading, math, and other student skill gaps (e.g., decoding, fluency, fractions), or instructional skill gaps for teachers.

Point us in a slightly more focused direction.

LEVEL 3
Street Data

Fine-grain and ubiquitous.

○ Help us understand student, staff, and parent experience as well specific misconceptions and mindsets.

○ Help us monitor students' internalization of important skills.

○ Require focused listening and observation.

○ Inform and shape our next moves.

to clarify *why* and *how* her students were struggling, so she was left feeling powerless. She needed Level 2 and Level 3 data to inform her planning and instructional moves.

Apostol Colin's principal could have offered the benchmark data as a starting point to establish patterns of achievement before asking teachers to think about what other evidence they needed. Should Apostol Colin administer a running record—a literacy tool that helps teachers identify patterns in student reading behaviors—to diagnose precisely where a child's comprehension was breaking down? Should she closely observe a student while he solves a math problem, noting the strategies he employs and where he gets stuck? These are examples of Level 3 data that help teachers navigate the complex path to learning.

As we change the conversation about data, here are a few principles to keep in mind:

Local accountability Work to create a culture of local, peer-to-peer accountability for results. Design opportunities for students to publicly demonstrate and reflect on their learning. Structure regular opportunities for staff to analyze student work. Cross-reference Level 3 data with Level 1 and 2 data to check for alignment and rigor.

Timeliness The data is most useful when it gets in the hands of educators quickly. Build teachers' capacity to collect daily informal data about student misconceptions. Coach teachers to listen carefully to student dialogue in the classroom. Give everyone a clipboard, and invite him or her to capture quotes and observations.

Experiential data Value people's experiences—students and adults—as a form of evidence. Listen keenly to how people tell the *story* of their experience, and pull out common words and narrative patterns. We'll talk more about this in Chapter 7.

Formative vs. punitive Don't use data as a hammer; use it purely for improvement, and you'll see how much more open teachers become to its positive potential.

Alternative assessments Multiple forms of data tell a story about students that paper-and-pencil assessments can't. Stretch yourself and your team to consider other measures, such as portfolios, graduation capstone projects, and performance-based assessments, that offer a fuller picture of who each student is.

Use the tool in Table 1.3 to identify your purpose in looking at data before selecting the data you need.

TABLE 1.3   A FRAMEWORK FOR LEVELS OF DATA

	Level 1: Satellite Data	Level 2: Map Data	Level 3: Street Data
Definition	Large grain size. Helps illuminate patterns of student achievement and equity. Points us in a general direction for further investigation.	Medium grain size. Helps identify reading, math, and other skill challenges (e.g., decoding, fluency, fractions). Points us in a slightly more focused direction.	Fine-grain and ubiquitous. Helps identify specific student misconceptions and monitor internalization of key skills. Requires careful listening.
Evidence of Student Learning	Standardized and external test scores (SBAC, SAT, PSAT, statewide graduation exams, district benchmarks, etc.)	• Reading Lexile levels • Oral fluency assessments to estimate correct words per minute • Student perception surveys • Performance-based assessments (portfolios, senior defenses, etc.) • Scholastic Reading Inventory (SRI) or other similar assessments	• Student nonverbal cues • Student interviews and focus groups • Teacher observation notes from guided reading or guided problem solving to gauge a student's misconceptions • One-on-one running records • Student work artifacts • Observation of students engaged in sorting activities to check misconceptions and internalization
Evidence of Teacher Effectiveness	Standardized and external test scores, disaggregated by teacher	• Administrator observation notes from formal observation and evaluation • Teacher performance-based assessments (portfolios, end-of-year reflective presentations, etc.)	• Teacher interviews and focus groups • Teacher nonverbal cues during lessons • Leader's notes from listening to teacher discourse in one-on-one meetings • Notes from regular, informal observations • Video clips of students engaged in a task

Note. Adapted from the Scaffolded Apprenticeship Model (SAM), Baruch College. For a downloadable tool to apply the Levels of Data framework, go to my website: shanesafir.com/resources

Of course, better data alone won't transform our schools. To improve outcomes, we have to strengthen the instructional core—the "black box" where teacher, student, and content intersect.[19] In his synthesis of over 800 studies of what works best in education, professor and researcher John Hattie found that leaders have little *direct* effect on student learning.[20] They can, however, create the right set of conditions for good instruction by discerning which initiatives matter and which do not; defining, as the Arts Academy staff did, local measures of success; building the capacity of teachers and teacher leaders; and working hard to foster a collaborative culture.

 MAKE IT MINDFUL

- What do you want every exiting student to know and be able to do?
- What values do you want students to develop?
- What types of data will you use to measure success?
- If you transform your school or system, what will parents, teachers, and students be saying 3 years from now?

BECOMING A LISTENING LEADER

Reflecting on the dynamics of school leadership, my colleague Jessica Gammell noted to me, "The higher you move up the food chain, the more you're rewarded for compliance." To that I would add, "and the less you're rewarded for listening to your staff and community." Listening runs counter to the archetype of a charismatic leader who unites his or her community through dazzling speeches. But charismatic leaders often do more harm than good because they foster dependency and serve as symbolic role models who can never be replaced. Listening Leaders, by contrast, understand their central mission as building the capacity of others to help lead and sustain change.

This book will walk you through three developmental areas of Listening Leadership represented in the acronym ARC: awareness, relational capital, and complex change. ARC provides a road map for listening and leading in ways that fuel equitable school transformation. Figure 1.4 depicts the three areas as rocks in a cairn—a human-made pile of stones

FIGURE 1.4   THE LISTENING LEADER ARC

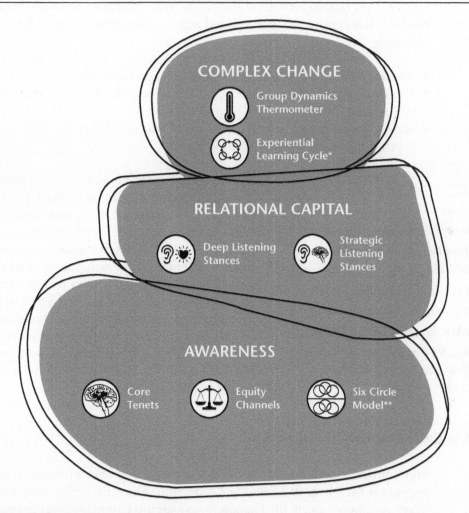

COMPLEX CHANGE

Group Dynamics
Thermometer

Experiential
Learning Cycle*

RELATIONAL CAPITAL

Deep Listening
Stances

Strategic
Listening
Stances

AWARENESS

Core
Tenets

Equity
Channels

Six Circle
Model**

*The experiential learning cycle is attributed to John Heron.
**The Six Circle Model was created by Tim Dalmau and Steve Zuieback, based on the work of Margaret Wheatley.

that serves as a landmark. (We'll explore this metaphor in Chapter 9.) Inside each rock are key frameworks that appear in that part of the book. It's important to note that each area builds on the previous one, providing a balanced collection of practical knowledge and skills.

Why do we need an entire book about listening, you might wonder? Human beings listen all the time—in personal, academic, and professional settings—yet not always with intention or rigor. Scholars have found that listening is a central yet undervalued aspect of leadership. Consider the following:

- We have learned 85% of what we know through listening.
- The average professional spends 33% of the workday listening and only 26% speaking.
- Very few professionals have had formal training to understand and improve listening skills and techniques.[21]

School transformation arises from the micro-interactions of each day—how a teacher talks to a student about her late arrival to class, how a parent is greeted when he enters the school building, or the ways in which you give and receive feedback.

We don't have models of Listening Leadership, nor have most of us learned *how* to listen well. No surprise, then, that listening functions like an underdeveloped muscle. But here's why it matters: School transformation arises from the micro-interactions of each day—how a teacher talks to a student about her late arrival to class, how a parent is greeted when he enters the school building, or the ways in which you give and receive feedback. These moments are the building blocks of a culture, and you can model a listening approach in each one.

A WORD ON MINDFULNESS

Mindfulness, a technique that has been used since ancient times, is an important backdrop to Listening Leadership. Since the 1970s, mindfulness has gathered steam internationally as a method for managing emotion and promoting physical and mental health. Programs based on Dr. Jon Kabat-Zinn's mindfulness-based stress reduction (MBSR) have found their way into prisons, hospitals, veteran centers, and schools. Research documenting the positive effects of mindfulness training continues to mount, pointing to improvements in focus, cognitive flexibility, stress reduction, emotional self-regulation, relationship satisfaction, and compassion.[22]

Listening allows us to practice two elements of mindfulness: *awareness*—bringing attention to the present moment by observing one's thoughts, feelings, and sensations without judgment—and *acceptance* of whatever is happening in that moment. At the same time, mindfulness enhances listening. Learning to step back from your autopilot thoughts in order to listen mindfully will help you transform any dysfunctional dynamics that get in the way of student learning. It will also help you cultivate empathy for yourself, emotional resilience, and an increasing ability to connect with others and across difference.

Mindful listening is the foundation of a comprehensive theory of change. By developing the competencies in this book, you will move the needle on

- Teacher retention: More teachers will stick around for the long haul if they feel respected, included, and heard.
- Teacher skill: Teachers will get better at their craft by working together in a safe, trusting climate where they're not anxious about the leader's next move.
- Family engagement: As you learn to listen, families will feel increasingly invested, welcomed, and willing to show up for you and your school or organization.
- Student-centered instruction: As you model the value of multiple perspectives and Level 3 street data, teachers will become more and more open to bringing student voice into the classroom culture.

THE ARTS ACADEMY REVISITED

Between 2009, when I first met the principal in our opening vignette, and 2013, the Arts Academy soared. In this 4-year window, the school received a number of positive parent reviews on an online school–quality website. Here are a few examples:

- "The Arts Academy has a strong set of teachers, an amazing principal, and a very involved parent community. During my four years so far there, I have seen things only get better for the kids, the school and the community."
- "The Arts Academy is a school with a fully engaged principal, completely committed staff, and an active family community.... Add to that, progressive ideals and a truly diverse student body, and it's near-perfect."
- "The Arts Academy is a great school with a hard-working and thoughtful principal, creative and dedicated teachers, and a giving and

involved parent community. We are a diverse group, with students from all different backgrounds and the principal and teachers work hard to create a welcoming, safe, and engaging learning environment for all the kids."

This is the very same principal whom veteran staff conspired to remove at the end of her first year! As a parent, I find these reviews compelling, and parent satisfaction is definitely an important measure of school improvement. But as an educator, I want additional data. California has long ranked public schools on an Academic Performance Index (API), scaled from 1 (low) to 10 (high), in two ways: against all other schools and against similar-demographic schools. I've always found the latter ranking more illuminating.

Between 2010 and 2013, the Arts Academy raised its similar-schools status from a 4 to an 8, an impressive increase. It's particularly significant that Latino and students of low socioeconomic status—two groups that had historically lagged behind—kept pace with the school's growth. On one standardized measure, Latino students even exceeded the overall proficiency level of 76% with 92% proficiency.

I'm convinced that the leader's shift in mindset and approach is what tilled the soil for the Arts Academy to bloom. Through listening, she created conditions for equitable school transformation that jump off the pages of the parent reviews. In 2012, she retired with great pride in the school and the work that her team had accomplished together.

What do you want your legacy to be? How do you need to grow as a leader to manifest this vision? If you were to invest in your own development, what might be true a year or 3 years from now? Here is the naked truth: No curriculum, program, or policy will save your team, school, or system. Only you, as a leader, can transform the current reality by learning to listen to your most vital resource—your people. The next chapter will reveal the exciting role of the brain in this process.

KEY TAKEAWAYS

- In the current climate, leaders at all levels are under tremendous stress and are pulled between competing archetypes (Manager, Driver, and Peacekeeper). Listening Leadership integrates the best of each approach into a powerful new way of being and leading.
- Communities have the ability to solve their own problems and grow their own solutions.

- The dominant language of school improvement, Discourse I, often serves to maintain the status quo and perpetuate inequity; Listening Leaders model a shift to Discourse II.
- Listening will help you address critical challenges including persistent inequity, student and adult trauma, the need for integrity in the face of pressure, and disconnected data.

LISTENING LEADER INQUIRY

Question: What do I do when my interest in Listening Leadership is at odds with the style and philosophy of other leaders I'm working with?

My thoughts: First of all, I would encourage you to think of Listening Leadership as a developmental process rather than as a model one adopts or rejects. Remember that many leaders have been influenced by the policy climate toward a more managerial or top-down style. Can you expose your colleagues to the principles and premises of Listening Leadership? Engage them in conversations about how and why to incorporate elements of this model? Ultimately, although you don't need to follow an identical playbook, you do want to have a baseline level of philosophical alignment with other leaders. You may benefit from a team retreat to hash this out.

Question: Taking feedback is hard for me—and apologizing to my staff, forget about it! Publicly apologizing will decrease my credibility and make me look weak. What are your thoughts?

My thoughts: Taking feedback is hard for most of us; I completely empathize. For me, the toughest part of being a school leader was that I felt as though I had to get everything "right," and didn't have room for my own mistakes and learning. In *Thanks for the Feedback: The Science and Art of Receiving Feedback Well*, author Douglas Stone writes, "Nothing affects the learning culture of an organization more than the skill with which its executive team receives feedback."[a] Welcoming feedback—and sometimes apologizing—is anything but weak; these moves model strength, integrity, and a willingness to grow. To prepare yourself to hear difficult feedback, try the following: Take a few deep breaths, have a supportive colleague or coach with you, tell yourself "it's just data for improvement," and identify one or two points that you want to work on.

Question: Standardized tests aren't going away, and I *do* feel accountable to them. If we don't raise scores, I could lose my job. How am I supposed to practice the data principles you offer?

(Continued)

My thoughts: This is a familiar bind for most leaders, and one of the persistent causes of inequity. Higher performing, affluent schools tend to enjoy more autonomy over curriculum and instruction, whereas schools in poor communities are constricted and held more accountable for specific results. I have found that as a school shows evidence of deep student learning, standardized test data become more of a secondary indicator of success rather than the whole story. At June Jordan School for Equity, all of our students engaged in a performance assessment process to exit 10th and 12th grades. They selected, revised, presented, and defended their best work before a group of teachers, students, and a significant adult in their lives. When we began to invite district officials to listen in, our relationship with the district shifted; no observer could deny the powerful learning demonstrated by students. This public process helped us negotiate a more comprehensive definition of success with the district.

Question: It's hard to stay true to my values on a day-to-day basis, given how many external mandates and pressures I juggle. Any advice?

My thoughts: Slowing down to listen to your own thoughts and feelings, and to set regular leadership intentions, will help you stay grounded in your values. This can be as simple as establishing a Daily Five ritual: Start your day with 5 minutes of writing or meditating on the question, *How will I model my values today?* Or find a colleague for a weekly Integrity Walk during which you spend 30 minutes walking and reflecting on the past week. Ask each other, "In the past week, where did you have success and where did you struggle to practice your values?" "What can you learn from either moment?" Finally, remember that integrity flows from listening to the voices of our students and families—the focus of Chapters 7 and 8.

* Stone, D., & Heen, S. (2014). *Thanks for the feedback: The science and art of receiving feedback well.* New York, NY: Viking, p. 10.

NOTES

1. Hargreaves, A., & Fullan, M. (2012). *Professional capital: Transforming teaching in every school.* New York, NY: Teachers College Press.
2. Metropolitan Life Insurance Company. (2013). The MetLife survey of the American teacher. New York, NY: Author.
3. Baldwin, J. (1962, January 14). As much truth as one can bear. *New York Times,* p. BR11, 38.
4. Eubanks, E., Parish, R., & Smith, D. (1997). Changing the discourse in schools. In P. M. Hall (Ed.), *Race, ethnicity, and multiculturalism: Policy and practice* (pp. 151–168). New York, NY: Routledge.
5. Gershenson, S., Holt, S. B., & Papageorge, N. W. (2015). *Who believes in me? The effect of student–teacher demographic match on teacher expectations.* Kalamazoo, MI: W. E. Upjohn Institute for Employment Research.

6. Brown, B. (2015). The anatomy of trust. Supersoul.TV. Retrieved from http://www.supersoul.tv/supersoul-sessions/the-anatomy-of-trust

7. Mintrop, H. (2012). Bridging accountability obligations, professional values and (perceived) student needs with integrity. *Journal of Educational Administration, 50*, 695–726.

8. Magee, M. (2016, May 4). More leeway on standardized testing. *San Diego Union-Tribune*. Retrieved from http://www.sandiegouniontribune.com/news/2016/may/04/standardized-testing-cindy-marten-san-diego/

9. Goleman, D. (1995). *Emotional intelligence*. New York, NY: Bantam.

10. Goleman, D. (2004). What makes a leader? *Harvard Business Review 82*(1), 82–91. (Original work published 1998)

11. Labby, S., Lunenburg, F. C., & Slate, J. R. (2012). Emotional intelligence and academic success: A conceptual analysis for educational leaders. *International Journal of Educational Leadership Preparation, 7*(1), 1–11.

12. Stone, H., Parker, J. D., & Wood, L. M. (2005). Report on the Ontario Principals' Council leadership study. Consortium for Research on Emotional Intelligence in Organizations. Retrieved at www.eiconsortium.org/pdf/opc_leadership_study_final_report.pdf

13. Maudling, W. S., Peters, G. B., Roberts, J., Leonard, E., & Sparkman, L. (2012). Emotional intelligence and resilience as predictors of leadership in school administrators. *Journal of Leadership Studies, 5*(4), 20–29.

14. American Psychological Association. (2016). Trauma. Retrieved from http://www.apa.org/topics/trauma/

15. Emdin, C. (2016, March 22). How can white teachers do better by urban kids of color? *Colorlines*. Retrieved from http://www.colorlines.com/articles/how-can-white-teachers-do-better-urban-kids-color

16. Emdin, C. (2016). *For white folks who teach in the 'hood ... and the rest of y'all too: Reality pedagogy and urban education*. Boston, MA: Beacon Press, p. 23.

17. Treatment and Services Adaptation Center. (n.d.). Secondary traumatic stress. Retrieved from https://traumaawareschools.org/secondaryStress

18. Popham, W. J. (2016, April 4). The fatal flaw of educational assessment. *Education Week*. Retrieved from http://www.edweek.org/ew/articles/2016/03/23/the-fatal-flaw-of-educational-assessment.html

19. Originally developed by Hawkins, D. (1974). *The informed vision*. New York, NY: Agathon Press. Elaborated on by Cohen, D., Raudenbush, S., & Ball, D. (2003). Resources, instruction, and research. *Educational Evaluation and Policy Analysis 25*, 119–142.

20. Hattie, J. (2013). *Visible learning: A synthesis of over 800 meta-analyses relating to achievement*. New York, NY: Routledge.

21. Janusik, L., Fullenkamp, L., & Partese, L. (n.d.). Listening facts. Retrieved from http://d1025403.site.myhosting.com/files.listen.org/Facts.htm; Weinrauch, J. D., & Swanda, J. R. (1975). Examining the significance of listening: An exploratory study of contemporary management. *Journal of Business Communications 13*(1), 25–32; Flynn, J., & Faulk, L. (2008). Listening in the workplace. *Kentucky Journal of Communication, 27*(1), 15–31.

22. Studies drawn from Davis, D. M., and Hayes, J. A. (2012, July/August). What are the benefits of mindfulness? American Psychological Association. Retrieved from http://www.apa.org/monitor/2012/07-08/ce-corner.aspx

Part 1

AWARENESS

AWARENESS

Chapter 2

The Core Tenets of Listening Leadership

Preview: Listening Leadership begins with understanding how our brains shape human dynamics and how this understanding can be the key to school transformation.

This chapter is designed to help you:

- Understand why listening is an effective and brain-savvy approach to leadership.
- Learn the core tenets of Listening Leadership and the brain "mandates" they suggest.
- Diagnose brain-based stress triggers and response patterns in your school or organization.

THE LEADER WHO WANTED TO WRITE PEOPLE UP

Estella was the principal of a thriving school in a high-poverty community when Jason became her supervisor. A woman of color with a PhD, a knack for raising private dollars to support her school, and a deep commitment to equity, Estella was well regarded across the district. Jason was a White man with similar values around equity, whose leadership of a successful elementary school had earned him a promotion to the central office. Knowing that he had credibility as a school leader, Estella felt excited to work with him.

A few months into Jason's first year on the job, Estella's students prepared for a state-mandated test. She had positioned a young teacher as the testing coordinator and was pleased to watch him breathe new life into the dry test-prep curriculum. Just before the exam, however, the teacher made an administrative error. While counting test booklets, he forgot to tally answer sheets, and on testing day, he realized they were short by 25.

In a panic, he ran to Estella and confessed his blunder: "I screwed up. I've called, emailed, and texted the district testing director, but I haven't heard back." While Estella reached out to Jason and several principal colleagues in an effort to locate more sheets, her assistant principal discovered that the school could readminister the test a few weeks later for a small fine. In Estella's mind, end of story: The teacher had apologized profusely to all affected parties, and they had a plan. Relieved, she emailed Jason to let him know the problem was resolved and offered to host any students from other schools who needed to make up the test.

The next day, Jason showed up in her office, asked how this had happened, and requested the teacher's name. Here is Estella's reflection on that moment: "I was about to tell him, but then I stopped and thought, *Huh . . . why is he asking me this?* So I asked, 'Why do you want to know?' And his response was clear: 'Because you need to write him up.' That's when things got contentious." Estella refused: "I'm not writing him up. He made a mistake, it's fixed, and everything is fine now." Jason countered, "Well, you need to document what went wrong."

By this point, Estella's blood pressure had risen, her shoulders were tight, and her cheeks flushed as she braced for a fight. Confused by Jason's directive, she argued back, "I actually *don't* need to write him up. You write someone up when something dangerous happens or if you're laying the groundwork for a serious letter of concern. This is a good employee who made a mistake and fixed it. I don't expect it to happen again." In her mind, writing up an employee creates emotional distance, whereas developing employees requires trust and proximity.

Eventually, Jason and Estella parted ways without resolution. She felt that she had handled the situation appropriately and that disciplining the teacher would destroy their nascent relationship. *This teacher trusts me and owes me one now,* she thought to herself. *If I were to write him up, he probably wouldn't come to me to help him solve other problems.*

A few weeks later, Jason and Estella met again, at which point it became clear that he was no longer suggesting disciplinary action; he was mandating it. When she maintained her position, Jason said: "Well, I would hate to have to write *you* up." At this point, Estella felt exasperated and simply replied, "Well, I would hate for you to write me up too." Recently, she reflected, "I couldn't believe we were having this conversation." What had begun as a novice teacher's slip-up had evolved into a battle of wills between two positional leaders.

Estella never disciplined her teacher, and Jason eventually turned a blind eye to the situation. Although he remained her boss for another year, she made a silent commitment not to reach out to him again for support. She simply didn't trust him. Jason and Estella held conflicting beliefs about supervision and leadership. More to the point for this chapter, each was driven by primal human needs that are rooted in the brain and overlaid with differences in race, ethnicity, gender, and role. As a new district leader, Jason wanted to position himself as an expert and authority figure who could manage his direct reports. His needs bumped up against Estella's equally strong desire for independence, fairness, and an intact relationship with her teacher.

Ultimately, Jason's approach failed. This chapter will help us understand why.

LISTENING IS BRAIN-SAVVY

Schools are rife with stories like Estella and Jason's, beneath which lie not only issues of power and identity, which we will delve into in Chapter 3, but also the inescapable chemistry of the human brain. Estella's fraught relationship with her supervisor diverted cognitive and emotional resources that she needed in order to lead her school. Had Jason learned to listen differently, he and Estella might have formed an alliance around their shared equity values.

This chapter illuminates the brain's ability to derail communication in the process of school transformation. I offer five key tenets of neuroscience and pair each one with a brain "mandate" to guide your day-to-day actions and decisions. Table 2.1 provides a summary of the tenets and mandates.

Although as leaders we listen all the time, we rarely accord this act the attention it deserves. Effective listening is a complex process that requires us to visualize and hear the speaker's message, locate it in working memory, perceive it through our own frame of reference, interpret verbal and nonverbal cues, and respond.[1] Many factors affect a listening exchange: age, race, culture, gender, and other identity features; the listener's attitude; and the social context of the communication, such as role differences, setting, and time.[2]

TABLE 2.1 CORE TENETS OF LISTENING LEADERSHIP

Core Tenet	Brain Mandate
1. Our brains are wired for survival first.	**Feed the lizard.** • Understand basic human needs, from food and movement to laughter and joy. • Address people's basic needs, even if they appear trivial to you. • Create a visually appealing environment.
2. Our brains react to survival threats through fight, flight, or "tend-and-befriend."	**Calm the amygdala.** • Bring awareness to your own thoughts, feelings, and triggers. • Be attentive to the emotional states and needs of others. • Learn to listen in ways that calm the emotional brain.
3. Social threats signal survival threats to our brains.	**Reimagine rewards.** • Begin to track what functions as a threat or reward for various people. • Expand the types of rewards you provide, from thank-you notes to verbal appreciations to simply taking time to listen and connect with someone.
4. Every brain grows in the right conditions.	**Water for deep roots.** • Invest time and resources to make professional learning meaningful. • Organize professional learning around inquiry questions—collective and teacher driven. • Interrupt biased discourse, which insinuates that students of color, English language learners, or special education students are less intelligent.
5. Organizations have core memories.	**Embrace "storientation."** • Reflect on and share your story as a leader. • Be curious about the stories of others. • Pay close attention to organizational narratives, both positive and negative.

Listening is a brain-savvy leadership approach for several reasons:

• It requires us to slow down and access our thinking brain.
• It quiets our emotional brain and allows pertinent new data to enter.
• It forges alliances by coupling our brain with the speaker's.
• It helps us calm the speaker's emotional brain and prime him or her for learning.

In Jason and Estella's case, differences in race, gender, and positional power may have contributed to communication miscues, which a listening orientation could have helped to bridge. Before we dive into the core tenets, let's pass quickly through the neighborhoods of the brain.

 MAKE IT MINDFUL

Consider how much conscious attention you bring to the phases of listening. Here are tips to boost your mindful listening:

- Flag *key points* for yourself during a conversation: "I want to remember and store this important piece of information."
- Write down a speaker's *key words* to firm up your memory.
- Ask yourself, *How might I be perceiving the speaker or the speaker's message through my own cultural or gender biases and frame of reference?*
- Pay attention to the speaker's nonverbal cues as well as his or her words. (Learning to notice and strengthen your listening skills is the crux of Chapters 4, 5, and 6.)

THE NEIGHBORHOODS OF THE BRAIN

Think of the brain as having three main neighborhoods to become familiar with as a leader: the brain stem, the limbic system, and the neocortex. (See Figure 2.1 for a graphic representation.) The brain stem, sometimes called the **lizard brain** for its resemblance to the entire brain of a reptile, is the oldest, most primitive neighborhood. It houses autopilot functions like breathing, heartbeat, blood pressure, digestion, and reactions to incoming stimuli. When the lizard brain gets a distress signal, it ratchets up heart rate and other physiological systems to prepare for survival.

The **limbic system**, also known as the emotional brain, constitutes the middle neighborhood. This region controls our feelings, impulses, and drives, and harbors **implicit biases**—the unconscious beliefs and attitudes that contribute to inequity in schools.[3] Our limbic networks shape how we interpret and react to our environment, processing incoming signals within one fifth of a second to decide if we are facing a danger or a possible reward.[4] Once the limbic brain has encoded a stimulus—a person, or even a physical stimulus like a new computer system—as a threat, it's hard to undo that association. Hence, in Estella's case, she held on to a negative

FIGURE 2.1   THE NEIGHBORHOODS OF THE BRAIN

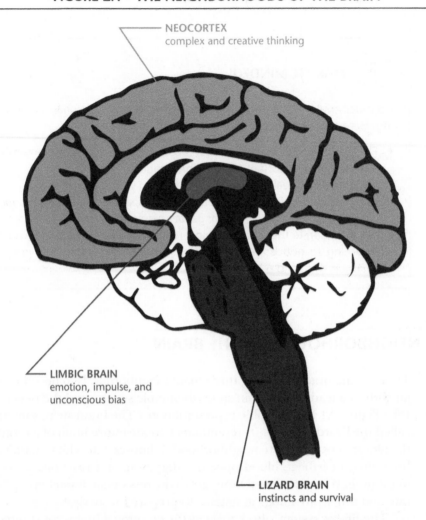

NEOCORTEX
complex and creative thinking

LIMBIC BRAIN
emotion, impulse, and
unconscious bias

LIZARD BRAIN
instincts and survival

perception of Jason after their conflict. In this chapter, we are going to focus on one key part of the limbic system called the amygdala.

The brain's most recently developed neighborhood is the **neocortex**, or prefrontal cortex. This "thinking brain" is unique to humans, allowing us to deliberate and respond thoughtfully. It is the cradle of imagination, organization, and planning. Referred to as the site of our **executive function**, the neocortex acts as the Oval Office of the brain. In our best

MAKE IT MINDFUL

Recall the last communication breakdown you experienced at work. Did you or the other person shut down emotionally, walk away, or blow up? If so, the lizard and limbic brains were working in tandem. As a leader, you have tremendous influence over the conditions that stimulate these regions, including the tone you set and the ways in which you listen to people.

moments, we sit at that presidential desk weighing our options and acting with strategic intent. Even though this slower pathway is always available, the fast-paced and emotionally charged reality of school life can cause the brain to bypass the neocortex and default to primal responses. Thankfully, we can retrain our brains by learning to slow down and listen before reacting.

Table 2.2 summarizes the main functions of each of the brain's neighborhoods.

TENET 1: OUR BRAINS ARE WIRED FOR SURVIVAL FIRST

Although the brain holds the keys to growth and learning, it can also interfere with our efforts at school transformation. Imagine the following scenarios. A student arrives at your office with a referral after yelling at her teacher. A colleague becomes so aggravated in a meeting that he gets up and walks out. A distraught parent begs you to give her son another chance

TABLE 2.2 THE MAIN REGIONS OF THE BRAIN

Region	Purpose/Functions
Brain stem, or lizard brain	• Houses autopilot functions like breathing, heartbeat, blood pressure, digestion, and reactions to stimuli
Limbic system, or emotional brain	• Controls subconscious feelings, impulses, and drives • Harbors unconscious biases • Drives how we interpret and react to our environment
Neocortex, or thinking brain	• Processes information slowly, allowing us to think critically, strategize, and respond in productive ways • Home of imagination, organization, and planning

to graduate. In each example, you face a person engulfed by emotions kindled inside the limbic system, in an almond-shaped object called the **amygdala**. We have to know how to listen and respond in brain-friendly ways, or we risk escalating the situation.

The amygdala stores memories of emotional experiences—positive and negative—and drives a fundamental principle of evolutionary biology: All human beings seek to avoid threats and pursue rewards. My colleague Zaretta Hammond likens the amygdala to a guard dog training the brain to remember people and situations that should be avoided.[5] When the amygdala perceives a serious threat, it leapfrogs over the thinking brain and sends alarm bells directly to the lizard brain in what's called an **amygdala hijack**, a term coined by author Daniel Goleman. The stress hormone **cortisol** floods the brain and shifts resources available for thinking toward survival.

There's a critical flaw in this process: Our emotional systems are predisposed to error and often resistant to change. When threatened, the brain struggles to discern the subtle signals that help us solve problems and gain insight. Instead, we tend to generalize more based on past experiences; connect things that are not actually connected; avoid taking risks; perceive small stressors as large stressors;[6] and behave impulsively in ways that we later regret. Without awareness, we may react in ways that undermine the culture we want to create. Here's the good news: As a leader, you can train your brain to recognize an amygdala hijack in yourself and others in order to choose a productive response. The first step to building a healthy culture is learning to "feed" the lizard brain in ways that keep the amygdala in check.

Here's the good news: As a leader, you can train your brain to recognize an amygdala hijack in yourself and others in order to choose a productive response.

Brain Mandate: Feed the Lizard

To leverage the power of listening, we must first feed the lizard. This means addressing people's basic needs, even if those needs appear trivial to you. If a printer is broken, make sure it gets fixed. If paper supplies are low, ensure they are replenished. If teachers feel stressed out because they don't know which summer dates to hold, set and communicate dates. If invoices aren't getting processed, reassign this task or have a hard conversation with the responsible employee.

Feeding the lizard also means paying attention to the physical environment, including halls, walls, meeting spaces, and classrooms. I recently visited a school that exudes *downtrodden* from the moment one sets foot on campus. The grass is dead, the paint is peeling, the digital bulletin board is broken, and there's no student work on the walls. These visual cues negatively prime the lizard brain to be on guard, which prevents students and adults from relaxing into learning. Positively prime the brain by creating a visually appealing environment.

Finally, understand the physical needs of human beings, from food and movement to laughter and joy. If you convene people for more than an hour, have snacks available to regulate their blood sugar. If you're designing a professional development (PD) session, try to build in at least one opportunity to move every hour (see Chapter 10 for many examples). All of the physiological and operational examples here sit at the bottom of Maslow's hierarchy of needs and represent low-hanging fruit you can pluck on the path to school transformation. Incidentally, feeding the lizard is an innate strength of the Manager, but often a weakness of the Peacekeeper. If you found yourself in the Peacekeeper quadrant in Chapter 1, you might focus your energy on this idea.

 MAKE IT MINDFUL

Take a close look at your work environment through the lizard's lens and ask yourself, *Is it welcoming? Are public spaces and workspaces clean and well organized? Are the walls and halls bursting with well-labeled student work? Are there vibrant paint colors and simple touches like plants, tapestries, and fresh coffee brewing that invite the lizard brain to rest?* If visual design isn't your thing, model a leader-ful organization and invite interested parties to form a design or beautification committee. Be sure to give them a budget!

TENET 2: OUR BRAINS REACT TO SURVIVAL THREATS THROUGH FIGHT, FLIGHT, OR "TEND-AND-BEFRIEND"

Our reactions to perceived threats are rooted in the brain, but they also stem from cultural conditioning, including our experiences around gender, race, socioeconomic status, culture, birth order, and family of origin. Think about yourself. When triggered, do you tend to lash out, walk away, or reach out to a colleague for support? Where did you learn that coping mechanism?

Lashing out and walking away are vintage **fight-or-flight** responses, the best-known patterns of reaction to threat. Remember Jason and Estella, our district supervisor and principal from the opening vignette? When Jason asked her to name the teacher in question, Estella almost answered before she recognized a threat signal and froze. Her brain cued "Danger!" to its reptilian region, which responded by increasing her heart rate and rushing blood to her cheeks. Her next move was to fight back with an assertive "no"—a classic fight response. When they later stopped having the conversation at all, they were both engaged in a form of flight.

Here is another story to illustrate flight. As a principal, I facilitated a Math Department meeting in which teachers were reviewing their students' grade data. Most people had a preponderance of A's, B's, and C's with a few D's and F's; however, one teacher—a veteran with a more traditional view of grading—had over 60% F's. As we began to discuss the data, he became visibly agitated, got up, and left the room. His social "safety"— namely, his credibility and status on the team—had been threatened, and self-preservation instincts told him to flee.

UCLA psychologist Shelley Taylor and her colleagues ran a study that led to an alternative stress paradigm that they call the **tend-and-befriend** model. The researchers found that although women show the same *physiological* reactions to acute stress that men do, they often respond differently by using caretaking behaviors to protect themselves and their loved ones—what Taylor named the "tend" element—or by forging strategic alliances with a larger social group, often other women— the "befriend" element.[7]

Although gendered patterns exist, we shouldn't stereotype men or women. I know many female leaders whose first move is to fight, and many men who are incredible at tending and befriending. We also can't filter out other aspects of identity, such as race and culture, when looking at how people experience and respond to social threats. Chapter 3 takes a deeper look at these intersections.

The bottom line is that self-preservation shows up differently in different people. Although there is no cookie-cutter response to stress, our underlying biology binds us all in the pursuit of survival and avoidance of danger.

MAKE IT MINDFUL

Think about a colleague, parent, or student with whom you have struggled in the recent past. Which of the four response patterns do *you* exhibit in this dynamic? Which does the *other person* exhibit? What behaviors or factors seem to trigger each of you?

Brain Mandate: Calm the Amygdala

Tenet 2 suggests a second brain mandate: Learn to listen in ways that calm the amygdala—both yours and others'. (Chapters 4 and 5 will provide concrete strategies.) Bring awareness to your thoughts and feelings. Become attentive to the emotional needs of others. Cultivate the ability to manage your own judgments and anxieties without superimposing them onto your interactions.

Listening facilitates alliances across difference.

You may be muttering to yourself, "But I'm not a therapist!" and you're right. However, keep in mind the symbiotic link between the brain's emotional and rational functions. You *are* a leader who wants people to get better at what they do. The only road to that destination is a healthy emotional climate in which people are relaxed enough to learn, grow, and collaborate. Exhibit 2.1 explores a story of how listening facilitates alliances by coupling two brains together.

EXHIBIT 2.1 LISTENING CONNECTS TWO BRAINS TOGETHER

The brain's basis for listening is so powerful that it shows up on MRI scans. During effective communication, information transfers between the speaker's and listener's brains in a process called **neural coupling**.[a] Let's visit David Reyes, a former principal who now leads a central-office team, to watch this process in action. In Reyes's new role, his first act was to hold 30-minute listening sessions with each team member to gather data and build relationship.

(Continued)

One day, he visited the office of a woman who had worked in the district for 40 years and seemed eager to share her experiences. When he walked in, his brain digested two pieces of information: pictures of her family on the wall and a long script in her hands filled with talking points. She said anxiously, "People have told me this half hour goes by really fast, so I wanted to make sure that I remember everything."

Rather than control the agenda, Reyes casually mentioned her photos. The woman began to speak of her deep pride in her children and the devastation she felt when one family member was tragically killed and another died of an illness shortly thereafter. By this point, Reyes was sitting quietly with tears in his eyes as their brains coupled through the power of her stories. In his words, "I just fell apart. It reminded me that we so often get caught up in our lists and checking things off that we don't take time to just listen to people—to hear them as people and not cogs."

After sharing these experiences, Reyes's colleague began to review her talking points, but only got through half before their time was up. She again looked worried, but Reyes reassured her, "We will sit down like this at least once a quarter." She breathed a sigh of relief. As they closed the meeting, he affirmed her vulnerability by saying, "My heart breaks around the loss of your loved ones. For you to share that with me in our first meeting, I'm floored." Her response was telling: "I just feel comfortable sharing with you. I feel like you'll hear me." It's worth noting that Reyes is a 40-something Latino man, and his colleague is a 60-something African American woman. Listening facilitates alliances across difference.

[a] Stephens, G., Silbert, L., & Hasson, U. (2010). Speaker-listener neural coupling underlies successful communication. *Proceedings of the National Academy of Science* *107*(32), 14425–14430.

TENET 3: SOCIAL THREATS SIGNAL SURVIVAL THREATS TO OUR BRAINS

We human beings are remarkably predictable in our longings. We want to belong, to feel valued and worthy of respect. We crave a sense of control and certitude in our lives. We want to be treated fairly. These *social* needs register in our brains akin to *survival* needs like physical safety, food, and water. Take feedback, for example. Author David Rock writes that the phrase "Can I give you some feedback?" is the equivalent of hearing footsteps behind you in a dark alley.[8] As leaders, we must recognize common threat triggers in schools and orchestrate a low-threat, high-reward environment.

In coaching school leaders, I have found Rock's **SCARF** model to be a helpful tool.[9] SCARF is an acronym for five social domains that have the potential to activate fight, flight, or tend-and-befriend responses. *Status* refers to a person's sense of value and standing in the organization. *Certainty* alludes to clarity over expectations, outcomes, and next steps. (The lizard needs this.) *Autonomy* speaks to the adult learner's need to feel control and agency in his or her work. *Relatedness* refers to a sense of emotional safety, belonging, and membership in the tribe, so to speak. *Fairness* represents the need to be treated justly by others, in particular by the leader.

This model offers a powerful lens for viewing every aspect of school life. Table 2.3 illustrates common ways that leaders activate threats and rewards in schools—either consciously or unconsciously.

TABLE 2.3   EXAMPLES OF THREATS AND REWARDS IN SCHOOLS

SCARF Domain	Threat Activation	Reward Activation
Status *Do others value me here?*	Being publically humiliated Being perceived as incompetent	Receiving public praise Being perceived as capable and smart
Certainty *Am I clear on what's expected of me and where we are headed as an organization?*	Getting mixed messages about a new initiative Not knowing what really matters to the leader	Clearly understanding how and when decisions are made Forming explicit agreements with the leader about next steps
Autonomy *Do I have a sense of agency in my work? Do I believe that my actions will make a difference?*	Being told what, how, and when to teach your subject matter Having a supervisor mandate something you don't agree wth	Being provided with several curriculum options Being trusted to make good decisions
Relatedness *Do I belong here? Am I safe here?*	Having to attend meetings with an "elephant in the room" Feeling as though there's an "in" group on staff that you don't belong to	Feeling that the leader is respectful and empathetic when you are struggling Feeling that the leader is curious and asks genuine questions about you
Fairness *Do I feel advantaged or disadvantaged? Does the leader single me out?*	A perception of bias or favoritism coming from the leader Being the one person not asked to give feedback to the leader	Being asked by the leader, "What support will you need to improve in the ways we've discussed? Allocating by the leader of an equitable supply budget to each department

Note. Inspired by the National Equity Project's SCARF game

Revisiting Jason and Estella, our supervisor and principal, we might wonder whether Jason's actions are driven by an expectation of *status* in his new role and deference from Estella. Although he was a successful principal, this is his first central-office gig, and he's quick to assert authority in the hopes of appearing promotion worthy. He also appears attached to *certainty* over the outcome of Estella's situation, taking the position that administrators *must* document staff errors, rather than entering into dialogue with her around possible solutions. Likely unaware of these subtle drivers, he takes a dogmatic approach rather than listening to Estella.

Estella is grappling with a need for *autonomy* over her school and *relatedness* with her teacher. She feels that Jason's approach lacks *fairness* and is unnecessarily punitive. Protective of her budding connection with a young colleague, she perceives Jason as trying to control a situation he doesn't understand, though she recognizes why he is predisposed to do this. In short, Jason is acting out the governing beliefs of the system in which they work.

 MAKE IT MINDFUL

Train your brain to slow down and detect social threats at work. If you witness or experience a strong emotional reaction, ask yourself, *Which SCARF area is being triggered right now: status, certainty, autonomy, relatedness, or fairness? What do I or the other person need in order to return to a sense of well-being?*

Understanding the impact of social threats will help you hold your positional power more carefully. Keep in mind that your title itself—be it "coach," "department lead," or "principal"—might trigger a social threat in a status-sensitive colleague. Know that your words and tone carry extra weight. Explore creative forms of reward like public praise, clear meeting outcomes, and offering teachers choice in professional learning.

Brain Mandate: Reimagine Rewards

Tenet 3 suggests that we must not only minimize threats but also reimagine rewards in the context of our adult communities. First and foremost, begin to *track* what functions as a threat or reward for various people. For one person, a reward might look like a promotion. For another, it entails public accolades. For others, you'll need to build a deeper relationship or provide more transparency around decision making. One leader I know leaves thank-you notes in mailboxes every time someone takes leadership outside of his or her official role. Another issues "wow" awards at meetings to celebrate teacher innovations.

These options will pop out like 3-D images once you start to pay attention. You need only cultivate awareness of the signals people send to know how to reward them effectively.

TENET 4: EVERY BRAIN GROWS IN THE RIGHT CONDITIONS

Now that we understand the brain's structure and primal tendencies, let's turn our attention to its finer roadways. The brain is composed of 100 billion cells called **neurons** that constitute our gray and white matter. (Figure 2.2 is an illustration of a neuron.) Neurons function in collaborative networks, transmitting and processing information through electrical impulses and the release of neurotransmitters across tiny gaps called

FIGURE 2.2   ANATOMY OF A NEURON

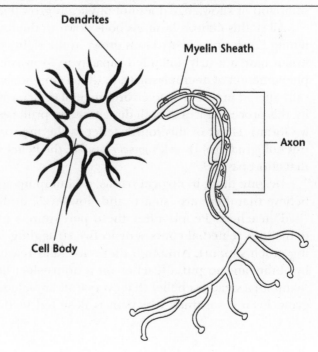

synapses. These networks grow stronger and more efficient as we use them, eventually banding together to establish a **neural pathway**—like a groove in the brain's relief map. Listening Leaders work hard to create the best conditions for these pathways to proliferate in the brains of students and staff.

Well-worn neural pathways allow us to act with **automaticity**—to do things intuitively without having to think about low-level details. For example, the first time I led a Socratic Seminar with my students, I had to walk myself through every last minutiae: how to organize the classroom space, what words I would use to introduce the activity, how I would teach students sentence stems for discussion, and the role I would play during the seminar, down to the type of notes I would take! After using this structure every week for a year, it became intuitive. Not only did *I* develop deep brain grooves around how to facilitate a Socratic discussion, but my students did too, and together we felt like a well-oiled machine.

Automaticity frees up brain space for higher order thinking. Whether you're designing a learning experience for students or for adults, be sure to couple new content with practice, reflection, and repetition. This cycle—learn, practice, reflect, and repeat—carves new neural pathways that enable complex and creative thinking. It also explains why traditional, sit-and-get instruction doesn't work for most learners. The passive consumption of knowledge does not physically grow the brain.

All of this neuron business boils down to the fourth core tenet of Listening Leadership: Every brain grows in the right conditions. In fact, our brains have a nearly unlimited capacity to form connections through the phenomenon of **neuroplasticity**, in which synapses and pathways are physically altered in response to environmental or behavioral changes. (In reality, this process moves in both directions: we prune as many connections as we form.) Think of this fourth tenet as the neuroscience companion to psychologist Carol Dweck's *growth mindset*, the belief that ability is fluid and that effort pays off,[10]

Despite these biological truths, we bump up against colleagues who believe that there are "smart" and "low-level" students, and "good" and "bad" teachers. People offer these perceptions to justify tracking students into remedial courses or to fire struggling teachers before offering much support. Although there are valid reasons to group students by ability and to put a teacher on a nonreelect list, Listening Leaders maintain a steadfast belief that every human being, and every brain, can grow. Even if we think a person is ill-suited to the work, we maintain

Listening Leaders maintain a steadfast belief that every human being, and every brain, can grow.

faith in his or her ability to evolve, and, when necessary, we coach him or her into a new career.

Let's apply Tenet 4 to Estella and Jason, our principal and principal supervisor from the opening vignette. Estella viewed her young colleague's error as developmental: In her mind, he would learn and grow from it. We don't know how Jason *viewed* the error, but we do know his preferred response: Write the teacher up. Did he believe that the teacher would improve through being disciplined? Neuroscience indicates the opposite: To develop, our brains need emotional safety, positive feedback, and room for error. According to John Hattie, a school climate in which "error and trust are welcomed as opportunities to learn" has a .72 effect size on student learning (.4 represents the hinge point above which any increase has a positive impact).[11] Believing that every brain will grow isn't just a nicety; it's a precondition for achievement.

Brain Mandate: Water for Deep Roots

Tenet 4 suggests the following brain mandate: Water (the brain) for deep roots. Listening Leaders create fertile conditions for the brain's gray matter to grow. This begins with rejecting an "everything but the kitchen sink" approach to PD and prioritizing depth over breadth. I work with many schools that are simultaneously incorporating four or five different instructional initiatives, and my first advice is always the same: Focus.

Look at your data and choose an instructional focus for the year. Identify key evidence (Levels 1, 2, and 3) to track the impact. Design professional learning around that focus, with lots of room for teacher voice and choice. One school I coached decided to engage teachers in a yearlong inquiry around this question: To what extent do we see evidence of meaningful engagement between students and tasks in our classrooms? The staff read relevant literature, observed each other's classrooms, and coplanned lessons to apply their learning.

Watering for deep roots also implies a dogged commitment to equity and to interrupting bias. If you hear *any* discourse that disparages the intelligence of students or grown-ups on campus, you must be courageous enough to interrupt it. Practice your values, and remind the speaker that every brain grows in the right conditions.

Chapters 6 and 10 will reveal concrete strategies for addressing this brain mandate, but for now, consider the following suggestions:

- Structure professional learning around a yearlong or semester-long inquiry question
- Support teachers to create their own inquiry questions related to the schoolwide focus
- Refine your ability to ask reflective questions in instructional or supervisory one-on-one meetings
- Build in lots of time for teachers to learn and practice new approaches
- Model a developmental, versus a punitive, climate in which it's safe to make mistakes

TENET 5: ORGANIZATIONS HAVE CORE MEMORIES

The human brain is hardwired to understand the world through stories. This is so true that psychologists often refer to stories as "psychologically privileged," meaning that our memory treats them differently from other types of information.[12] By organizing our life experiences into a story structure, we try to create order from what feels like chaos. Organizations are no different, except that now you have dozens or perhaps hundreds of people trying to form a *collective* story out of their reality.[13] This is a tough charge and prone to distortion.

Just as individuals have core memories, so do organizations. Inside every school or team are stories that give shape to a collective identity: "We are a team that . . ."; "We are a school where . . ." A key role of Listening Leaders is to curate hopeful stories while helping shape a narrative around difficult experiences. Here's the catch: The brain has a **negativity bias**, meaning that people give more weight to bad experiences than to good ones. In a fragile culture, negative core memories stack up and begin to infect the climate as well as the leader's credibility. In a healthy culture, positive core memories help people build resilience to weather tough times.

A key role of Listening Leaders is to curate hopeful stories while helping shape a narrative around difficult experiences.

Estella's tussle with Jason left her with a negativity bias toward him. On a larger scale, it seeded an organizational core memory that jeopardized Jason's reputation. Estella was socially networked with her fellow principals and other leaders across the system. After her first line of fight-and-flight responses, she approached a colleague for advice, asking, "How do I deal with this situation?" Because Estella and Jason never resolved their conflict, no counternarrative emerged to restore Jason's reputation. What if they had participated in a restorative conversation to rebuild trust? What if he had apologized for his missteps?

Understanding that organizations have core memories will help you reframe each interaction as a plot point in a larger story. The implications of this tenet are far reaching. An instructional leader's greatest challenge is transforming an unhealthy school culture into a healthy one that promotes lifelong learning for students and adults. This can't happen in a school where people are distressed and operating from overactive emotional brains.

Lead in ways that overcome the brain's negativity bias by immersing people in positive experiences. Create a culture of affirmation to release happy neurotransmitters, which tell our brains to remember and repeat the behavior that elicited the affirmation so that we can feel good again. Create a culture in which it is safe to make mistakes and take risks. You can translate threats into opportunities by listening and responding with awareness.

Brain Mandate: Embrace "Storientation"

Tenet 5 suggests a final brain mandate: embrace **"storientation,"** or close attention to the role of stories in equitable school transformation. Notice and curate three types of story: self, other, and organization. First, think about who you are as a leader and who you aspire to be. Consider the pivotal moments that have shaped your journey. Share pieces of your story with students, parents, and colleagues to model social-emotional intelligence and the power of vulnerability.

Second, demonstrate curiosity about the stories of others. Ask people who they are and what they care about. Tap into personal narratives as a source of connection and to activate a sense of reward.

Finally, pay keen attention to your organization's core memories. In *Primal Leadership*, Daniel Goleman writes that leaders "manage meaning" for a group, "offering a way to interpret, and so react emotionally to, a given situation."[14] Cue your brain to actively manage meaning for your team. Craft a hopeful, forward-moving story line. If you make a mistake, own it quickly and candidly lest it become a negative core memory. Find ways to visually curate and celebrate positive stories—for example, in a newsletter or on the school or office walls. Debbie Meier's wonderful book *The Power of Their Ideas* offers a storientation exemplar in the letters Meier wrote to her families as the principal of Central Park East Elementary School in Harlem, New York City. Exhibit 2.2 tells the story of one leader I coached who had to learn to overcome her staff's negativity bias.

EXHIBIT 2.2   OVERCOMING THE BRAIN'S NEGATIVITY BIAS

A few years back, I supported a school where teachers voiced concern over the lack of strong "systems." "What happens after I send a student to the office?" "How will class composition be decided each year?" "How is basic information communicated to us on a daily basis?" They were desperate for clarity around basic procedures.

This was the basic stuff, but teachers also lacked a vision of where the school was headed and what really mattered to their principal. So many initiatives were floating around the district that nobody knew what to pay attention to. Instead, they fixated on what felt controllable, such as not having enough sticky notes or the delivery mechanism for the bulletin.

In coaching the principal, I learned that she was so triggered by her teachers' complaints that she lacked empathy for them. She saw them as whiny, immature, and focused on "trivial" issues. In the battlefield of perceptions, however, the principal was losing. Her staff's experiences of uncertainty had begun to aggregate into a negative story about her. I needed to stage an intervention.

In one coaching conversation, I leveraged our growing trust to confront the principal on her dismissive attitude toward the teachers. "Listen," I said. "You may see the bulletin as trivial, but for the staff it's creating a level of uncertainty that distracts them from their work. Your job as the leader is to get on the balcony and see the whole picture. In this case, you have an opportunity to pluck a piece of low-hanging fruit by addressing concerns over the bulletin. If you do, I guarantee that you'll buy goodwill, enable your staff to think with you about higher level matters, and 'lower' everyone's **affective filter**." (*Affective filter* is a term coined by Dulay and Burt to describe the interplay of negative social and emotional factors that can interfere with our ability to process information. These factors include anxiety, insecurity, boredom, and irritation, among others.[a])

This push led to an "ah-ha" moment for the leader, who shed some tears as she realized that she needed to address these issues so that her school could move forward. She committed to listening to the staff, and when she did, the culture began to shift.

[a] Dulay, H., & Burt, M. (1977). Remarks on creativity in language acquisition. In M. Burt, H. Dulay, & M. Finnochiaro (Eds.), *Viewpoints on English as a second language* (pp. 95–126). New York, NY: Regents.

An Epilogue on Estella and Jason

Months after Estella and Jason's dispute, their relationship remained cordial but distant. Estella assumed that Jason stopped pushing his agenda because they had reached an impasse. To take on a well-established principal would have required him to spend a lot of political capital. As for the teacher in question, she says, "His apology was sincere. He's never done anything like that again and has been a team player, so my instincts were correct."

Right and wrong aside, Estella struggled with her own role in the dynamic with Jason and the district at large. Despite her surface "win," she felt discouraged: "The fact that I could say no to my boss came from a place of power and privilege. I've been a leader here, with a solid reputation, for nearly 10 years. If that weren't true, I might have been writing up a teacher who didn't deserve it." Estella had built up the political capital to say no to her supervisor, but she recognized that this experience was less about Jason as an individual and more about the dysfunctional system in which they both worked. In many ways, Jason was acting out the implicit philosophy of the system. At the end of the day, both leaders lost an important collegial relationship and a chance to learn and grow together in service of students.

Let's imagine a different school system in which leaders like Jason were trained and supported to become Listening Leaders. If Jason had been taught to listen with awareness of the brain, what new moves might have been available to him? Table 2.4 juxtaposes possible moves with elements from the chapter. Had Jason tried any of these moves, he would have modeled the behaviors of a Listening Leader.

TABLE 2.4   LISTENING LEADER BRAIN-FRIENDLY MOVES

Listening Leader Moves (What other moves could Jason have made?)	Awareness (What brain insight informs this move?)
1. Jason could have started his new role by proactively building a relationship with Estella. He could have visited her with the goal of listening to understand her core beliefs and values as well as to learn whether the school had basic needs that the district office could easily fulfill. He might also have looked for opportunities to leverage humor and build connection by offering her a small token of appreciation for her work—for example, a book, a plant, or a card.	• Reimagine rewards (listening connects two brains together). • Feed the lizard.

(Continued)

TABLE 2.4   (CONTINUED)

Listening Leader Moves (What other moves could Jason have made?)	Awareness (What brain insight informs this move?)
2. When Estella emailed Jason to open up the make-up testing day to other schools, he could have said, "Great problem solving!" before helping her identify what had initially gone wrong.	• Calm the amygdala; reimagine rewards (the importance of praise and affirmation). • Every brain grows in the right conditions.
3. Once they met, he could have shown curiosity about her perspective by listening and asking questions like "How did you choose to handle the situation?" "What beliefs and values informed that approach?" "What did you learn in the process?"	• Calm the amygdala by listening. • Water for deep roots with reflective questions.
4. He might have chosen his battles and ceded this decision to her as the site leader. In so doing, he could have expressed an alternative viewpoint while not undermining her authority: "Have you considered writing him up?" "Are you concerned that this type of mistake might happen again?"	• Calm the amygdala (the importance of autonomy). • Water for deep roots by offering new perspectives.
5. After their initial conflict, he could have reflected on the consequences of leaving the tension unresolved. He could have gone back to Estella to acknowledge the tension and reflect together on how they might rebuild trust: "I want to acknowledge that this was a hard and awkward conversation. It's important for me to be in good relationship with you; I value and respect you. Let's debrief what happened and how we can repair our relationship."	• Overcome the brain's negativity bias. • Embrace storientation by facilitating a healing experience rather than allowing a negative core memory to fester.

KEY TAKEAWAYS

- The brain has three main neighborhoods: the lizard brain, the limbic brain, and the neocortex. Understanding the function of each orients us in our listening.
- Listening Leaders create learning conditions that enable every brain to grow. (Water for deep roots)
- Human beings are hardwired to avoid threats at all costs. (Calm the amygdala)
- Social threats equal survival threats to the brain. (Reimagine rewards)
- Organizations harbor core memories. (Embrace storientation)

LISTENING LEADER INQUIRY

Question: I have one teacher colleague who I fundamentally do *not* believe can grow. He is stubborn, entrenched, and very ineffective in the classroom. How am I supposed to help him?

My thoughts: First of all, if you don't believe a person can grow, you won't be able to help him. I encourage you to question where your skepticism comes from. Does he trigger you personally in some way? If so, can you pair him with another leader or coach for support? If you have evidence that he's unwilling to develop, it's time for a hard conversation. This might look like a rigorous evaluation process, placing him in a peer assistance and review program, or taking an assertive coaching stance in which you give him limited time, clear goals, and support to improve. If you still believe that he can grow, you can model a listening stance by asking, "What's getting in the way for you?" "What makes it challenging to try out new practices?" "What support do you need to demonstrate growth this year?"

Question: I fear that I behaved like Jason in the story and have already created a negative reputation for myself among my staff. How do I get out of this hole?

My thoughts: It's never too late to become a Listening Leader. If you recognize gaps in your approach, own up to them and make a conscious shift. If you have particular relationships to repair, be brave and repair them. Sometimes the best thing to do is to approach a colleague you know you have harmed in some way and say, "I recognize that my tone, words, or actions were hurtful to you. That was not my intent, and I want to repair our relationship. What do you need from me to heal this situation?"

Question: How can I use my understanding of listening and negativity bias to overcome a sustained negative culture/climate?

My thoughts: See Chapters 10 and 11 for a host of concrete suggestions!

Question: There are times when we all become depleted as leaders. What are some quick ways I can "feed my lizard" and/or replenish in these circumstances?

My thoughts: It is critical to practice self-care as a leader. You will be a better colleague who gets more done and responds more thoughtfully if you set aside time to nourish yourself. What this looks like will vary depending on your personality. Are you an introvert? Maybe you need to set aside time for a weekly meditative hike or other experience in nature. Are you an extrovert? You may need to form a peer group of leaders who meet for happy hour once a week to debrief the work. If self-care seems impossible, set a small goal that represents progress—for example, *I'm going to eat breakfast every morning* or *I commit to attend one yoga class per week.*

NOTES

1. Wolvin, A. D. (2012). Listening, understanding, and misunderstanding. In W. F. Eadie (Ed.), *21st century communication: A reference handbook* (pp. 137–147). Thousand Oaks, CA: Sage.

2. Wolvin, Listening, understanding, and misunderstanding; Weick, K. E. (1995). *Sensemaking in organizations.* Thousand Oaks, CA: Sage.

3. Staats, C. (2014). *State of the science: Implicit bias review 2014.* Columbus: Kirwan Institute for the Study of Race and Ethnicity, The Ohio State University.

4. Zull, J. E. (2002). *The art of changing the brain: Enriching teaching by exploring the biology of learning.* Sterling, VA: Stylus; Hammond, Z. (2014). *Culturally responsive teaching and the brain: Promoting authentic engagement and rigor among culturally and linguistically diverse students.* Thousand Oaks, CA: Corwin Press, p. 40.

5. Hammond, Z. (2014) *Culturally responsive teaching and the brain.* Corwin.

6. Phelps, E. A. (2006). Emotion and cognition: Insights from studies of the human amygdala. *Annual Review of Psychology 57,* 27–53.

7. Azar, B. (2000). A new stress paradigm for women. *Monitor on Psychology, 31*(7), 42.

8. Rock, D. (2009). *Your brain at work.* New York, NY: HarperCollins, p. 190.

9. Rock, D. (2008). SCARF: A brain-based model for collaborating with and influencing others. *NeuroLeadership Journal, 1*(1), 1–9.

10. Dweck, C. (2006). *Mindset: The new psychology of success.* New York, NY: Ballantine Books.

11. Hattie, J. (2011). Feedback in schools. In R. Sutton, M. J. Hornsey, & K. M. Douglas (Eds.), *Feedback: The communication of praise, criticism, and advice* (pp. 265–278). New York, NY: Peter Lang, p. 273.

12. Willingham, D. (2009). *Why don't students like school?* San Francisco, CA: Jossey-Bass, p. 67.

13 Brown, J. S., & Duguid, P. (1991). Organizational learning and communities-of-practice: Toward a unified view of working, learning, and innovation. *Organization Science, 2*(1), 40–57.

14 Goleman, D. (2013). *Primal leadership.* Cambridge, MA: Harvard Business Review Press, p. 8.

Chapter 3

Listening for Equity

Preview: In this chapter, we cultivate awareness by tuning in to critical equity "channels."

This chapter is designed to help you:

- Explore how racial bias and cultural insensitivity can undermine a healthy staff culture.
- Tune in to structural racism, unconscious bias, and cultural difference.
- Gain powerful language and tools to listen and lead for equity.

THE FRAGILITY OF TRUST ACROSS DIFFERENCE

Joy returned to school after a tedious principals' meeting. Entering the building, she saw an image taped to her closed office door—visible to anyone passing by. Approaching, she found the cover of a recent issue of *Scholastic* magazine featuring a photo of a monkey-like creature with a long nose; attached was a yellow sticky note that read "Good morning!"

An African American woman in her 50s, Joy was immediately triggered. "What the hell?" she said to herself as she thought of the racist history of Black people being associated with monkeys. In the staff room, Joy found a group of teachers—including a White woman named Wendy who was the school's designated equity teacher leader—sitting around the table. "Does anyone know who put the *Scholastic* thing on my door?" The teachers chuckled and glanced sheepishly at one another. "Cause I'm really offended by it," she declared. The room fell silent as Joy walked out, shaking her head and unnerved by the lack of response.

Wendy sat frozen, her mind scrutinizing the ridiculous image she had shown several colleagues before placing it on her principal's door with the hope of making her laugh. In their 2 years as colleagues, she and Joy had discovered a similar sense of humor and playful banter. They had joined the staff together, finding an adult culture in upheaval, and would joke, "It was broken when we got it!" Under the previous top-down leader, the community splintered into warring factions: teachers against administration, competing parent groups, African American instructional aides in tension with the majority-White teaching staff.

In this contentious climate, Joy and Wendy bonded over their shared passion for equity. They spoke frankly about race and racism, exchanged personal stories, and brainstormed how to address teachers' unconscious biases toward students. They planned staff meetings to discuss the "preschool to prison" pipeline. After 2 years of Joy's inclusive leadership style, it felt as though a new era had dawned. As Wendy describes it, "A lot of trust had developed. We were out of the woods in terms of the posttraumatic stress teachers had experienced, and the school felt stable."

When Joy confronted the group in the staff room, Wendy at first thought that her boss was feigning anger, but she sensed that something was off. Then it clicked: "Oh my god, it's a monkey." In Wendy's words, "My whole emotional and mental state went into a blur. I realized that I had done something really bad even though I hadn't intended to. I felt extremely misunderstood—not a feeling of self-pity, but more of mortification and shame because I prided myself on doing so much reading and work with White teachers about race." She grabbed a rose from a lunchroom bouquet and went out to recess to find Joy.

"I'm so sorry," Wendy said. "I put the image there. I thought it would lighten up your day and make you laugh." As a White woman, Wendy hadn't considered how an African American colleague would experience the cartoon. Still reeling, Joy took a deep breath and replied, "I understand that was your intention, but having a picture of a monkey on my door for everyone to see was very offensive and degrading to me." After a tense exchange, they parted ways, and Wendy went to her classroom, shut the door, and sobbed. Later she reflected, "I felt badly that I had hurt someone with whom I had a lot of trust and solidarity."

Joy retreated into her office and shut the door as well. She felt utterly humiliated and lost and couldn't believe that Wendy would do something so thoughtless. Joy recently shared, "This was a person I had hired and believed in, someone who shared my vision of equity and social justice.

I had even appointed her as the equity teacher leader! How could she insult me like this?" Over the next few days, Joy grappled with how to address the incident. First she emailed Wendy articles about the profound history behind the image, but she heard nothing back.

A week later, Joy stood uncomfortably before her mostly White staff and said, "Today we're going to talk about cultural insensitivity, and how we sometimes inadvertently disregard a person's culture and identity." As her narrative unspooled, the room grew increasingly tense. By now, much of the staff held pieces of the backstory, and people began exchanging nervous glances. Joy closed by saying, "I felt offended by this incident, but I wanted to share it as an example of how we need to understand other people's backgrounds and think about the ramifications of our actions."

Suddenly, Wendy raised a shaking hand and stammered, "Listen, this was me. I didn't do it out of malice. I'm not a racist. I didn't realize the connotation it had." As Wendy continued, Joy thought to herself, *This isn't about being a "racist." It's about cultural insensitivity.* The room seemed to sway toward Wendy, and Joy was devastated: "The staff did a 180. They didn't give me the benefit of the doubt and jumped on her side." Wendy, in the meantime, felt "very betrayed" that Joy had presented the story without checking in with her first: "She didn't make any effort to preserve my dignity."

In the ensuing weeks, teachers and staff members circled their wagons around Wendy. A few people told Joy that she had handled the situation "inappropriately." She was stunned. How had she, an African American principal reeling from a racialized incident, become the culprit? As the weeks passed, the relationship between Joy and Wendy hovered at a tense register. Where would they go from here?

Joy and Wendy are former colleagues of mine who entrusted me to tell this vulnerable story as a text for learning. If we look at their story using the core tenets from Chapter 2, we see how both women's emotional brains were hijacked by the situation. We see variations of fight, flight, and tend-and-befriend behaviors across the school, and we see the urgent need to "water for deep roots" (Chapter 2 brain mandate) with respect to the staff's awareness around race and equity—to cultivate a shared language and understanding of the issues at play. This last point brings us to the heart of this chapter, which provides specific tools for examining racism, bias, and cultural difference in our schools.

TABLE 3.1   EQUITY CHANNELS

Channel	Brief Description
Awareness of structural racism	Tuning in to the overlapping social structures and systems that produce racialized outcomes, including education, employment, transportation, housing, health care, and criminal justice
Awareness of unconscious bias	Tuning in to the perceptions, attitudes, and stereotypes that unconsciously affect people's beliefs, actions, and decisions
Awareness of cultural difference	Tuning in and attributing positive value to cultural difference and embracing a learning stance with respect to culture

What does it mean to listen and lead for equity? What land mines await the equity-driven leader? How can we develop trust across difference, skill to engage in hard conversations, and courage to interrupt inequitable practices in the classroom and the staffroom?

What does it mean to listen and lead for equity? What land mines await the equity-driven leader? How can we develop trust across difference, skill to engage in hard conversations, and courage to interrupt inequitable practices in the classroom and the staff room? Because so much of school transformation hinges on racial and cultural inequity, we must develop a robust vocabulary around these issues. A rigorous and daily analysis of equity issues will complement our understanding of the brain as we work to create great schools for every child. Chapter 3 addresses this need by helping us tune in to three critical "channels" of awareness: structural racism, unconscious bias, and cultural difference. Table 3.1 offers a sneak preview.

TUNING IN TO STRUCTURAL RACISM

Racialized outcomes do not require racist actors.

—john a. powell, director of the UC Berkeley Haas Institute for a Fair and Inclusive Society

To build equitable schools and systems, we must first acknowledge the sociopolitical context in which they sit—those overlapping policies, practices, and institutions that uphold inequity.[1] We begin by tuning in to awareness of **structural racism**, namely, the ways in which systems of education, employment, transportation, housing, health care, and criminal justice conspire to produce racialized *outcomes*, regardless of the intentions of individual people.[2] Although these institutions affect poor White people as well as people of color, it is important to name the ways that race and class intersect to magnify the oppression of people of color in America.

Listening to this channel, we reject the myth of "color blindness" and acknowledge that people have unequal access to opportunity and freedom. In her powerful book *The New Jim Crow: Mass Incarceration in the Age of Colorblindness*, civil rights advocate Michelle Alexander discusses the metaphor of a birdcage (see Figure 3.1) to help us conceptualize structural racism:

> If one thinks about racism by examining only one wire of the cage, or one form of disadvantage, it is difficult to understand how and why the bird is trapped. Only a large number of wires arranged in a specific way, and connected to one another, serve to enclose the bird and to ensure that it cannot escape.[3]

Working together, these wires generate racialized outcomes for different groups, even in the absence of explicitly racist actors.[4]

Sometimes the "bird" does escape, but at a steep emotional or physical price. I think of the food deserts of East Oakland where my partner taught for many years and had to drive several miles to purchase a healthy lunch, a reality that neighborhood families continually endured. I think of June Jordan School for Equity students whose families left San Francisco due to rising housing costs, but still commuted 3 hours per day to access a quality education. I think of Michael, a homeless White student who lived with his mentally ill mother in a bus that relocated every day, but who still woke up, got dressed, and took himself and his siblings to school.

Structural racism helps us view schools as **opportunity structures** that create and distribute society's benefits and hardships.[5] Table 3.2 tells this story by contrasting professor john a. powell's hometown of Detroit and the prosperous community where his stepdaughter attended high school. Similarly, my children attend an opportunity-rich public school in Oakland, California; parents raise funds for special programs, children stroll to school through a quiet neighborhood, and experienced teachers stay for many years. Although the student body has historically been both racially and socioeconomically diverse, gentrification is shifting the landscape toward affluent, predominantly White families. Here structural racism is playing out at the intersection of housing and education.

FIGURE 3.1   THE BIRDCAGE AS A METAPHOR
FOR STRUCTURAL RACISM

TABLE 3.2   A TALE OF HIGH-OPPORTUNITY AND LOW-OPPORTUNITY
STRUCTURES

High Opportunity	• The year powell's stepdaughter finished high school, 100% of students graduated and 100% went on to college. • Most students will never drive by a jail. • Bus services are free. • The city has a relatively easy time attracting capital investment. • It is very safe and full of beautiful parks. • It's easy to purchase fresh, healthy food.
Low Opportunity	• Less than 25% of students in Detroit finish high school. • More than 60% of men will spend time in jail. • Soon, there may be no bus services in some parts of town. • It is not very safe, and there are few parks. • It's quite difficult to access fresh, healthy food.

Note. Adapted from the work of john a. powell, director of the UC Berkeley Haas Institute for a Fair and Inclusive Society

This channel interrupts the dominant narrative that explains inequity through individual traits or effort—"If only students had more grit, character, or self-discipline"; "If only families worked harder or invested in their children's education." Such statements distract educators from addressing root causes, such as the unequal distribution of resources within and across school systems. In a powerful modeling of Discourse II to call out the impact of structural racism, pedagogical theorist Gloria J. Ladson-Billings charges America with accumulating an "education debt" to generations of students of color and students trapped in poverty.[6]

Schools can operate as spaces of transformation that interrupt racialized patterns of success and failure, or as spaces of reproduction that sustain inequality.

Schools can operate as spaces of transformation that interrupt racialized patterns of success and failure, or as spaces of reproduction that sustain inequality. Transformational schools move the equity needle by weakening or eliminating the education wire on the birdcage, cracking open space for the bird to wiggle out.

When tuning in to structural racism, I remind myself that . . .

- People are differently "situated" with respect to opportunity, contrary to the fantasy of a color-blind or meritocratic society.
- Our societal structures and institutions are designed to produce racialized inequitable outcomes in schools.
- As powell writes, "racialized outcomes don't require racist actors." You don't have to be "a racist" or have racist intent to contribute to and reinforce structural racism.
- Schools are microcosms of the sociopolitical context.

- Structural racism shapes unequal access to opportunity, including experienced teachers, rigorous instruction, clean and healthy facilities, and enrichment programs.
- Racially unequal outcomes are more than the sum of individual and group behavior.
- A person's social location—or where he or she is situated with respect to race, class, and gender—influences his or her experience in the school system.
- I *can* influence outcomes by making structural changes in my school or organization and by building authentic partnerships with families and community.

When tuning in to structural racism, I ask the following questions . . .

- What opportunity structures are available to my students and their families?
- What opportunity structures do they lack access to?
- To what extent does our staff live within the same social and structural reality as our students? If there's a gap, how does it manifest in the classroom and in staff perceptions and discourse around students and families?
- What is *my* social location, or access to opportunity, as a leader? How does that influence how I'm perceived and positioned with students, families, colleagues, and supervisors?
- How is our school situated within local opportunity structures and in the broader community?
- What role has our school played historically in helping families gain access to opportunity?
- How can our school play a role in supporting families to gain access to opportunity?

For a printable version of this tool, go to my website: shanesafir.com/resources.

Joy and Wendy's Story: Tuning in to Structural Racism (Channel 1)

Joy and Wendy's school enrolls a racially and economically diverse student body, but sits in a wealthy, predominantly White neighborhood. Many students of color take district buses or travel across town to get to school, and the majority-White staff did not fully reflect the student body at this time. As the school's first African American principal, Joy began to address this demographic gap by recruiting more teachers of color. The school was well positioned to benefit from her commitment to equity and her insight as a woman of color in leadership.

However, when Joy chose to publicly reflect on the painful incident, the staff rallied around Wendy, dropping into an individualistic narrative and insisting that Wendy was "not a racist." Tuning in to structural racism could have helped the staff understand that a racialized outcome—in this case, Joy's trauma in confronting the image—does not require a consciously racist actor, and that impact matters more than intent. Had she not been emotionally hijacked herself, Wendy could have demonstrated cross-racial allyship by helping educate her White colleagues on the historical subtext and connotations of the image.

Instead, their coalition dissolved in the wake of the incident and in the face of Wendy's shame and Joy's hurt. Rather than reckoning with the ingrained nature of structural racism, the staff defended Wendy and lost an opportunity to learn and grow together.

TUNING IN TO UNCONSCIOUS BIAS

Unconscious bias, also called implicit bias, refers to the attitudes and stereotypes that unconsciously affect a person's perceptions, actions, and decisions.[7] Did you know that the vast majority of our thoughts live in the brain's unconscious networks? We are continually bombarded by biased messages from the dominant culture that communicate to the unconscious about the relative worth and humanity of women, people of color, and other groups. In the absence of awareness and a conscious equity stance, the brain begins to code other people as more or less valuable and more or less threatening. Concretely, the prefrontal cortex lights up when we view someone as "highly human," but fails to activate when we dehumanize people.[8] Unconscious biases cut off the circuits that enable empathy and connection.

On a day-to-day level, unconscious biases are often the culprit behind **microaggressions** in schools—routine verbal, nonverbal, and environmental slights or insults that communicate hostile, degrading, and negative messages to people of color.[9] (Table 3.3 provides examples of microaggressions and the messages they communicate.) In cutting to deep layers of identity, these incidents diminish a person's sense of safety and well-being. For all educators, and particularly those from the dominant culture, it's important to pay attention to the message *received* and its effect on the recipient, rather than to the message *intended* by the speaker. "But I didn't

TABLE 3.3   RECOGNIZING MICROAGGRESSIONS AND THEIR IMPLICIT MESSAGES

Theme	Example	Message
Alien in One's Own Land When Asian Americans, Latino Americans and others who look different or are named differently from the dominant culture are assumed to be foreign-born	"Where are you from or where were you born?" "You speak English very well." "What are you? You're so interesting looking!"	You are not a true American. You are a perpetual foreigner in your own country. Your ethnic/racial identity makes you exotic.
Color Blindness Statements that indicate that a White person does not want to or need to acknowledge race.	"When I look at you, I don't see color." "There is only one race, the human race." "America is a melting pot." "I don't believe in race." Denying the experiences of students by questioning the credibility and validity of their stories.	Assimilate to the dominant culture. Denying the significance of a person of color's racial/ethnic experience and history. Denying the individual as a racial/cultural being.
Pathologizing Cultural Values/Communication Styles The notion that the values and communication styles of the dominant/White culture are ideal/"normal."	To an Asian, Latino or Native American: "Why are you so quiet? We want to know what you think. Be more verbal." "Speak up more." Asking a Black person: "Why do you have to be so loud/animated? Just calm down." "Why are you always angry?" anytime race is brought up in the classroom discussion. Dismissing an individual who brings up race/culture in work/school setting.	Assimilate to dominant culture. Leave your cultural baggage outside. There is no room for difference.

Note. From *Microaggressions in Everyday Life: Race, Gender and Sexual Orientation,* by Derald Wing Sue, 2010, Hoboken, NJ: Wiley. Reprinted with permission.

mean it that way!" can easily become a safety valve for maintaining White racial equilibrium and Discourse I.

As we tune in to this channel, several findings emerge. First, all of us harbor unconscious beliefs that affect our perceptions of others—and often of ourselves. Harvard psychologist Mahzarin Banaji and her colleagues developed the Implicit Association Test to assess for unconscious associations in areas like race, gender, age, and appearance.[10] They've collected data from millions of anonymous test-takers, with illuminating

Become aware of your biases so that you can interrupt them. Before entering a conversation with a parent or colleague who may trigger you, take a 10-second pause to ask yourself: What are my biases toward this person? How can I disrupt those automated thoughts so that I can genuinely listen to him or her?

findings. For example, people over 60 and 20-year-olds show an equally strong bias toward youth—probably because the elderly are a stigmatized group. Along the same lines, close to 80% of White and half of African American participants show a pro-White bias even after claiming no racial preference.[11]

Second, it's important to distinguish implicit biases from willful acts of discrimination; the former are the brain's distorted attempt to find patterns amid a flood of incoming, often highly distorted data. This fact points toward a key solution: Become aware of your biases so that you can interrupt them. Before entering a conversation with a parent or colleague who may trigger you, take a 10-second pause to ask yourself: *What are my biases toward this person? How can I disrupt those automated thoughts so that I can genuinely listen to him or her?* As a principal, I recall practicing this with a parent who often demanded my attention and triggered a flight response. When I was able to pause, I noticed that I had written her off as "needy" without truly listening to her needs. This allowed me to show up with more presence and compassion.

Finally, we can't afford to ignore the far-reaching effects of unconscious bias in schools:

Disproportionality in discipline Policies that appear racially neutral on their face, but result in the overrepresentation of students of color— particularly Black boys—in suspensions, expulsions, and referrals for subjective infractions like "defiance"

Disproportionality in special education Misguided placements and the overrepresentation of culturally and linguistically diverse students in special education

Detrimental teacher mindsets and beliefs Underestimating the intellectual capacity of culturally and linguistically diverse students, and often girls, inside the classroom

Unfair tracking of students School policies that disproportionally place students of color in low-level classes, or limit their access to honors and Advanced Placement courses

Discourse I Ways of talking about students and families that diminish, pathologize, or even criminalize them

Inequitable staff power dynamics Marginalization of, and glass ceilings imposed on, staff of color and women; on the flip side, men and/ or White people being given credit for other people's ideas

How can we lead for equity in the face of these systemic challenges? We must understand that biases stem from developmental experiences— where one grows up, lives, and socializes. A study by the PRRI found, for example, that White Americans have social networks that are 91% White. (Among African Americans, 83% of social networks are also African American, and for Latinos, 64% are Latino.)[12] One result of this pattern is that our most diverse schools are often staffed by White teachers who grew up in segregated communities. Where structural racism maintains racial separation, people's lived realities can produce exaggerated perceptions of difference and high levels of threat and fear.

Here's the good news: If biases have been learned, they can surely be unlearned. As a leader, you can engineer experiences that build bridges and challenge misconceptions.

Here's the good news: If biases have been learned, they can surely be unlearned. As a leader, you can engineer experiences that build bridges and challenge misconceptions. Embrace storientation by helping your staff safely share their stories across difference. Support people to increase awareness of their identity, including areas of power, privilege, and disadvantage. Promote an understanding of intersectionality, or the ways in which race, class, and gender overlap to create systems of oppression and discrimination. Model the value of an inclusive society with every interaction and message.

When tuning in to unconscious bias, I remind myself that . . .

- Schools aren't race neutral or "color blind," as seductive as that thinking can be. We are not in a postracial era, and we are all vulnerable to implicit biases.
- Bias is a universal human condition that we must recognize and manage; it is not a personal defect.
- We all carry biases from swimming in the waters of a racialized society.
- Implicit biases can be internalized by nondominant groups (i.e., people of color, women, etc.) and feed a pattern of **negative self-talk**—internal commentary on one's failings.

- Focusing on individual acts of racism, or weeding out the "bad people," won't solve the fundamental problem.
- Implicit bias is an involuntary reflex rooted in the unconscious mind and distinct from explicit, targeted racism.
- As a shortcut the brain takes to process data, implicit bias relies on common stereotypes.
- Implicit bias and structural racism work together to produce racist outcomes even without racist intent.
- I can slow down and tune in to my own biases. With awareness, I can replace biases with listening and with affirming thoughts.
- I can track classroom behaviors that interrupt bias and those that spiral into bias.
- I can track and interrupt microaggressions in the classroom and the staff culture.
- Becoming aware of implicit biases is a key element of emotional intelligence.
- The first step to interrupting implicit bias is to listen with empathy (we will unpack the leadership stance of mature empathy in Chapter 5) and develop a nuanced understanding of who a person is.

When tuning in to unconscious bias, I ask the following questions . . .

- Where do I see implicit biases playing out in our school culture?
- What fear or apprehension do I have about addressing implicit bias?
- How can I serve as an ally to colleagues, students, and families who experience bias in our school?
- What have been my own experiences of implicit bias, as victim or perpetrator?
- What assumptions have been made about me that represent an incomplete or distorted story?
- When I think of a staff member with whom I've struggled to build trust, what assumptions might I have made about this colleague or she of me? How might implicit bias be at play?

Joy and Wendy's Story: Tuning in to Unconscious Bias (Channel 2)

We all have unconscious biases—it's part of being human—and, even when we bring awareness to them, we can't always know how these biases affect our actions. Regardless of Wendy's intentions, her decision to leave the image on Joy's office door hijacked Joy's emotional brain, which was already on guard. In her words, "This was a horrible experience for an African American administrator who is always dealing with identity threats. How many times have I met a White parent and introduced myself as the principal only to have them say with surprise, 'Oh, *you're* the principal?!?'"

As the incident became public, Discourse I kicked in to consolidate a single story: "Wendy isn't a racist," and "Joy is being too sensitive." Swept up in a collective amygdala hijack, the staff lost its ability to be reflective— to ask, What could we learn from this moment, together?

How can such a school tune in to unconscious bias to prevent and address such incidents? A more diverse staff, or a staff with increased awareness of this channel, might have paused to listen deeply to Joy's experience and to engage in the necessary, if difficult, conversations around bias. Chapter 10 depicts this type of staff culture in the context of tensions around gender and gender bias.

TUNING IN TO CULTURAL DIFFERENCE

As we strive toward equity, we have to turn up the volume on culture. In 2014, the overall number of students of color in public K–12 schools surpassed the number of White students, while the teaching force continues to hover at around 83% White.[13] This demographic gap can lead to cultural disconnects and biases in the classroom that impact students' opportunities to learn. By building our own and our colleagues' awareness of cultural difference and by prioritizing the hiring of a diverse staff, we can create more inclusive school environments.

Listening Leaders tune in to cultural difference and have the capacity to recognize and respond positively to difference, read subtle cultural cues and adjust their moves, [and] embrace humility and a learning stance with respect to culture.

Listening Leaders tune in to cultural difference and have the capacity to

- Recognize and respond positively to difference
- Read subtle cultural cues and adjust their moves
- Embrace humility and a learning stance with respect to culture

This isn't about memorizing every nuance of every culture you encounter. It's about opening your thoughts, feelings, and behavior beyond the psychological limits of one culture.[14] It's about listening in ways that foster **cultural synchronicity**—the ability to connect across difference so that you avoid cultural miscommunication cues that act as social threats to the brain. And it's about recognizing that cultural proficiency is a lifelong process that takes active work because culture, language, and context are constantly shifting.

In schools, we may focus on visible and audible manifestations of culture, such as food, dress, customs, and language. We celebrate diversity or host international days, which are perfectly legitimate and worthy activities. As we increase our awareness, we notice cultural differences in ways of communicating, negotiating personal space, relating to time, or expressing respect. All of this matters, but the Listening Leader's most important focus is on tuning in to what my colleague Zaretta Hammond calls **deep culture**—ways of seeing and experiencing the world that stem from unconscious assumptions, mental models, and worldviews.[15] It is our deep culture that governs how we learn and process new information.

The reality is that even though there are clearly patterns within any cultural group, there are also endless permutations of deep cultural schema. The nuances of culture can vary from street to street and block to block! Listening is the pathway to understanding those subtleties in your own context.

 MAKE IT MINDFUL

Think of someone with whom you've struggled to build an alliance. What do you understand about her cultural schema, or frame of reference? What are her driving beliefs and values and her ethical worldview, or sense of right and wrong? What tacit knowledge does she hold about the world? Now consider: To what extent are you culturally in sync with this person?

In addition to cultivating self-awareness, the Listening Leader recognizes the presence of a **dominant culture in schooling** that tends to promote

- Individualism and individual achievement over team success
- Independence and self-reliance over interdependence
- Technical, or "hard" skills, *over* relational, or "soft" skills
- Competition over collaboration
- Quiet, stillness, and compliance over talk, movement, and critical thinking

These individualistic values have roots in the Industrial Age when public schools were designed like factories, and businesses needed compliant workers. My colleague Abby Soriano, an instructional coach in San Jose, California, refers to the dominant culture in schooling as akin to a vestigial organ the body no longer needs, but which remains present. Not only has our economic reality transformed, but also these ways of being and learning are culturally incongruent for the majority of students (and many educators!) in contemporary classrooms.

A friend of mine quit her job at a charter school after a supervisor insinuated that her focus on relationships and community was preventing a "sense of urgency," and demanded that she use "bell-to-bell instruction." A woman of color with an equity lens, this teacher possesses a profound sense of urgency, but her instructional methods—relationships first, responsive pacing, collaborative group work—were out of sync with her White, middle-class supervisor. Joking that she didn't want to strap on a headpiece and become a Zumba instructor, she left the school just as test scores came out showing that 100% of her students had passed her subject area's high-stakes test. By failing to tune in to cultural difference, this leader lost a strong teacher.

Cultural proficiency is not so much a skill you acquire as an orientation—a way of being that listening supports. A Listening Leader is:

- Committed to self-awareness, consistently examining his or her worldview and biases
- Committed to social awareness, embracing the fundamental unity of all human beings while appreciating differences
- Committed to an antiracist agenda, which includes combating racism and "all forms of prejudice and discrimination, through the development of appropriate understanding, attitudes, and social action skills"[16]

Tuning in to culture will help you manifest all three of these commitments and cultivate synchronicity across difference.

When tuning in to cultural difference, I remind myself that . . .

- Culture shapes every person's lens—it's the basis for our schema and mental models of the world.
- To listen and lead across difference, we must first recognize and understand our own cultural worldview. Only then can we begin to understand

the perspectives of our students and families. (This may take more intentionality and conscious work for White educators, who come from a dominant cultural perspective.)

- There is a dominant culture in schooling that may appear neutral, but that privileges students from White, affluent, and/or culturally assimilated backgrounds.
- As equity-driven leaders, we must approach cultural difference with humility and a learning stance.
- Listening Leaders recognize, affirm, and validate cultural differences.
- Listening Leaders are actively antiracist; they combat explicit and implicit forms of racism.
- Listening Leaders build unity and partnerships across difference.

When tuning in to cultural difference, I ask the following questions . . .

- How am I situated with respect to the dominant culture?
- How are my students, families, and colleagues situated with respect to the dominant culture?
- Whom have I promoted or cultivated into leadership roles? Do I lift people up who are culturally different from me?
- With whom do I struggle to form alliances in my school community? With whom do I easily form alliances?
- When faced with a dilemma, to whom do I turn first in my community?
- Whom else could I challenge myself to turn to as I grow my cultural awareness?
- When listening to parents and colleagues, how often do I think explicitly about my cultural lenses and biases?
- How do I view and define the culture of my school?
- Do I see evidence of dominant cultural norms in the classroom and/or schoolwide behavior expectations?
- What behavior patterns are privileged in my school's culture? Which are ascribed a negative value?

Joy and Wendy' Story: Tuning in to Cultural Difference (Channel 3)

Despite their convergent beliefs around equity, Joy and Wendy came from different cultural backgrounds and worldviews. Joy believed that Wendy's action stemmed from a blind spot: "Had she been an African American, she would have immediately recognized that the monkey image is a negative stereotype. She would not have placed it on a door for everyone to see."

At the same time, Joy felt empathy toward Wendy, asserting, "It's hard to know the nuances of everyone's culture. I admit that I don't!" She shared a story about a recently arrived Muslim student from Iraq who spoke limited English. One day, he walked into the office holding a tooth that had just fallen out, and Joy said, "Oh Mousa, you lost your tooth! How wonderful! Let me get you a little holder to save it in for the tooth fairy." The child looked perplexed, which Joy thought indicated a language barrier. To be sure he understood, she grabbed an Arabic-speaking fifth grader to translate the message. The older student informed Joy, "Um, we don't have tooth fairies. We just throw the tooth away."

Joy had to laugh at herself: "Hello! Not everybody has a tooth fairy. It's a different culture. I'm assuming he's going to follow the American custom: Some random person breaks into your house at night and leaves a gift." Tuning in to culture, Joy modeled humility and self-reflection—the reality that "we all make these errors." What if her staff had taken a similar approach with respect to Wendy's painful mistake? What if she and Wendy had supported the staff to develop equity literacy by reading and discussing the history of the image? What does it take to listen and learn across difference? Exhibit 3.1 explores the spectrum of cultural proficiency through a story.

EXHIBIT 3.1   MOVING TOWARD CULTURAL PROFICIENCY

Emmanuel is a Filipino American math teacher at a high school that serves recent immigrants, including a large Yemeni Muslim population. Per the tenets of Islam, Muslim male students must wash their hands and feet before prayer. One day, Emmanuel walked into the school bathroom and saw a group of boys standing around the sink laughing, with water all over the floor. He assumed they were goofing around and made his presence known by standing in the doorway and giving them the teacher Look.

A colleague passed by and said, "You know, they're washing their feet for prayer." This immediately shifted Emmanuel's perspective, but he also knew that the students were fooling around during the ritual, as teenagers frequently do. With new insight, he changed tactics and said "Salaam" (hello in Arabic) as a gentle reminder of *why* they were washing their feet. Instead of saying "Behave yourselves," he tried to communicate "Do this with the right intentions." "Remember your purpose." Following are four ways Emmanuel could have responded to this situation that represent a spectrum of cultural proficiency.

Spectrum of Cultural Proficiency	Possible Action
Cultural denigration See the difference, eradicate it.	Emmanuel might have asked the school to prohibit foot and hand washing because it's "not American."
Cultural insensitivity See the difference, fail to understand it, shame it.	Emmanuel might have chased them out of the bathroom and said, "Stop playing with the water. You're making a mess in here!"
Cultural acceptance See the difference, respond imperfectly in ways that maintain the status quo.	This is basically what happened, in Emmanuel's opinion. Although he saw the difference and allowed the boys to proceed, he realized that the current context for the ritual was inadequate and quite unsafe. The boys were permitted a few minutes out of class to prepare for prayer, but they had to stand and hoist bare feet into a waist-high sink while standing on a wet and slippery school bathroom floor.
Cultural advocacy See the difference, value the difference, change the context.	After this experience, Emmanuel decided to advocate for a bathroom station at which the students could wash their feet safely and with dignity. Looking online, he found two universities that provided such facilities. (He also found many examples of intolerance with signs that said "No foot washing allowed.") Emmanuel dreamed up a solution that would cost less than $100: Purchase a rubber floor mat to prevent tripping. Purchase plastic tubs and chairs. Add a hose extension from the sink to allow for easy access to water. Place Arabic decorations on the wall to create a culturally resonant space and to remind the boys, "This is why you are here." These moves would express, "We're a culturally proficient school that does things for the right reasons. We understand this ritual is important to you, we value you, and we welcome you to pray safely."

Note. Inspired by and adapted from the work of R. B. Lindsey, K. Nuri-Robinsm, and R. D. Terrell in *Cultural Proficiency: A Manual for School Leaders*, 2003, Thousand Oaks, CA: Corwin Press.

LESSONS LEARNED: JOY AND WENDY

Joy and Wendy eventually sat down to have a hard conversation about the incident. At one point, Wendy asked her principal, "Did you ever think of my feelings when you told that story at the staff meeting?" Joy responded frankly: "To tell you the truth, Wendy, I never thought about your feelings. I was just speaking my truth." She was surprised that the staff had reacted by defending Wendy. In her words, "I thought I had built trust, but all of a sudden I felt really alienated. *Maybe these people don't trust me,* I thought. *Maybe this is fake congeniality.*"

At the same time, Joy realized that her own emotional distress had made it hard to empathize with Wendy or to anticipate the staff's response. She later shared, "What keeps resonating with me is that I needed to look at the situation from multiple perspectives, and I didn't because it was such a deep, hard, emotional situation." During the conversation, Wendy had her own epiphany after she said out loud to Joy, "I guess I'm color blind to the fact that you're African American. I just see you as a friend." The moment she uttered these words, Wendy realized that she had just unconsciously reinscribed her own bias and privilege as a White woman. In her eagerness to be an ally, she had lost the social context of what the monkey image could mean to a Black woman leader. She had essentially deracialized Joy, effacing critical elements of her identity.

After this talk, the two women spoke to their staff together and emphasized the importance of being professional and open, and maintaining communication with one another. Although they maintained a cordial relationship, their friendship and trust never fully recovered. What did they each learn as leaders who care about equity?

Here are Joy's lessons learned:

Don't let it go. "If somebody makes a comment and you feel uncomfortable, say something. Even if it's just, 'I'm not really comfortable talking about kids like that.'"

Invest in people's cultural competence. Don't shy away when an opportunity presents itself. If a colleague does something culturally insensitive, have the conversation. Invite the person to reflect publicly *with* you on the experience.

Don't fight the power. In the heat of her anger, Joy forgot that her positional power could trigger threat responses in staff. She reflected, "Staff members were uncomfortable when they heard the story because they felt that the 'boss' could possibly 'turn' on them if they made a similar misstep. I may think that all staff members are my friends, but I can't ever forgot that they see me as the 'boss' first."

Here are Wendy's lessons learned:

Take a risk and be vulnerable. "In hindsight, I would have proactively explained to the staff what had happened to open up an important conversation." Despite how vulnerable she felt, she would have supported her White colleagues to address the issues at hand rather than rally to her defense.

Own your privilege. In hindsight, Wendy recognized that the way the incident played out reinforced her privilege as a White woman and cast *her* as the victim (a phenomenon known as "white fragility," which I'll discuss in the Listening Leader Inquiry section). She would have named this dynamic instead of "taking center stage" in the conversation.

Acknowledge the conditions that make equity conversations difficult. Wendy felt that she and Joy could have named the emotional challenges of equity work: "We're in the context of a highly stressful profession and calling. When you give yourself to the mission of equity, it's a prerequisite to understand that this is a life-and-death situation for some kids. If you don't believe that, you can live in blissful ignorance."

There is so much to mine from Joy and Wendy's story: We need to create resilient adult communities where people have the courage to address incidents of bias, microaggressions, and cultural insensitivity—and still come out the other side. We need to view trust and commitment to equity as fragile resources that leaders must constantly renew. And we need to invest in the equity literacy of our colleagues. It will be hard to do this deep work if we are in the grip of an amygdala hijack, so please practice self-care. Find allies outside of your context to "get real" with—people who will listen to you, validate you, and then ask tough questions that require you to rethink your assumptions or approach.

For Listening Leaders of all backgrounds, there may also be a lesson around the importance of cross-racial alliances. How do we hold each other accountable for missteps without getting tangled in guilt and shame? How do we model for students the need to have courageous conversations alongside the need to acknowledge one another's humanity and imperfection? The National Coalition on Equity in Education writes,

> To make progress on this very complex problem [educational inequity] it will be necessary to improve alliances between educators from different ethnic and racial groups, between males and females, between those with disabilities and those without, and between people of different class backgrounds.[17]

This won't be easy; it is messy, taxing, yet critical work.

At the end of the day, we must remember that impact matters more than intent. Racism and bias infuse the air we all breathe, and we must hold ourselves and our colleagues accountable for actively filtering this air. Bias can't be cured, but it can be disrupted through listening and by developing layered stories about each other that reflect our full humanity. Listening cracks open the cognitive and emotional space to understand one another.

KEY TAKEAWAYS

- Without a shared language to address equity issues in our schools, we will undermine the fragile currency of trust and marginalize the experiences and voices of people of color.
- Tuning in to structural racism allows us to see how institutional structures and systems interact to produce racialized outcomes, regardless of the intent of individuals.
- Tuning in to unconscious bias helps us understand that bias is pervasive and destructive and that we can interrupt it with awareness and conscious reconditioning.
- Tuning in to cultural difference allows us to be humble and take a learning stance around the complexity of culture and context.

LISTENING LEADER INQUIRY

Question: What if I engage my team in an equity conversation and people fall apart emotionally?

My thoughts: Emotion is a natural outgrowth of hard conversations about inequity. Listening Leaders create space for people to express emotion; in particular, they don't allow the **tone policing** of people of color who speak up about racial injustice. (Chapter 10 discusses tone policing in the context of group dynamics.) They also pay attention to White fragility—a state in which even a small degree of racial stress feels intolerable to White people and triggers defensive reactions like arguing, silence, or walking out of the room.[a] These behaviors, though likely driven by the emotional brain, serve to maintain Discourse I and restore White racial equilibrium. Although there's no easy "fix" to this dynamic, I would recommend that you focus on building the racial literacy of your team. Read and discuss this chapter and other writing on equity. Use Robin DiAngelo's article to teach the term *White fragility* and bring consciousness to this pattern of behavior. As you build shared language, invite your team to form agreements for how they want to communicate when the conversation gets hard. Chapter 10 includes sample agreements.

Question: I'm the only woman leader on a team of men. I often feel undermined by my male colleagues in ways that are subtle and I think unconscious. What should I do?

My thoughts: As you note, this is a tough situation because of the unconscious nature of the behavior. I would encourage you to identify at least one male ally who you believe will listen to your experience and act as a thought partner. Invite this person into a confidential conversation, share your concerns, and think together about how to address the dynamics. I would also consider asking your team to explore a text that discusses issues of gender bias in the workplace.

Question: I love the idea of shifting the discourse and tuning in to the channels. What advice do you have for someone who is not the positional leader of the entire school? If I am a coach or an AP, how can I influence these conversations without seeming insubordinate?

My thoughts: Great question. Professional learning communities (PLCs) are the optimal spaces in which to engage in these conversations. Ideally, you are in a position to create opportunities for your colleagues to apply the equity channels to dilemmas they face with students and families. For example, have people read and discuss this chapter to build shared language. Next, invite them to share their own experiences around these issues. (Chapter 10 offers meeting routines for this type of work.) Then organize small-group discussions in which people take turns sharing a dilemma while their colleagues each pay attention to one of the channels and pose questions from that angle. The consultancy protocol, or Helping Trios, described in Chapter 10 is a helpful structure for this process.

Question: Implicit bias occurs all the time in my school. I want to make sure that I am tuning in and responding to this, but I don't want people to feel like I am "policing" them. How can I hold true to this focus while maintaining an environment in which people don't feel constantly threatened or launched into "flight" mode?

My thoughts: It isn't always on *you* as a leader to interrupt bias. You need a cadre of equity leaders across your organization who begin to form an aligned vision around this work. Consider forming a study group to build the equity literacy of emerging leaders. Read Zaretta Hammond's wonderful book *Culturally Responsive Teaching and the Brain* together or Michelle Alexander's stunning *The New Jim Crow: Mass Incarceration in the Age of Colorblindness*. Also consider the role of self-reflection in fostering critical consciousness around bias. As you develop common language and knowledge around equity, create opportunities for people to reflect with peers around their own experiences of implicit bias as well as critical incidents in the classroom or staffroom. The next chapter provides prompts for how to approach this, and Chapter 9 offers key steps in an equity-driven change process.

[a] DiAngelo, R. (2011). White fragility. *International Journal of Critical Pedagogy, 3*(3), 54–70.

NOTES

1. Hammond, Z. (2014). *Culturally responsive teaching and the brain: Promoting authentic engagement and rigor among culturally and linguistically diverse students.* Thousand Oaks, CA: Corwin Press, p. 28.
2. powell, j. a. (2009). *Structural racialization: A lens for understanding how opportunity is racialized* [PowerPoint slides]. Retrieved from http://www.slideshare.net/kirwaninstitute/2009-07-911isaiah2
3. Alexander, M. (2012). *The new Jim Crow: Mass incarceration in the age of color blindness.* New York, NY: New Press, p. 184.
4. powell, *Structural racialization.*
5. Grant-Thomas, A., & powell, j. a. (2006). Toward a structural racism framework. *Poverty & Race, 15*(6), 3–6.
6. Ladson-Billings, G. (2006). From the achievement gap to the education debt: Understanding achievement in U.S. schools. *Educational Researcher, 35*(7), 3–12.
7. Staats, C., Capatosto, K., Wright, R. A., & Contractor, D. (2015). *Status of the science: Implicit bias review 2015.* Columbus, OH: Kirwan Institute for the Study of Race and Ethnicity.
8. Paterson, E. (2012). *Implicit bias.* Oakland, CA: Equal Justice Society. Retrieved from https://equaljusticesociety.org/law/implicitbias/
9. Garibay, J. C. (2014). *Diversity in the classroom.* Los Angeles: UCLA Diversity & Faculty Development.
10. Project Implicit. (2011). *Implicit Association Test.* Retrieved from https://implicit.harvard.edu/implicit/takeatest.html
11. Project Implicit. (2011). FAQs. Retrieved from https://implicit.harvard.edu/implicit/demo/background/faqs.html
12. Cox, D., Navarro-Rivera, J., Jones, R. P. (2016, August 3). *Race, religion, and political affiliation of Americans' core social networks.* PRRI. Retrieved at http://www.prri.org/research/race-religion-political-affiliation-americans-social-networks/
13. National Center for Education Statistics. (2013). Enrollment and percentage distribution of enrollment in public elementary and secondary schools, by race/ethnicity and region: Selected years, fall 1995 through fall 2023. *Digest of Education Statistics.* Washington, DC: Author. Retrieved from http://nces.ed.gov/programs/digest/d13/tables/dt13_203.50.asp; Maxwell, L. A. (2014). National enrollment hits majority-minority milestone. *Education Week, 34*(1). Retrieved from http://www.edweek.org/ew/articles/2014/08/20/01demographics.h34.html
14. McAllister, G., & Irvine, J. J. (2000). Cross cultural competency and multicultural teacher education. *Review of Educational Research, 70*(1), 3–24.
15. Hammond, *Culturally responsive teaching and the brain,* p. 23.
16. Bennett, C. I. (1995). *Comprehensive multicultural education: Theory and practice* (3rd ed.). New York, NY: Allyn & Bacon, p. 263.
17. National Coalition for Equity in Education & Cary, V. (2004). Equity perspectives: Creating space for making meaning on equity issues. Retrieved from National School Reform Faculty at http://www.nsrfharmony.org/system/files/protocols/12_perspectives_equity_1.pdf

Chapter 4

Getting Ready to Listen

Preview: Quality listening builds trust, a precondition for equity conversations and authentic collaboration. But listening can't be a haphazard act; it requires conscious, focused preparation.

This chapter is designed to help you:

- Examine the role of trust in equitable school transformation.
- Consider how your responses to people's daily "bids" for attention affect trust.
- Learn to explore different perspectives on a single interaction.

LISTENING BELOW THE GREEN LINE

Bianca became the director of professional development in a large school district after serving for many years as a site administrator. In her new role, she inherited a high-profile coaching initiative that was about to merge with the teacher induction program. This meant bringing together two teams—instructional coaches and mentors—with distinct histories, identities, and cultures. It also meant forming new relationships with coaches whom she had supervised as teachers.

Bianca felt nervous. She saw coaches and mentors as emerging leaders with a high level of expertise, which called for a different leadership approach than she was used to taking with teachers. In her words, "I was fearful because the coaches had been together and established a group dynamic. . . How do I join the group without disrupting what they've created, but still adding who *I* am and what I bring to the table?" How would she demonstrate credibility while honoring their skills?

She worried that her reputation would precede her: By her own account, Bianca's principalship had earned mixed reviews. Overwhelmed at first, she fell into the Manager archetype—focusing on tasks over relationships and compliance over vision. As a Latina leader, she also faced virulent racism that ultimately affected her ability to lead. In one jarring incident, a teacher left an anonymous note in her mailbox telling her to "stop speaking Spanish to students" and "go back to Puerto Rico." After that she felt so emotionally unsafe at work that she found herself evading many of the adults she was supposed to be supervising.

As Bianca entered her fifth year as principal, the superintendent asked me to coach her, and she welcomed the support. She wanted to be effective and knew that she needed to acquire new skills. Observing her in action, I saw that she was hard working, sharp, and dedicated, but underprepared for the social and emotional demands of the job (much as I had been myself as a young leader). We worked together for 2 years, allowing us to deepen the coaching over time. At first we focused on developing her leadership team, sitting shoulder to shoulder to plan meetings that would foster a culture of trust and collective responsibility. Soon we began to explore the more sensitive aspects of leadership: How did the staff experience her? What kind of leader did she want to be, and how did she need to "show up" differently? How would she confront entrenched belief systems among teachers?

One day, Bianca came to me feeling unsettled by a tense interaction with a teacher from the leadership team. He had confronted her in the hallway with a concern, and she was caught off guard. Instead of pausing to listen, she had brushed him off and visibly offended him. She knew that she had compromised hard-won trust and was now wrestling with regret and confusion. Sensing an opportunity to grow, she asked me to help her replay the interaction. What could she have done differently?

We had only 45 minutes together, but our relationship allowed me to jump right into the hard conversation. I started by asking her to consider several angles on the interaction. Through this process, Bianca discovered that she had been harboring an unconscious belief about leadership that she resented but couldn't let go of: She felt as though she had to immediately solve every problem that crossed her radar. She realized that this idea was largely self-imposed, but she didn't seem able to shake it. Driven by this invisible rule, Bianca had boxed herself into two options: fail at the impossible task of solving everyone's problem or dodge people in an effort to avoid failing.

I offered her this: What if you had paused to listen with care and attention, document the concern, and reassure the teacher that you would look

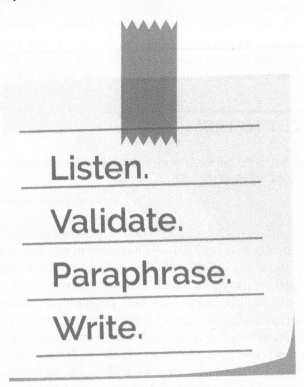

Listen.

Validate.

Paraphrase.

Write.

into it and get back to him? Just imagining this shift, Bianca released a visible sigh of relief. As we talked, she jotted down four words that would live on a sticky note in her notebook for the rest of the year: "Listen, Validate. Paraphrase. Write." The note stood as a visual reminder of how she wanted to act when approached in the future. By slowing down to reflect, Bianca built new muscle as a leader.

By the time she assumed the district role, Bianca had become much more conscious of her leadership moves and messages. She took time to mentally rehearse before difficult interactions, previewing the situation through different lenses. To build trust with the coaches and mentors, she set up one-on-one meetings with each person before school started. Though she was nervous about these meetings, she had strategies to manage her anxiety.

First, just being aware of it gave her some critical distance and the freedom to say to herself, "Hey, this is a new role for you. Take it easy on yourself." Second, as she met with coaches, she realized that they were actually quite open, which allowed her to "relax a little bit" into the listening. Once she did that, she found they had excellent questions and suggestions for how to build an effective team with great interpersonal dynamics. Finally, she considered the practical issues involved in merging the two separate programs, including how much time it would take to accomplish the process, who would supervise it, and how create to trust and a team identity. Bianca was ready to listen.

NO SHORTCUT TO TRUST

Relational trust is the connective tissue that binds individuals together to advance the education and welfare of students.

—ANTHONY S. BRYK AND BARBARA SCHNEIDER[1]

Equitable school transformation is possible only in the presence of trust. In its absence, hard conversations about equity will send people running for the hills (flight!), resisting and pushing back (fight!), or organizing frequent parking lot cabals (tend-and-befriend). A low-trust climate exacerbates implicit biases and puts people in a constant state of high alert—an exhausting situation for the body and brain. The truth is, there's no shortcut to building trust; it takes time, intentionality, and a willingness to slow down and genuinely listen. It also calls for awareness of the many factors that influence what may seem like a simple interaction.

Why is trust so vital in schools? I once coached a leader who grumbled about the "relentless needs" of teachers and parents. When I suggested that communication and relationships are hallmarks of the job, she said with a smirk, "Maybe this isn't the right job for me." Here's the problem with that half-joking reply: Relationships aren't a warm and fuzzy goal of softhearted leaders. They are the connective tissue that makes learning possible for students and adults. If you want people to take risks and grow together, you have to invest in cultivating trusting relationships.

Decades of research back up the pivotal role of trust in school change efforts. Surveying over 400 Chicago elementary schools, Anthony Bryk and Barbara Schneider completed one of the most comprehensive studies on this topic. Across the board, they found a strong correlation between trust and a "reform orientation." Trust, they concluded, builds resilience to take on the tough work of change, reduces the vulnerability teachers often feel, and fosters the prerequisite emotional safety to experiment with new practices.[2] Another study by the duo found that relational trust is built through day-to-day exchanges in a school community—what I call micro-interactions. Trust forms through "mutual understandings that can only arise out of sustained associations."[3] That means we have to behave in consistently trustworthy ways

TABLE 4.1   RELATIONAL TRUST VS. CONTRACTUAL TRUST

Relational Trust	Contractual Trust
• Stems from underlying expectations that are grounded in beliefs and agreements about how people need to work together • Can be only informally monitored • Withdrawn when people's expectations are violated	• Stems from explicit expectations that are defined by the parties through formal transactions (i.e., a contract or legally binding agreement) • Can be formally monitored • Subject to legal or contractual redress

over time in order to retain strong staff. In other words, listening to build trust is an ongoing process, not a one-shot deal.

Think of your school or team as an ecosystem that requires healthy, interdependent relationships to thrive. As a leader, you are the central organism in this ecosystem; people's level of connection with you will have secondary effects on their sense of status and fairness. If a colleague feels estranged from you, they may wonder, *Does this leader value me? Does he think I'm terrible at my job? Why does he talk to other staff members more than to me?* In this uneasy state, the person is less likely to show up as an ally and change agent.

There are different types of trust, and Bryk and Schneider argue that **relational trust** is better suited to the social complexity of schools than something they call **contractual trust**. Table 4.1 gives a brief summary of each form.

BIDS AND BETRAYALS

When you're a leader, people make constant "bids" for your attention. Your inbox overflows with unmet needs. Someone is always knocking on your office door, and it can feel terribly overwhelming. I recently met with a colleague who holds a high-level central-office position; after taking an hour-by-hour inventory of his previous week, he discovered that he had spent 50 hours in meetings alone! Meanwhile, emails flooded in, and the queue of stakeholders-in-need lengthened every day. That's why it's critical to bring awareness to how you respond to these constant demands.

Psychologist John Gottman has shown that

> human links are cemented by the way we respond to each other's bids for attention. Do we put aside texting on our smart phones, look away from Facebook or the television screen, and turn our attention to each other and empathize? If so . . . we'll stick together, and be the happier for it.[4]

(In an aside, Gottman found that happy couples have one thing in common: The partners turn *toward* each other approximately 20 times more during daily, mundane interactions than struggling partners do. This pattern actually tracked to divorce rates.)

Each bid you receive is an opportunity to build trust or to betray, as well as an opportunity to activate a reward or a threat for the other person.

Each bid you receive is an opportunity to build trust or to betray, as well as an opportunity to activate a reward or a threat for the other person. If we choose *not* to connect when we have the opportunity, we run the risk of creating a small betrayal that seeps into the organizational culture like a microtoxin. By contrast, when we pause to engage a bid, we activate a reward and generate the "cuddle hormone" **oxytocin**, which tells the amygdala to stand down.

I recently led an all-day learning session for 30 administrators. At lunch, I was sitting on my own preparing for the next activity when a participant approached me to chat. I had two choices: tell him that I was busy or put down my task and engage. Calling on the mindfulness I've nurtured over years (and wish I had possessed as a principal!), I chose the latter.

He asked me about Oakland, where I live, and began to talk about the restaurants that he and his wife frequent there. Then he shared that he keeps moving "further north" every year, starting from his birthplace of Mexico City. Suddenly, a lively conversation ensued about my travels to Mexico, my love for Mexico City, and our respective bicultural families. I lost a good 10 minutes of prep time, but I gained synchronicity with a participant who was now more invested in my session because we had connected. Besides, it was delightful! My own brain clearly released oxytocin and a hit of dopamine, the motivating chemical that reinforces behaviors that make us feel good.

What if each time someone approached you at work, you viewed it as a bid for care or attention? Even those times that feel shrouded in criticism or negativity: Can you find a bid lurking there? Bids come in all shapes and sizes. A student wants to show you her A grade on a hard math test. A colleague stops by to unload after a difficult class period. A fellow leader asks for support around a dilemma. A parent pulls you aside to share a concern about his child. How you respond to these offers matters . . . a lot. You have the potential to reward people by listening or to threaten their sense of connection and value. You hold a fragile ecosystem in balance.

When my son entered first grade, he displayed some audio processing issues that concerned his father and me. One morning, I bumped into his principal on the schoolyard. She and I hadn't had a particularly warm relationship in the past, but I took a risk to share my concerns, and she listened with care. Were she holding the rubric in Exhibit 4.1, she would have seen the following indicators:

- I was willing to meet. In fact, I initiated the conversation (a bid!).
- My tone of voice and body language (nodding) indicated openness to her ideas.
- I shared emotion, in this case distress about my child, which indicated a willingness to be vulnerable.
- I disclosed enough information to push past a safely superficial mode of conversation.

EXHIBIT 4.1   EARLY INDICATORS OF TRUST

When working toward trust, it's helpful to know what signs to look out for. I have found the following indicators helpful to track.

Relational Trust Indicators	Description
Willingness to meet	• If you ask to meet with a person, is she open and willing? • Does she make excuses, cancel, or reschedule more than once? • Or has she approached you first with a "bid" for care or attention?
Tone	• In conversation, how would you characterize the person's tone: flat, agitated, or animated? Do you detect warmth and openness? Passion? • Tone as a trust indicator is very culturally bound. It's important not to misread someone's tone based on your own sense of normal. • Avoid the trap of "tone policing," defined by blogger Maisha Johnson in this way: "when marginalized people speak up about our struggles, and people from more dominant groups focus not on *what* we said, but *how* we said it."[a] If someone shares a concern in an animated or upset tone, that could very well be a sign of her willingness to trust you. Your job is to listen, validate the *content* shared, and work to understand the underlying need being expressed.

(Continued)

EXHIBIT 4.1   (CONTINUED)

Relational Trust Indicators	Description
Body language	• How would you describe the person's body language: open, guarded, or closed? • An open stance, uncrossed arms, or a smile may signal emerging trust. • Again, use caution so as not to misread physical cues based on your own cultural norms. In some cultures, for example, it is considered disrespectful to make eye contact or to stand close to another person. If you're uncertain how to read a nonverbal signal, take an inquiry stance and do some research.
Emotion	• Does the person express emotion or vulnerability? This could appear as tears, yelling, laughter, or even shaking. • The willingness to share emotion, though uncomfortable for some of us to receive, can indicate increasing trust.
Level of sharing	• What's the content and depth of what is shared? • Does the speaker keep her sharing superficial, or does she disclose information that entails a level of risk?

[a] Johnson. M. (2015). What we can all learn from Nikki Minaj schooling Miley Cyrus on tone policing. *Everyday Feminism*. Retrieved from http://everydayfeminism.com/2015/09/lessons-on-tone-policing/

Had she brushed me off or responded with the faintest hint of judgment, I would have retracted my trust. Again, every exchange counts as you grow a healthy relational ecosystem.

UNDERSTAND YOUR LIVING SYSTEM

The "hallucination" was that if you changed the structure of the organization—assigned people to have the primary responsibility for a key initiative—the organization would then positively respond to the change.

—STEVE ZUIEBACK[5]

To nurture trust, we have to become aware of the various forces that influence each leadership interaction. The **Six Circle Model**, developed by Steve Zuieback and Tim Dalmau based on the work of Margaret Wheatley, offers a powerful lens for viewing our schools, teams, and organizations as living systems in which a small leadership move can have big ripple effects (see Figure 4.1).[6] This framework groups the technical dimensions of an organization into three circles "above the green line"—Structures, Patterns, and Processes—and locates the relational, or cultural, dimensions in three circles "below the green line"—Information, Identity, and Relationships.

FIGURE 4.1   THE SIX CIRCLE MODEL

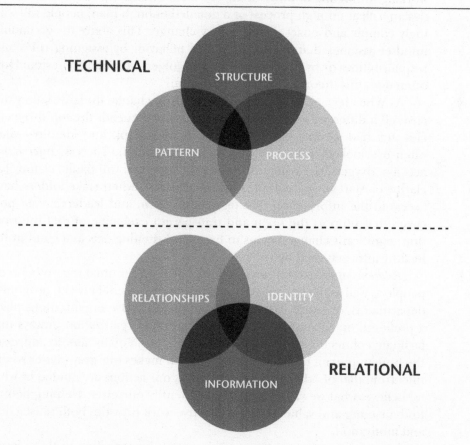

Note. Developed by Tim Dalmau and Steve Zuieback based on the work of Margaret Wheatley

Above the green line sit the concrete and measurable aspects of the work—what we *do* on a daily basis. *Patterns* include the cyclical results, messages, and behaviors in the system, both planned and unintended (e.g., achievement data, teacher turnover rates, or chronic truancy). *Structures* describe how the parts of the system, such as teams and roles, are organized in relation to one another. Examples of structures include organizational charts, systems of supervision, master schedules, and strategic plans. *Processes* describe the operational protocols through which things get done in the system, such as evaluation, hiring, and decision making.

While observing organizations in the process of change, Wheatley realized that most leaders approach change with a technical orientation—by working within one or more of the top three circles. We imagine that if we design a clear enough process or a detailed enough plan, people will willingly comply and enact the necessary change. This above-the-green-line mindset assumes that we can influence behavior by assigning roles and responsibilities or by itemizing every goal, objective, and action step. How often does this theory of action break down?

As Wheatley and others studied successful change initiatives, they discovered a different set of influences operating beneath the top three circles that had to do with information, relationships, and identity—vital, often overlooked, resources that fuel organizational success. *Information* acts like oxygen in a system. In its absence, people will panic, clamor for clarity, or start to make things up. By contrast, when stakeholders have access to the information that matters to them, and leaders create processes that support the open and transparent exchange of that information, significant change begins to happen. Listening acts as a conduit for healthy information flow.

Relationships represent the quality of trust and mutual regard between people as well as the level of connection and alignment between programs, departments, or teams. Wheatley found that effective organizations place a premium on relationships, and structure the organization in ways that facilitate connections across teams and divisions. Finally, *identity* addresses the human pursuit of meaning—that which makes our gray matter so distinct from that of other species. As people, our actions are guided by what we believe, what we value, and how we identify ourselves. Helping people find meaning and value in their collective work provides both satisfaction and motivation.

Listening Leaders embrace storientation by attending to three levels of identity:

Self Who am I, as a person and as a leader? Who do I want and need to become?

Other Who is this person I am listening to? How does he see himself and his place in the work? What does he stand to lose if he decides to go along with a program of change?

System/collective Who are *we* as a school, team, or organization? What shared purposes, values, and principles will motivate people to work together toward equity?

In Wheatley's model, all six circles are essential for equitable school transformation, but in most reform efforts, leaders focus on the top three circles. As you practice the strategies in this book, you'll grow attuned to the technical and relational dimensions of change.

MINDFUL LISTENING

Between stimulus and response there is a space. In that space is our power to choose our response. In our response lies our growth and our freedom.

—VIKTOR FRANKEL[7]

Applying mindfulness to our listening will help us create healthy below-the-green-line conditions and gather pertinent above-the-green-line data. By slowing down to observe the present moment—our breath, our autopilot thoughts and feelings, and other people's dispositions—we multiply the options available to us. Leadership can be emotionally draining. Engaging with people all day long—juggling competing social and operational needs—may leave us exhausted, depleted, and resistant to feedback. How to rejuvenate and get ready to listen? Table 4.2 outlines three steps toward mindful listening.

TABLE 4.2   MINDFUL LISTENING STEPS

As you get ready to listen, follow these three steps.	
1. Look in the mirror.	Cultivate self-awareness.
2. Step into the other person's shoes.	Gently and consciously shift your awareness toward the other person's perspective.
3. Step up to the balcony.	Imagine yourself as a neutral observer as you watch and listen to yourself and the other person interacting.

Photo taken by the author on I-80 East approaching the San Francisco–Oakland Bay Bridge

Step 1: Look in the Mirror

It requires a lot of vulnerability to look in the mirror, to not look away or blame the mirror, but to own it and decide to wake up the next day and be the author of meaningful change.

—DEBORAH MEISTER, Instructional Coach

We human beings are prone to view the world egocentrically, through the prism of our own experiences. But without checks and balances, we lose the ability to describe and assess what is *actually* happening in a given moment. Looking in the mirror—cultivating self-awareness—is the first step toward mindful listening.

Begin to track your thoughts, feelings, and reactions to others. Carry a little journal to jot down the emotional peaks and valleys of your day and the questions that arise. Develop a clear understanding of your identity: where you are privileged, where you are not, and how the power dynamics of identity shape your biases. Learn to actively manage your biases and triggers by slowing down, breathing, and engaging your thinking brain to replace reactive thoughts with questions like *What is coming up for me right now? Why am I reacting so strongly to this individual?*

MAKE IT MINDFUL

Step 1: Look in the Mirror

Scenario: Take a moment to think of a recent or upcoming opportunity to listen—one that causes you some angst. (You'll carry this scenario through all three steps of mindful listening.) For example, perhaps you've just met with a parent who was upset about how you handled a discipline issue with her child. Or you're scheduled to debrief a really terrible lesson with a new teacher. Or your last meeting with a grade-level team was derailed when a colleague started complaining about students, using subtly biased language. You know you need to follow up with him, but aren't sure how. Now look in the mirror and consider the following:

Race and culture

How do you identify racially and culturally? From your frame of reference, what communication styles—verbal and nonverbal—are normative?

Gender

What is your gender or gender identity? How does your gendered life experience shape the ways in which you communicate with others?

Role

To what extent does your organizational role or position provide status and other rewards? When does your role seem to generate a threat to those with whom you work?

Emotion

How comfortable are you with open displays of emotion and with various emotions? What was the role of emotion in your family of origin? How do your family and cultural background influence your relationship to emotion?

Remember Bianca, the principal turned district leader who now manages a team of coaches? As Bianca prepared for her one-on-one meetings with the coaches, she looked in the mirror and reflected on what it meant to be a woman of color leading a diverse team of mostly female colleagues. She noticed her own anxiety about taking on the district role and wondered if her reputation as a principal would precede her. Looking in the mirror helped her to consciously manage these fears and learn to listen better. It also gave her the freedom to be imperfect and to allow herself room to grow.

Step 2: Step Into the Other Person's Shoes

In Step 2, gently shift your awareness toward the perspective of the other person. I want to acknowledge that this is neither intuitive nor easy and will require conscious mental preparation. Try to see, hear, and perceive the interaction through her lenses. Listen through her ears and feel her feelings and emotions. Run through your previous interactions as you try to understand her needs and disposition. If you close your eyes and review all the subtle data you have about this person, can you gain a sense of what's important to her right now? Does she want to be heard and validated, to increase her status in your eyes, or to find a solution to a problem?

 MAKE IT MINDFUL

Step 2: Step Into the Other Person's Shoes
Return to your scenario. Try to see *yourself* through the other person's eyes—your posture, facial expressions, words, and messages. How do you come across? Are you taking his perspective into account? Now explore the same four areas of reflection from his vantage point:

Race and culture
How does the other person identify racially and culturally? What communication styles might he consider normative? Does his "normal" match yours?

Gender
How might gender influence the way the other person communicates with you?

Role
How might the other person's role or position in the system impact his emotional safety or trigger social threats?

Emotion
How comfortable is this person with open displays of emotion and varied emotions?

As Bianca prepared to listen, she thought deeply about the coaches on her team. She reflected on her history with the ones she had supervised before, and considered what fears and preconceived notions they might hold about her. She also stepped into the shoes of the new mentors who had been transferred into the initiative without much input. She wondered if they might feel undervalued by the district. Finally, she considered the racial, cultural, and gender identities of each team member, thinking in particular about how to ensure that the few men on the team would feel included.

Step 3: Step up to the Balcony

In Step 3, imagine yourself as a neutral observer—a camera or a fly on the wall—as you watch and listen to yourself communicating with the other person. Better yet, picture yourself on a balcony watching two people interact on the dance floor below. This critical distance will allow you to gain perspective on a situation that may feel overwhelming when you're in it.[8]

 MAKE IT MINDFUL

Step 3: Step up to the Balcony
From the balcony, use the Six Circle Model to think about what's happening between you and the other person on the dance floor. Below the green line, consider:

Information
How does information move through the system where these two people work? Is either person missing critical information that he or she needs?

Relationships
What is the quality of trust between these colleagues? What is the level of connection between their respective teams or roles?

Identity
How are their identities similar and different? To what extent are they aligned around an organizational identity—a sense of shared purpose and meaning?

Think too about the above-the-green-line factors at work:

Structures
How do organizational structures facilitate or inhibit healthy communication between these two people?

Processes
What internal processes exist to support a healthy dynamic (e.g., conflict mediation, restorative conversations, or regular sharing of work in meetings)?

Patterns
Is this interaction unique, or does it represent a pattern within the organization—a sort of cultural script that plays out time and again?

As you watch the scene, try to see yourself in the interaction as objectively as possible and consider our areas of inquiry: race and culture, gender, role and position, and emotion.

Before her one-on-ones, Bianca used the Six Circle Model to gain a systemic perspective on the merger of the two teams. Looking above the green line, she thought about the *structures* of support each group had received, the *processes* they were accustomed to, and the *patterns* of skill and orientation to the work that each group had developed. Looking below the green line, she considered issues of *identity*—the coaches' and mentors' professional identities as well as the teams' collective identities. She thought about *relationships*—how to navigate issues of status, fairness, and relational trust between the teams. And she thought long and hard about the flow of *information*: What message would she convey about the merger? What informal channels of communication existed on the team? Who was likely to talk to whom?

To take up the mantle, she had to be alert and aware on multiple levels. By anticipating these influences, Bianca was better prepared to listen objectively without taking things personally. Exhibit 4.2 represents the listening protocol Bianca designed for her one-one-ones.

THE PROBLEM OF RUMINATION

Mindful listening increases one's capacity to connect with others across differences in gender, race, culture, and age. If we know this is a powerful practice, the question becomes, What gets in the way of mindful listening? For me, the intense stress of leadership created a habit of *rumination*—the tendency to get absorbed in one's thoughts, sensations, and interpretations rather than being present in the situation.[9]

EXHIBIT 4.2   BIANCA'S PROTOCOL FOR EARLY ONE-ON-ONES

My goal: to gather data and feedback around how instructional coaches
see their role and what support they need to be successful

My talking points (how I'll frame the purpose of these meetings):

- My intention is to be a listening, learning leader.
- I really appreciate you taking on this key role, especially in these times of change.
- My goal for our first meeting is to get to know you better and understand your perspective.

My questions:

1. How are you feeling about being a coach this year?
2. What are you most excited about doing this school year?
3. How would you describe your relationship with your teachers/coachees last year?
4. I want to ensure that our meeting time feels valuable to you this year. How do you learn best?
5. What are your hopes and fears about your role?
6. What do you think the role of a coach should be?
7. What would success look like for you at the end of this school year?
8. What support do you need from me to do your best work as a coach?
9. What's the most important thing I should know about you as an educator and coach?

One day, in my second year as coprincipal, I was marching down the hallway to some meeting or another with my head down. I didn't see our student advisor Toni, who was also a key parent leader, as she approached. Toni stopped me in my tracks and pulled me aside. "Shane, I need to share something with you," she said in a loving tone. "I feel like you don't pay attention when I walk by. It's like you're in your own head so much that you don't notice me. You seem aloof, and I just needed to get this off my chest." *Aloof?* I thought to myself. I saw myself as a warm and caring leader and felt ashamed that a valued colleague would see me so differently.

That night, I went home and reflected on the conversation. *When had I become so preoccupied that I couldn't make eye contact with people? What was so important that I couldn't pause to greet my colleagues?* As sobering as this moment was, it served as a wake-up call to slow my pace, set aside my preoccupations, and connect with what matters most in school transformation: human beings. Toni's "intervention" cracked open the space between stimulus and response in which I now had more freedom to choose my moves.

Research shows that people are highly attuned to the emotional state of people in leadership positions—and that those emotions can be contagious. If the principal walks around aloof or anxious, staff and students will respond in kind, which can undermine the culture of the whole organization. The most effective leaders are able to understand and manage their own emotions as well as the emotions of others—a lesson I had to learn over time.[10]

To model empathy and receptivity, we have to fend off distraction by our own fears, plans, or sorrows. Use the Mindful Listening Tool in Exhibit 4.3 to combat rumination and get yourself ready to listen.

EXHIBIT 4.3   MINDFUL LISTENING TOOL

Use this tool to pivot through the three steps in any challenging situation you face.

Steps	My Notes and Reflections
1. Self-awareness: Look in the mirror.	
• What social threat does this situation activate for me (e.g., I feel disrespected, undervalued, treated unjustly)?	
• Who am I in this interaction (identity) through the lenses of race, culture, gender, age, and role?	
• What unconscious biases may be at work in my brain?	
• How am I holding my body, face, what tone of voice am I using?	
• What messages might I be conveying to the other person, consciously or not?	
• How do I want to show up in this interaction?	
• What do I value most in this interaction?	
• What is my truest intention?	

Getting Ready to Listen

Steps	My Notes and Reflections

2. Other awareness: Stand in the other's shoes.

- What social threat might be activated for the other person?
- Who is *he or she* in this interaction through the lenses of gender, race, culture, age and role?
- What unconscious biases may be at work in his or her brain?
- What do his or her body, face, and tone convey?
- What does the person seem to care about most in this situation?
- Who does he or she need me to be in this interaction?

3. System awareness: Step up to the balcony to analyze the various forces at play.

- How would you describe this interaction?
- What nonverbal behaviors stand out to you?
- What indicators of trust do you see? Is there evidence of rapport, genuine listening, and mutual regard?
- How are issues of identity, power, or bias at play?
- Does the interaction reflect other patterns, or cultural scripts, in the system?
- What structural factors could be influencing it (e.g., time, teaming, org chart)?
- Could these two individuals find a common goal?

Given all of this, how would you like to show up?

Jot down any new insights you may have now:
For a printable version of this tool, go to shanesafir.com/resources.

A SEAMLESS TRANSITION

By preparing to listen, Bianca—former site administrator, now district leader—had primed her brain to take in important, yet subtle, data when she met with each coach. In these meetings, she paid attention to all three levels of awareness: self, other, and system.

Having studied the brain research in Chapter 2, she found the idea of social threats popping up in her head like thought-bubbles as she listened. With one coach, she immediately sensed that the person's main concern was about status. With another, she felt that the person needed immediate certainty on some issues: *She's anxious about the induction process and has so many questions that she can't move ahead.* She listened for recurring words and sentiments and asked each person, "What would success look like for you at the end of this year?"

Within a week, she had completed 15 meetings of about 45 minutes each—this during a time of year when tasks pile up on desks and inboxes brim with requests. (Chapters 6 and 11 will offer more detailed guidance on how to facilitate different types of one-on-ones.) I asked her, "How would you convince another leader to invest 2 or 3 days in this process? What was the payoff?" Her response:

> Oh my god, the payoff was huge! As a leader, these meetings began to solidify the stance that I would take with the team. It gave them confidence that things are going to be okay under this new leadership. At the end of each conversation, I felt truly appreciated for having taken the time—from people who gave me hugs to those who thanked me for "being responsive" or just "being there."

By preparing to listen, Bianca created the conditions for a powerful and positive rechartering of a crucial instructional team. Just before schools opened their doors, she convened the entire team for the first time. Still nervous about the group dynamic, Bianca found herself facing a room of open, relaxed colleagues. She fielded questions as coaches and former mentors grappled with their blended role and began to lean on each other for support. One coach shared her satisfaction with the process: "We were all on pins and needles . . . and then pleasantly surprised! The group has come together seamlessly."

What made a potentially volatile situation come together "seamlessly"? Bianca prepared herself to listen mindfully. She overcame her own fears and laid a foundation of trust and mutual understanding for the work ahead. One team member reflected, "The idea of our new boss saying, 'Tell me who you are. I want to know each of you as individuals.' That set a great tone." A few days before school began, Bianca glowed with a new-found optimism that had eclipsed her anxiety. She had carved out a relational foothold with an important team and was clear about her next steps. Moving forward, she would schedule regular listening sessions to continue building trust but also to monitor the work. She would shift the conversations toward learning, asking coaches to reflect on their early conversations with teachers. Listening would be a formative assessment tool as she gauged the initiative's success.

Conversation by conversation, Bianca was becoming the leader she had always wanted to be.

KEY TAKEAWAYS

- There's no shortcut to trust. It's a precondition for hard conversations about equity and a core factor in school improvement.
- Notice when someone approaches you with a "bid" for care or attention; this is an opportunity to activate a threat or reward—to connect or betray.
- The Six Circle Model helps us understand our schools as living systems with technical (structure, pattern, and process) and relational (identity, relationship, and information) elements.
- Get ready to listen mindfully, following three steps: Look in the mirror, step into the other person's shoes, and step up to the balcony.

LISTENING LEADER INQUIRY

Question: I'm an introvert by nature. How do I overcome my own anxiety and fear to build strong relationships with others?

My thoughts: Preserving "alone time" to replenish yourself is crucial. It may also be helpful to share with your team that you are an introvert and what that means to you. Explain your hopes and intentions around building relationships, but also the reality that you may struggle from time to time. People appreciate honesty and vulnerability in a leader; it's humanizing.

Question: How can leaders balance the real demands of a to-do list with the need to respond to bids? Can you offer a few tips from your personal experience?

(Continued)

My thoughts: Here are a few ideas to consider:

Schedule talk time hours. Structure predictable times when staff members can bring specific concerns to you or just engage in open dialogue. Explain the purpose of this time, and advertise it in staff meetings and/or a newsletter.

Hold a weekly snack-and-chat. To reduce the amount of individualized bids and provide meaningful and thoughtful responses, host a weekly group chat at which you provide snacks to feed the lizard (see Chapter 2).

Do morning rounds. Circulate to classrooms in the morning to check in casually with teachers, interact with them in their space, and proactively support bids.

Do a walk-and-talk. A simple way to unlock your brain, move your body, and respond to a bid all at once is to invite the person who approaches you to take a walk-and-talk. I recently did this with an urban high school principal whom I coach. As we circled the long block around her school, we not only had a great coaching conversation, but she found and redirected several students back to school! Walking together can accomplish more than sitting in an office, with you behind the desk or even in a nearby chair. Walking side by side breaks down the physical power structures and creates a more equal conversation plane. For some people, not having to engage in direct eye contact makes it easier to be candid.

Defer, delete, or delegate. Do you make a "top three" list of priorities for any given week? If not, try making one each Monday. Once you do, comb through your to-do list looking for items that *don't* fit those priorities. For each one you discover, think about how to defer, delete, or delegate it.

Keep channels of communication open. Make sure that people know there are many ways they can consult with you outside of official meetings. Suggest they email you with follow-up questions; let them know they can text you. That doesn't mean you have to be available 24/7, but it sends the message that you're there if they need you.

Take care of yourself! You'll be a better leader who gets more done and responds more thoughtfully if you take time for yourself, as discussed in Chapter 2. Setting even small goals can help: *I will reach out to a leader colleague for support each time I find myself at an impasse, or I will reserve Sundays for family time and commit to turning off my cell phone all day.*

Question: Mindfulness sounds like a good idea, but how can I incorporate it into my day-to-day leadership?

My thoughts: Mindfulness can be a formal or informal practice. Formal practices include structured mental exercises, such as concentrating on your breath, walking slowly and consciously, or bringing awareness to what you perceive through your senses, as well as noticing your mental judgments and "scripts" about other people. You can embed informal practice in virtually everything you do as a leader. Here are a few simple ways:

- Start each morning with a 1-minute meditation. Do this alone or with a colleague, a team, or even a group of students. (Visit my website, shanesafir.com/resources, for sample short guided meditations.)

- Host a lunchtime mindfulness group. Set up chairs in a circle and set a timer for 10 minutes. Open the group with a poem, a quote, or just an invitation for participants to close their eyes and begin to notice their breath and any physical stress they're carrying.

- Do a walking meditation at school or in the office. Set a 5-minute timer and bring your awareness to the visual and audio signals around you. Notice the walls, notice people's body language, notice who is talking with whom. Just notice.

- Start your meetings off with 3 to 5 minutes of mindfulness. Chapter 10 includes a story of a staff meeting that begins like this.

NOTES

1. Bryk, A. S., & Schneider, B. (2003, March). Trust in schools: A core resource for school reform. *Educational Leadership, 60*(6), 40–45. Retrieved at http://www.ascd.org/publications/educational-leadership/mar03/vol60/num06/Trust-in-Schools@-A-Core-Resource-for-School-Reform.aspx
2. Bryk & Schneider, Trust in schools.
3. Bryk, A. S., & Schneider, B. (1996). *Social trust: A moral resource for school improvement.* Chicago, IL: University of Chicago Center for School Improvement, p. 6.
4. Korda, J. (2015, July 22). Meditation can hold feelings, but only other people heal our pain. *Huffpost Religion.* Retrieved from http://www.huffingtonpost.com/josh-korda/meditation-can-hold-feeli_b_7840596.html
5. Zueback, S. (2012). *Leadership practices for challenging times: Principles, skills and processes that work.* Washington, DC: DG Creative, pp. 2–3.
6. Wheatley, M. J. (1992). *Leadership and the new science.* Oakland, CA: Berrett-Koehler.
7. Adapted from Frankl, V. E. (1959). *Man's search for meaning.* Boston, MA: Beacon Press.

8. Heifetz, R., & Linsky, M. (2002). *Leadership on the line: Staying alive through the dangers of leading.* Boston, MA: Harvard Business School Press.

9. Sauer, S., & Kohls, N. (2011). Mindfulness in leadership: Does being mindful enhance leaders' business success? In S. Han & E. Pöppel (Eds.), *Culture and neural frames of cognition and communication* (pp. 287–307). Berlin, Germany: Springer-Verlag.

10. Goleman, D., Boyatzis, R., & McKee, A. (2013). *Primal leadership: Unleashing the power of emotional intelligence.* Boston, MA: Harvard Business Press.

Part 2

RELATIONAL CAPITAL

Chapter 5

Practicing Deep Listening

Preview: Now that you've prepared to listen, it's time to practice. Try using the Deep Listening stances in this chapter to build trust, connections, and relational capital.

This chapter is designed to help you:

- Understand how listening grows relational capital, the foundation of equitable school transformation.
- Learn to read and respond to nonverbal cues.
- Discover subtle ways to convey empathy and calm the amygdala.
- Leverage the stance of affirmation as a way to reimagine rewards and prime the brain for learning.

THE FALLOUT OF FAILING TO LISTEN

In my second year as a principal, I forgot how to listen. One day, Sandra, a veteran teacher and informal staff leader, dropped by my office to let me know. "Shane," she said, "people aren't happy with the professional development we've been doing. They're spending all their time in cross-content groups, analyzing lessons that don't feel relevant. What they need is to collaborate within their own departments."

"But it's a strong PD plan," I countered, "supported by a big grant. We can't spend all of our time planning curriculum. We also need to reflect and learn *across* disciplines. Isn't that the goal of professional development?"

Sandra sighed, scrunched her brow with restrained exasperation, and said, "Well . . . Right now people need time to plan together. They feel like you're not listening."

Just like that, my leadership identity had the wind knocked out of its sails. *Not listening?* I *prided* myself on being a Listening Leader. Having tuned my ears in the organizing process that gave birth to June Jordan School for Equity (JJSE), I held a deep belief in listening. Once the founding staff was hired, I met with each teacher to ask why he or she had chosen to work at JJSE, what his or her hopes were for our first year, and what he or she needed from me to be successful. In our first year, I checked in with people regularly, organized staff retreats to fortify trust, observed classrooms religiously, and provided feedback around areas that teachers themselves had selected. I even hired a masseuse to pamper the staff at our midyear retreat!

Things went well that first year. By the spring, JJSE had caught the attention of local foundations, and a program officer invited me to submit a proposal focused on innovative professional development (PD). My timeline was tight. I collected input from a few staff members before sketching out what felt like a promising, research-based model: Teachers would collaborate in cross-disciplinary professional learning communities (PLCs), using peer observation and video to reflect on one another's practice. I shot off the proposal, and within a month, we had received a sizeable grant.

In our second year, though, several events occurred that had a dramatic effect on my leadership. On a personal note, I had fallen ill that summer and had to return home from a trip to Southeast Asia for major surgery. When the new school year began, I made an effort to pull back physically and emotionally. I knew that the 16-hour days and intense pace of year one had affected, if not caused, my illness. But in seeking personal balance, I failed to anticipate the psychic distance I would create between me and my staff.

A campus relocation only heightened the pressure. When the district moved JJSE from San Francisco State University to a site across town in the southeast corner of the city, we lost our highest-achieving 20% of students and gained an equal number of students with high academic and social-emotional needs—a welcome shift given our mission, but a demanding one nonetheless. At the same time, we doubled our staff and student body. This meant that I needed to listen to and build relationships with twice as many human beings in the exact moment when I was trying to set healthier boundaries.

In hindsight, I recognize another, more subtle condition informing the listening gap that Sandra had named: I hadn't done enough "innervisions" work around my identity, power, and privilege as a leader.[1] Our founding team had worked hard to hire and retain a diverse staff on multiple measures—race, gender, age, experience, culture—which meant that as a leader, I needed to understand and be responsive to a wide spectrum of life experiences and perspectives. But I hadn't really looked in the mirror to ask hard questions like, *What does it mean to be a White woman leading a multiracial staff? What cultural and implicit biases do I need to examine and check to become an effective equity-driven leader? How do power and privilege show up in my leadership style, and where do I experience disadvantage?*

Sandra's words echoed in my ears: "People feel like you're not listening." I wanted to lead with humanity. I wanted to lead responsively. But under duress and lacking a coach or mentor, I started to slip into a nose-to-the-grindstone routine. I became more of a Driver than a Listening Leader. The more I felt accountable to the funder for our PD grant, the more tone deaf I became to the needs of my staff.

It's hard to acknowledge moments of failure. I've watched as, under the cloud of accountability (and a fear of losing status), leaders go to excruciating lengths to mask their weaknesses. But I knew it was time to figure out where I had gone wrong. It was time to rebuild what I call relational capital.

RELATIONAL CAPITAL

Relational capital is the term I use to describe the resource that leaders accrue when they take time to listen to and convey authentic care and curiosity toward others. And it's a precursor to many conditions for equitable school transformation: risk-taking, productive conflict, hard conversations, adult learning, and collaboration, among others. If relationships function as currency in schools, relational capital is like a big savings account of trust and goodwill (see Figure 5.1). Every time someone makes a bid for your attention, you have the opportunity to invest in this account. Conversely, when you need to push people or enlist them in a change agenda, you have the opportunity to make a withdrawal; there's cash in the bank, so to speak.

Looking back at my conversation with Sandra, I see a number of missed opportunities for creating relational capital—and some ways to rebuild it. In Chapter 4, we took a balcony view of our listening interactions "on the dance floor." This chapter and the next will focus on the role of learning

FIGURE 5.1   LISTEN TO BUILD RELATIONAL CAPITAL

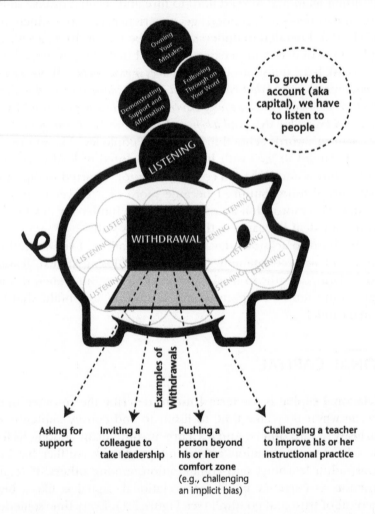

to listen on the floor itself. We'll be ferreting out the finer details of communication, such as:

- How to interpret a speaker's explicit and implicit messages
- How to hold your body and face as you interact with others
- How to craft your words to convey empathy and affirmation
- How to ask compelling reflection questions
- How to inspire a person to take action
- How to connect a one-on-one conversation to a larger vision of success

TWO TYPES OF LISTENING: DEEP AND STRATEGIC

There are two basic types of listening—Deep Listening and Strategic Listening—though often you need to do the two in succession. Buddhist monk and spiritual leader Thich Nhat Hanh defines **Deep Listening** as "the kind of listening that can help relieve the suffering of the other person . . . compassionate listening. You listen with only one purpose: help him or her to empty the heart."[2] If someone comes to you in distress, do your best to switch off your "fix-it" brain and allow the person to release emotion. Often, that's all he needs! I like to think of this practice as listening without an agenda.

Strategic Listening, by contrast, supports us to influence a person's thinking or behavior. (Hanh calls this "correcting wrong perception.") It still requires care and compassion—we can't influence a person if we view him with judgment or disdain—but the idea here is to help create the mental space that can lead to more thoughtful action. When we practice Strategic Listening, we prompt the speaker with carefully crafted reflection questions, which ultimately help him take steps to change some aspect of his mindset, behavior, or approach.

The rest of this chapter is about how to become a good deep listener; Chapter 6 is devoted to Strategic Listening. My hope is that you'll end these two chapters feeling energized and ready to practice new strategies. Table 5.1 is a preview of the Six Stances of a Listening Leader, which span these chapters. (Appendix B also offers a summary of the stances.)

PRINCIPLES OF DEEP LISTENING

Deep Listening is rooted in a few core principles that are countercultural in the education field, where we tend to privilege above-the-green-line approaches. (Recall the circles of structure, pattern, and process discussed in Chapter 4.) The idea of listening to allow a person to "empty his or her heart" may seem wildly disconnected from the urgency of improving test scores, implementing initiatives, or strengthening classroom practice. Particularly for Drivers and Managers (archetypes described in Chapter 1), Deep Listening may feel awkward and uncomfortable at first, and that's okay. You do not need to become a different person to develop a humanizing practice of Deep Listening. Exhibit 5.1 will help you assess your current go-to listening style.

TABLE 5.1   THE SIX STANCES OF A LISTENING LEADER (A PREVIEW)

Key Stances	Description	Examples/Places to Practice
Deep Listening Stance 1: Attention to nonverbal cues Deep Listening Stance 2: Mature empathy Deep Listening Stance 3: Affirmation	Listening with no agenda to allow a person to release emotion; supports healing and builds trust *(Note: Constructivist Listening, a routine profiled in Chapter 10, is a powerful structure for Deep Listening.)*	Teachers arrive at the staff meeting upset about a student fight at lunch. A parent comes to you in distress about her child. A colleague stops by to vent his frustration over a recent policy change.
Strategic Listening Stance 1: Orientation to vision Strategic Listening Stance 2: Reflective inquiry Strategic Listening Stance 3: Bias toward action	Listening in ways that influence the thinking, practice, or behavior of the other person	Supervisory one-on-one meetings Postobservation debriefs Coaching conversations

Note: Active listening, which means stopping to paraphrase and/or check your own understanding, is a key component of both Deep and Strategic Listening.

EXHIBIT 5.1   WHAT'S YOUR LISTENING STYLE?

People develop different listening habits over the course of a lifetime. Here are four primary styles, as originally identified by Watson, Barker, and Weaver:[a]

1. A people-oriented style, which focuses on the emotional and relational aspects of a communication
2. A content-oriented style, centered on processing complex information
3. An action-oriented style, where the listener prefers clear, efficient information
4. A time-oriented style, where the listener has a preference for short, limited messages

Women are often more likely to be people oriented, and men are often more likely to be action, content, or time oriented.[b] What do you notice about your default settings as a listener?

[a] Bodie, G. D., Worthington, D. L., & Gearhart, C. C. (2013). The listening styles profile-revised (LSP-R): A scale revision and evidence for validity. *Communication Quarterly*, *61*(1), 72–90.

[b] Johnston, M. K., Weaver, J. B., Watson, K. W., & Barker, L. B. (2000). Listening styles: Biological or psychological differences? *International Journal of Listening 14*(1), 32–46.

I offer you this idea to consider: Human beings and their concerns are the central text of equitable school transformation. This includes students, their families, and your colleagues. Every time you slow down to pay heed to those concerns, you add a bit of relational capital to the bank. And when

When you practice Deep Listening with teachers, you model the values of a culturally responsive, humanizing classroom that places students—not curriculum or content—at the center of the learning enterprise.

you practice Deep Listening with teachers, you model the values of a culturally responsive, humanizing classroom that places students—not curriculum or content—at the center of the learning enterprise. The power of this practice cannot be underestimated.

Table 5.2 frames four principles of Deep Listening, connected to common leadership pitfalls I have observed in the field (or have been guilty of myself).

TABLE 5.2   DEEP LISTENING PRINCIPLES AND PITFALLS

Principles of Deep Listening	Common Leadership Pitfalls
Power lies in the relationship.	• Thinking that a well-planned initiative will drive change on the ground • Forgetting that people have to "buy in"—not just to an idea, but also to *you* as a leader
Meet people where they are, not where you want them to be.[a]	• Leading from a self-proclaimed "sense of urgency" and pushing people to move faster than they are ready to
Emotional distress interferes with caring behavior and clear thinking.[b]	• Viewing emotion as "unprofessional"; judging or dismissing people's feelings • Failing to manage your own distress or allow for others to release their emotions
Everyone is a potential ally.	• Aligning oneself with one faction or another in the political landscape instead of building bridges • Failing to listen and learn from those you perceive as adversaries

[a] This principle and the first come from my work with the San Francisco Organizing Project, which is a branch of the Pacific Institute for Community Organizing (PICO; http://www.piconetwork.org/).
[b] This principle comes from curriculum on Constructivist Listening from the National Equity Project (NEP; https://blog.nationalequityproject.org/).

 MAKE IT MINDFUL

• Take a moment to reflect on the principles of Deep Listening. Grab a colleague with whom to discuss them. Which ones resonate? What connections do you make to your own leadership?
• Now think of a person in your school or team whom you know you need to listen to differently—a student, colleague, or parent, or even a supervisor. Hold this person in mind as we explore the stances.

DEEP LISTENING STANCE 1: ATTENTION TO NONVERBAL CUES

Nonverbal communication relies on wordless signals that illuminate people's emotions, social needs, and cultural norms. Chris Emdin talks about how nonverbal forms of communication function as shared cultural knowledge, or social capital, helping students (and urban youth in particular) navigate any challenges they bump up against in the classroom.[3] Learning to interpret and respond to nonverbal cues is a critical component of becoming a culturally responsive leader.

Because these signals are transmitted at the brain's reptilian level, we could playfully call this stance "read the lizard" instead of "feed the lizard." (You may recall the "feed the lizard" section of Chapter 2, which instructed us to take care of people's basic needs.) As you cultivate nonverbal literacy, you'll become an expert at assessing subtle clues to a person's disposition, and your next move on the dance floor will flow from that assessment.

What percentage of meaning do you think is conveyed by our words? In reality, it's less than 10%. As illustrated in Figure 5.2, even though we

FIGURE 5.2   NONVERBAL COMMUNICATION

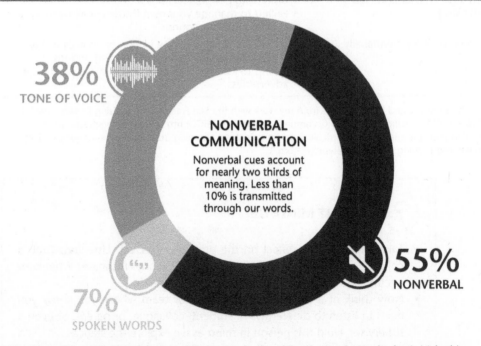

38%
TONE OF VOICE

NONVERBAL COMMUNICATION
Nonverbal cues account for nearly two thirds of meaning. Less than 10% is transmitted through our words.

55%
NONVERBAL

7%
SPOKEN WORDS

Note. Adapted from *Silent Messages: Implicit Communication of Emotions and Attitudes,* by A. Mehrabian, 1981, Belmont, CA: Wadsworth.

may spend a lot of time crafting our words, nonverbal cues account for over half of the meaning transmitted, and tone of voice accounts for nearly 40%.[4] In some cultures, those percentages may be even higher. Whereas in Western contexts, such as the United States and Canada, people tend to rely on verbal information to communicate meaning, places like Japan and Saudi Arabia require more inference and less talk.[5] My sabbatical year of teaching in Amman, Jordan, gave me insight into this difference and exposed my own reliance on verbal cues. I remember sitting in English Department meetings where little was said, but volumes were conveyed through facial expressions and tone.

Nonverbal cues are crucial for understanding the dynamics of role and power within school settings. British social psychologist Michael Argyle analyzed the communication of power, or what he called "submissive/dominant attitude." He found that nonverbal cues had 4.3 times the effect of verbal cues in communicating hierarchy, with physical posture being the most efficient way to reinforce status differences.[6]

 MAKE IT MINDFUL

The next time you interact with a colleague or parent, notice how you are holding your body and the subliminal messages you may be expressing. Consider the physical organization of the interaction: Are you sitting or standing? Is there a table or desk between you and the other person? Are you leaning in or sitting back with crossed arms? Are you making eye contact, or distracted by your phone or computer? Consider the dynamic that you *want* to have with this person—collegial, hierarchical, distant, trusting?—and adjust your stance accordingly. Inviting a person to take a short walk while you talk can be a simple way to level the playing field and lower the anxiety that a formal setting can produce.

Gender also acts as a major influence in nonverbal communication. Orick and other researchers note that women tend to show they are listening through eye contact, affirmative nodding, and responsive comments like "Right" or "That makes sense."[7] (Men often misconstrue these behaviors as tacit agreement with the speaker.) Men, by contrast, make less frequent eye contact; use little to no nodding; and may engage in movement, such as walking around a room. Are any of these descriptions familiar?

It can be helpful to remember that nonverbal communication takes place mostly at a subconscious level. Remember this the next time you feel triggered by a colleague's frown or a student's eye-rolling; the person is probably unaware of the offending signal. Bringing awareness to your own and others' nonverbal communication will help you practice mindful listening.

 MAKE IT MINDFUL

Ask a colleague's permission to video-record the first 5 to 10 minutes of your one-on-one meeting. Watch the video and analyze your nonverbal cues. What messages are you conveying nonverbally?

Here's a piece of good news: Training in listening and nonverbal communication significantly increases cross-cultural sensitivity.[8] You don't need to become a neuropsychologist to build muscle at reading and responding to nonverbal signals. Table 5.3 provides a starter kit of common cues and ways to interpret them.

Applying This Stance to My Conversation With Sandra

When Sandra approached me with concerns about our PD, I should have paid attention to her nonverbal signals. Looking back, I recall that her brow was furrowed and that she spoke in a slow, deliberate cadence. This might have indicated a hesitation to come forward, or a lack of trust in my willingness to hear her out. I remember that when I responded defensively, I watched her nod with an ever-so-slight smile on her lips. In retrospect, I see that this likely meant that I had confirmed her fears: I wasn't doing a great job of listening.

I also could have gathered nonverbal data while observing the cross-content PD. I remember sitting in on those meetings and sensing that something wasn't quite right. Even today, I have a mental image of checked-out facial expressions and passive body language—teachers slumped compliantly in their chairs. All signs pointed to a mismatch between the PD model and the needs of my adult learners. I wish I had developed the skill to interpret and respond to this evidence.

TABLE 5.3   INTERPRETING NONVERBAL CUES

Common Cues	Might Indicate . . .
FACIAL EXPRESSION	
Frowning	Confusion, frustration, lack of resolution
Smiling	Happiness, joy, intellectual breakthrough
Laughter	A rush of dopamine, a social or intellectual breakthrough, bonding
Verging on tears	Emotional overwhelm, fatigue, intense joy
Flushed	Shame, embarrassment
BODY LANGUAGE	
Nodding slightly	Thinking about or considering an idea
Hunched over	Feeling emotionally shut down or tired
Open shoulders and stance	Feeling confident and open
Leaning in	Wanting to connect or create an alliance
Stepping back	Discomfort with proximity; retraction from a comment that didn't sit right
Crossed arms	Frustration, skepticism, low trust
EYE CONTACT[a]	
Direct	Engaged, interested, curious, nervous
Averted	Bored or uncomfortable; not wanting to confront
Gazing at someone or something else	Cognitively distracted or emotionally distressed and looking for relief
Pupils dilated	Fear, anxiety
Increased blink rate	Anxiety; sudden perception of threat
BREATHING PATTERNS[b]	
Slow and rhythmic	Relaxed, feeling safe
Quick and/or short	Agitated, feeling threatened
PHYSICAL SPACE	
Keeps a distance	Low trust and/or cultural norm
Leans in or steps closer	High trust and/or cultural norm
VOICE AND TONE	
Loud and animated	Excited, feeling inspired, cultural norm
Soft and gentle	Nervous, feeling timid, cultural norm
Quivering	Scared of retribution, not feeling safe

[a] A note on the cultural nuances of eye contact: This nonverbal cue functions differently in different cultures. For example, in the Middle East, direct eye contact is less common and sometimes considered inappropriate. In East Asian countries, pointing one's eyes downward can signal respect for an elder. It is important not to jump to conclusions about what someone is trying to convey based on eye contact alone.

[b] Ting-Toomey, S. (1999). *Communicating across cultures.* New York, NY: Guilford Press.

DEEP LISTENING STANCE 2: MATURE EMPATHY

Empathy is the ability to perceive a situation from another person's perspective and vicariously experience his or her emotions—skills we rehearsed in Chapter 4. The stance of **mature empathy** is based on an understanding of how **mirror neurons** operate in interactions between leaders and stakeholders. These unique brain cells fire not only when we perform an action but also when we *observe* the same action (or emotion) performed by someone else. In other words, our neurons "mirror" the other person's behavior as if we ourselves had initiated it. Mature empathy allows us to form a mental picture of the other person's experience and demonstrate compassion by mirroring the person's nonverbal cues, using active listening stems, and validating what he or she shares.[9]

This stance is incredibly important for leaders who are navigating differences of race, culture, gender, age, and socioeconomic status; it can mitigate unconscious biases, build trust, and check the tendency to project one's own cultural norms onto others. As a young teacher in the Law Academy, I took my students on frequent field trips. One day, we traveled to a local law school's moot court room to rehearse for our upcoming mock trial. After boarding the bus, my student Alberto plunked himself down, wrapped his head with bulging earphones, and hunched over to stare out the window. I had asked students to finish prepping with their trial teams, so I approached Alberto with a gentle reminder to remove his headphones and join his group, at which point he grew agitated and told me that I should leave him alone. Well, you can imagine how my teacher hackles rose! I demanded that he show more respect.

Alberto did need to show respect, and I ultimately "won" the battle. But I recognize now that I missed an opportunity to cultivate trust through mature empathy. I didn't pause to formulate an idea of Alberto's experience: He was a Latino boy from a neighborhood with a strong gang presence, riding a city bus through other gang territories. He must have felt incredibly vulnerable, and needed some way to insulate and protect himself. By responding with authority before compassion, I failed to build a bridge to his reality.

On the flip side, mature empathy does *not* mean that we let teachers or students off the hook for poor behavior or performance. Gloria Ladson-Billings calls this the *pobrecito* (**"poor little one" in Spanish) syndrome** and rightly calls it out as a manifestation of unconscious bias in schools.[10] Despite the common rhetoric of "high expectations for all," the *pobrecito* syndrome manifests in a low bar of success for some students, often children of color. The authors of a report on transforming perceptions of Black men and boys describe how teachers, "worried about facing us in parent teacher meetings, will give our sons good grades for work that is not their best effort."[11]

The *pobrecito* pattern—close kin to the White savior complex I referenced in the Preface—reproduces educational inequity just as much as punitive responses. In fact, these two P's, the punitive and the *pobrecito*, prop up inequity in schools, just as structural racism and unconscious bias prop up the larger sociopolitical context. As leaders, we can easily fall into the *pobrecito* trap with teachers by making excuses for, or turning a blind eye to, mediocre practice.

Mature empathy doesn't mean trying to fix or solve other people's problems; on the contrary, it reminds us when to remain an empathetic listener without offering a lot of advice. This can be really difficult for leaders who are used to solving problems! Many people will directly ask, "What do you think I should do?" Although we may want to offer a quick fix— "If I were in your shoes, I would just . . ."—such advice fails to build that person's confidence in his or her own judgment and ability. If we always jump in to save the day, we risk cultivating dependency and learned helplessness. One of the gifts of a Listening Leader is the ability to empower others to make clearer and better decisions.

The stance of mature empathy works best when bolstered by active listening and validation moves. **Active listening** simply means paraphrasing and summarizing what the speaker has said. (See the tips here and Appendix B for examples.) *Validation* entails recognizing and legitimating a person's thoughts and feelings, whether you can relate to them or not. Think of these techniques as verbal companions to mirror neurons—ways of echoing back and normalizing the range of human experience. Active listening also helps us derive accurate meaning from what we hear, while validation calms the speaker's amygdala and activates the emotional reward of feeling seen, heard, and understood.

I recently led a retreat for a high school redesign team caught in the crossfire of district reorganization. Some members had just been moved to another division, but hadn't yet been told. When the team's director flashed a PowerPoint slide with these people's names conspicuously absent, the wheels came off the bus. One young woman spoke up in a distraught tone, "This *really* doesn't feel good. To see our names missing and to not have known before . . . I'm not feeling this." Because I was facilitating the session, all eyes fell on me: How would I respond? Would I shut her down? Back up the director? Ignore the comment? "I want to thank you," I said, "for taking a risk to put your feelings out there. It takes a lot of courage to

publicly name discomfort with a decision, and I commend you for that."
It was a simple validation move, but it allowed the room to uncoil itself as
she flashed me a grateful smile.

Being a leader who constantly fields other people's needs and concerns can be exhausting. Figure 5.3 comically depicts the cliff's edge to
which this state of affairs can bring us at times. The practice of mature
empathy will help you balance compassion with boundaried support: you
are saying, in effect, "I care about you and will listen to you, but I also want
to help you solve your own problem."

FIGURE 5.3   MATURE EMPATHY CARTOON

"So, does anyone else feel that their needs aren't being met?"

Tom Cheney/The New Yorker Collection/The Cartoon Bank

TIPS FOR USING THIS STANCE

Here are some ways to practice mature empathy:

1. Pause to form a mental picture of the other person's experience.

2. Notice and manage your own anxieties so that they don't distort your listening.

3. If you feel triggered, take a deep breath and try to step into the other person's shoes.

4. Employ active listening stems like these:

   - What I hear you saying is . . .
   - Am I missing anything?
   - In other words . . .
   - As I listen to you, I'm hearing . . .
   - Is there anything else you feel I should know?

5. Take advantage of mirror neurons to reflect back the speaker's tone, body language, and facial expressions.

6. Validate the person's experience, even if you don't share it.

   - I can see that you're distressed, and that makes a lot of sense given the circumstances.
   - I really hear and see what you're struggling with. You're not crazy!
   - That must be tough. I'm so grateful that you trusted me enough to share this.
   - I hear your concern about . . .

7. Ask what the person needs from you; don't assume.

   - Can you tell me what you need in this moment?
   - What can I do to support you?

Applying This Stance to My Conversation With Sandra

When Sandra approached me, I was so bothered by the staff's resistance that I failed to render a mental picture of their experience. Had I practiced mature empathy, I would have validated Sandra's mettle in coming forward to share these concerns, and I would have seen how overwhelmed the staff felt by teaching at a new school with a complex approach to teaching and learning. Instead, I was triggered by the message and shut down

---

EXHIBIT 5.2   MATURE EMPATHY STEMS

How are you doing, really?

How are you feeling about . . .?

What's going on for you right now?

I sense that you're feeling . . . Is that accurate?

Tell me a little bit more about why this is challenging for you.

It seems like this is bringing up a lot of emotion for you. Can you share
    what is coming up?

I have a hunch that there's something you are not saying . . . Do you want
    to put it out there?

When you think about . . . what thoughts or feelings come up for you?

I heard you say . . . Can you share a little more about what that means to you?

---

emotionally. It took me several days to overcome my amygdala hijack and
become genuinely curious about the feedback. By then, I may have lost
some relational capital.

DEEP LISTENING STANCE 3: AFFIRMATION

Negative feedback sticks to our brains like Velcro, with the potential to unleash toxic chemicals into the body, contract our muscles, cloud our cognition, and fuel negative self-talk.

The stance of **affirmation** allows us to reward the emotional brain (limbic system) and prime the thinking brain (neocortex) for learning. Negative feedback sticks to our brains like Velcro, with the potential to unleash toxic chemicals into the body, contract our muscles, cloud our cognition, and fuel **negative self-talk**—a running internal commentary on one's flaws and inadequacies. By contrast, affirmations—both verbal and nonverbal—release "happy chemicals" like **dopamine** and **serotonin** that serve to build a person's confidence, reinforce positive behaviors, and lay the groundwork for improved performance. Researchers from psychology and other fields suggest ratios for the number of positive to critical feedback interactions ranging from 3:1 to 5:1, a simple rule of thumb I often share with teachers and leaders.[12]

Practicing this stance doesn't require grand gestures. Researcher Mary Rowe defines **micro-affirmations** as "tiny acts of opening doors to opportunity, gestures of inclusion and caring, and graceful acts of listening." These acts are often "ephemeral and hard-to-see, events that are public and private, often unconscious but very effective, which occur wherever people wish to help others to succeed."[13] Micro-affirmations can take many forms,[14] such as

- Offering support (e.g., attentive listening, a warm smile, or a hug) when a person is distressed or has experienced a setback
- Providing clear, fair, specific, and timely feedback that helps a person build his or her confidence and capacity
- Leaving a note of appreciation in a teacher's box
- Facilitating a meeting ritual in which staff have the opportunity to appreciate one another (see Chapter 10)

Great teachers practice micro-affirmations all the time, mindfully finding ways to affirm *every* child in the classroom. Author and STEM educator Chris Emdin has students create a classroom handshake to reinforce successful interactions as a "silly humorous variation of the cultural phenomenon that creates a bond."[15] In my work with school leaders, I coach them to pay attention to these subtle features of classroom culture as well as to track the ratio of positive to negative feedback doled out to various students.

As human beings, we crave positive feedback from people we respect. Recently, my son, Maximo, learned how to make fresh-squeezed orange juice and slice bananas. He wanted to apply his newfound skills, so he brought a sampling of each item to his father and me. Before we could say a word, he started jumping up and down with a huge grin on his face and said, "Clap for me, and say thank you!" This precious moment reminded me that even when we feel good about our own behavior, we still want to be seen and affirmed by others. Maximo was craving affirmation.

Grown-ups need this reinforcement just as much as children do. My colleague Preston Thomas started and led an innovative school called Life Academy of Health and Biosciences for many years (I taught there briefly and later coached the Humanities Department and school leaders), where he made sure that every teacher had a weekly check-in with either him, the assistant principal, or a coach.

After learning about the importance of the 5:1 feedback ratio, he decided to implement this concept with teachers. He remembers one teacher who designed dynamic lessons but didn't have any type of a seating system or methodology. Students clustered with their friends in ways that seemed to Thomas to create unproductive group dynamics. In one of their early check-ins, Thomas asked the teacher why she allowed students free rein in their seating choice: "They're seniors," she said. "They should choose where they want to sit." *Okay*, he thought to himself, and decided that rather than fight this battle immediately, he would begin to emphasize her strengths.

We need to constantly look for and call out positive things people do, from the mind-blowing to the mundane. . . . By naming the positive, we begin to open up cognitive space for new learning.

Every time they met, he would name a specific asset and tell her exactly what he appreciated about it. He noticed that the next time he would visit her classroom, she would be doing those things he had affirmed even better! After several of these cycles, he offered some gentle feedback on the seating dynamics: "Hey, I noticed some interesting patterns of gender and race distribution in the class today. What do you think?" She was very receptive and open to the feedback and later thanked him for helping her adjust her seating chart. Thomas believes that had he launched into this feedback early on, she would have been defensive. Affirmation paved a path to feedback.

Overcoming the brain's negativity bias isn't a one-shot deal. Like all new learning, it requires repetition and rehearsal. We need to constantly look for and call out positive things people do, from the mind-blowing to the mundane. To a teacher: "Wow, I really appreciated that you spent 5 minutes with Joanna helping her grapple with that text." To a parent: "I'm so grateful that you took the time to meet with me and share your concerns." To a student: "I'm proud of you for how much effort you put into this assignment! Keep it up." By naming the positive, we begin to open up cognitive space for new learning.

 TIPS FOR USING THIS STANCE

Here are some ways to practice the stance of affirmation:

1. Set your brain to notice the positive—from the small to the significant.
2. Pick out specific behaviors or actions to reinforce with verbal affirmation.
3. Use nonverbal cues like touch and facial expressions to convey affirmation.
4. Tap into endorphins by inviting people to walk and talk rather than always meeting in a room.
5. Model affirmation repeatedly to flood people's brains with positive neurotransmitters.
6. When you see early indicators of trust, ask permission to give feedback.

EXHIBIT 5.3   AFFIRMATION STEMS

I really appreciate how you . . .

I'm impressed by how you . . . Here is the direct impact that I witnessed . . .

I want to share a strength I've noticed in your teaching . . .

What do you see as some of your strengths as a [teacher, leader, parent, etc.]?

What are you feeling most confident about in your practice these days?

What is one specific piece of that lesson that you want to lift up and celebrate?

Applying This Stance to My Conversation With Sandra

As I mentioned earlier, the teachers at JJSE were working hard to implement a challenging instructional model. At one point, a colleague told me in passing, "People just want to feel appreciated." At the time, it seemed almost childish to me, but I can see now how wrong I was. When Sandra approached me about the PD, I needed to thank her for the honest and thoughtful feedback, affirm the staff's hard work and dedication, and make adjustments to demonstrate that I had listened. I also needed to communicate clearly and transparently what those adjustments would be and why we were shifting course, modeling mature empathy.

Looking back, I see that my conversation with Sandra was a hard, but necessary, moment that forced me to confront the gap between my intentions and my actions. I was lucky to have an outspoken teacher who was willing to help me fill that gap. Although people who approach you with tough feedback might trigger a fight-or-flight response, use your mindfulness skills to slow down and listen to what they have to say; a frank colleague might have just the insight you need to shift your team culture. A quality coach can also serve this purpose.

With a bit of time, I was able to take in Sandra's feedback and modify the PD plan in response. I recently found a note in my end-of-year report to the funder: "Placed all teachers in cross-disciplinary groups for video-based discussions. Due to teacher feedback, switched from cross-disciplinary to content-based groupings." This small piece of data reminds me that we have to treat ourselves with compassion as well. I was a second-year leader in a complex school environment juggling lots of moving parts; I, too, needed support.

With the benefit of hindsight and many years of experience, I now see the role that Deep Listening could have played in strengthening my leadership: By accruing relational capital, this practice earns you the right to push people outside their comfort zones and creates a platform for hard conversations about equity, instructional practice, and school culture.

KEY TAKEAWAYS

- Listening helps us build relational capital with stakeholders.
- Know your purpose in each listening interaction: Deep Listening, Strategic Listening, or a mix of both.
- Pay close attention to nonverbal cues, your own and others'. (Deep Listening Stance 1)
- Practice mature empathy (Deep Listening Stance 2) by forming a mental picture of the other person's experience, activating mirror neurons, and modeling active listening and validation.
- Practice affirmation (Deep Listening Stance 3) in verbal and nonverbal ways to release positive neurochemicals that prime people for learning.

LISTENING LEADER INQUIRY

Question: What can I do when I listen to my staff and I have a hard time empathizing with what I'm hearing?

My thoughts: We are only human. Of course, there will be times when you struggle to empathize with people. I would encourage you to first determine what kind of listening you need to practice. Is it a moment for Deep Listening, where the person is venting his frustration and may not actually *mean* everything he says? Or is it a moment for Strategic Listening, where you may want to push the person's thinking and language? Even if it's the latter, can you take an inquiry stance? By that I mean, try to be curious about where the person is coming from. Sometimes, negative comments are a smokescreen for insecurity or fear; if you can expose those underlying feelings, the speaker may be able to shift into more thoughtful dialogue.

Question: Should the person speaking know which intention I have as a listener? Should we signpost how we're listening and why?

My thoughts: For me, this very much depends on the speaker's needs and current disposition. If the speaker seems distressed, I may ask, "What kind of listening do you need me to do right now? Do you want to just vent, or do you want a thought partner?" These questions empower him or her to coconstruct the purpose of our interaction. As far as explicit signposting is concerned, this is most useful when talking with other leaders who could benefit from learning the listening skills you are modeling. Transparent listening allows you to name the moves you're making and *why*, which can transform a conversation into a teachable moment. For example, suppose I am an assistant principal meeting with the third-grade team leader. Once I've read the teacher's nonverbal cues to discern that she is in distress, I might say to her, "Okay, I'm going to practice Deep Listening right now—meaning I'm just going to give you a chance to share whatever you're feeling. If and when you want me to ask questions to inform your next steps, just let me know."

NOTES

1. Emdin, C. (2016, February 23). *Teaching, learning, and becoming: Innervisions in the key of life.* Keynote at the 18th National Symposium on Teacher Induction, Bellevue, WA.
2. Hanh, T. N. (2012). Thich Nhat Hanh on compassionate listening [Video file]. *SuperSoul Sunday.* Retrieved from http://www.oprah.com/own-super-soul-sunday/Thich-Nhat-Hanh-on-Compassionate-Listening-Video
3. Emdin, C. (2016). *For white folks who teach in the hood . . . and the rest of y'all too,* Boston, MA: Beacon Press.
4. Mehrabian, A. (1981). *Silent messages: Implicit communication of emotions and attitudes.* Belmont, CA: Wadsworth.
5. Wolvin, A. D. (2012). Listening, understanding, and misunderstanding. In W. F. Eadie (Ed.), *21st century communication: A reference handbook* (pp. 137–147). Thousand Oaks, CA: Sage.
6. Argyle, M. (1988). *Bodily communication* (2nd ed.). Madison, CT: International Universities Press.
7. Orick, L. M. (2002). *Listening practices of leaders* (Unpublished doctoral dissertation). University of New Mexico, Albuquerque; Tannen, D. (1994). *Talking from 9 to 5: How women's and men's conversational styles affect who gets heard, who gets credit, and what gets done at work.* New York, NY: Ballantine Books; Marsnik, N. (1993). The impact of gender on communication. *Journal of the International Listening Association* (Suppl. 1), 32–42.
8. Timm, S., & Schroeder, B. L. (2000). Listening/nonverbal communication. *International Journal of Listening 14*(1), 109–128.

9. Aragno, A. (2008). The language of empathy: An analysis of its constitution, development, and role in psychoanalytic listening. *Journal of the American Psychoanalytic Association, 56,* 713–740.

10. Ladson-Billings, G. (2012, March 8). *Pushing past the achievement gap.* [Lecture]. Oakland High School, Oakland, CA.

11. Perception Institute. (2013). *Transforming perception: Black men and boys.* New York, NY: American Values Institute, p. 4.

12. Gottman, J. M. (1994). *What predicts divorce? The relationship between marital processes and marital outcomes.* New York, NY: Erlbaum; Losada, M. (1999). The complex dynamics of high performance teams. *Mathematical and Computer Modeling, 30*(9–10), 179–192. doi:10.1016/S0895-7177(99)00189-2; Losada, M., & Heaphy, E. (2004). The role of positivity and connectivity in the performance of business teams. *American Behavioral Scientist, 7,* 740–765. doi:10.1177/0002764203260208

13. Rowe, M. (2008). Micro-affirmations and micro-inequities [Editorial]. *Journal of the International Ombudsman Association, 1*(1), 45–48.

14. These ideas were adapted from Rowe, Micro-affirmations and micro-inequities.

15. Emdin, *Teaching, learning, and becoming.*

Chapter 6

Practicing Strategic Listening

Preview: With the practice of Deep Listening, you created a reserve of relational capital. Try using the Strategic Listening stances in this chapter to build the capacity of your colleagues to teach and serve every student who enters the building.

This chapter is designed to help you:

- Understand why Strategic Listening is critical for developing adult learners.
- Digest clear, concrete principles for the practice of Strategic Listening.
- Prepare to model an orientation to vision, reflective inquiry, and a bias toward action.
- Plan out a high-leverage conversation with a colleague, using the Six Stances of the Listening Leader.

THE IMPACT OF THE RIGHT QUESTION

I coached Abby in her third year of teaching ninth-grade English in a high school with many English language learners (ELL students). Her style leaned toward direct instruction, and she did a great job of modeling literacy strategies. One day, I observed her leading a mini lesson on paragraph revision. As I sat beside an ELL student named Daniela, I noticed that her "paragraph" was one long run-on sentence. Abby stood confidently before the class demonstrating how to revise a paragraph while Daniela struggled to makes heads or tails of hers. With the student's permission, I made a copy of the paragraph.

"Ugh," Abby sighed when she saw it, her facial expression shifting from neutral to dejected. "What do I do with this? She doesn't know what a period is." Daniela had a clear learning gap around punctuation and syntax.

"Well," I said, "you get to teach her! What do you know about her schooling experiences in Honduras? What are her strategies for approaching a task like this? You set a goal to individualize instruction this year, and this seems like an opportunity to practice. Why not pull Daniela aside tomorrow to coach her on this paragraph?"

"But we have a quiz!" Abby responded. "There's never enough time."

"Why," I pushed gently, "does she need to take the quiz more than she needs to sit with you, her amazing teacher, and learn how to structure a paragraph?" It was a simple question, but I saw signs of awakening spread across Abby's face.

"You're right," she finally said, issuing a sigh of relief. "I never considered my ability to make choices like this. Tomorrow, I'll work with Daniela one-on-one."

BUILDING CAPACITY THROUGH LISTENING

Leaders have to set a tone and have the skillset or the toolkit, if you will, to have those difficult conversations with staff . . . those real probing, pushing yet caring kinds of conversations, be it individually, across grade levels, across subject areas, or with an entire group of faculty and staff.

—DR. TYRONE HOWARD, professor of education at UCLA and director of the Black Male Institute

Sometimes the right question cracks open a whole new way of seeing things. My conversation with Abby boiled down to a simple inquiry: "Why?" By probing her assumption—that instruction requires keeping all students on pace all the time—I allowed her to free herself from a constraining mental model. It's important to note that this conversation took place well into the school year, when we had already built a strong relationship. At this point, I was attuned to Abby's nonverbal signals and had leveraged mature empathy and affirmation to build relational capital with her. She was ready to be pushed and challenged.

This chapter invites you to practice Strategic Listening by taking a coaching stance in your formal and informal conversations—to listen before telling and to probe before suggesting. Whether you're a formal coach, an administrator, or a teacher leader, you need to listen and create conditions for people's brains to grow—to water for deep roots, as we

TABLE 6.1   THE SIX STANCES OF A LISTENING LEADER

Key Stances	Description	Purpose
Deep Listening Stance 1: Attention to nonverbal cues	Listening with no agenda to allow a person to release emotion; supports healing and builds trust	Deep Listening
Deep Listening Stance 2: Mature empathy		
Deep Listening Stance 3: Affirmation		
Strategic Listening Stance 1: Orientation to vision	Active listening to influence the thinking or behavior of another person	Strategic Listening
Strategic Listening Stance 2: Reflective inquiry		
Strategic Listening Stance 3: Bias toward action		

discussed in Chapter 2. The Strategic Listening stances (see Table 6.1 for a reminder) will support you to facilitate

- Coaching conversations with colleagues
- Data-driven dialogue
- More meaningful conversations within the evaluation process
- Supervisory meetings that lead to growth and strategic action
- Courageous conversations around unconscious bias, microaggressions, and other barriers to equity

Whereas Deep Listening feels like a slow partner waltz, Strategic Listening requires you to be an active dance coach—helping people rethink their routines, stumble through new steps, and reflect on their progress. (Refer to Appendix B for a more comprehensive summary of the Six Stances of a Listening Leader.) An instructional coach recently asked me, "Why can't I just *tell* people how to improve? Isn't that more efficient than all of this listening business?" My reply was, "Does it work?" In my experience, *telling* grown-ups to change fails 9 times out of 10 because it violates the adult learner's need for autonomy and self-direction. By learning to pose the right questions at the right time, you will open up cognitive windows to new learning.

PRINCIPLES OF STRATEGIC LISTENING

In Chapter 2, we discussed the role of practice and repetition in the development of new neural pathways. Here we add another condition that is particularly important for the adult learner: choice. Researcher Lorraine Slater writes that a leader's preconceived agenda may interfere with listening and in turn will stand in the way of capacity building. When an agenda is in place, the principal may delegate unwanted tasks to others rather than listening well and attempting to figure out what would really inspire an individual.[1]

The Strategic Listening stances offer a corrective to this pattern. According to theorists Stephen Brookfield and Malcolm Knowles, the optimal adult learning environment is self-directed, collaborative, and inquiry based and allows educators to design and explore their own practices.[2] Strategic Listening conversations, facilitated by you in a one-on-one or team setting, represent the building blocks of such an environment. These well-planned sessions allow you to engage with colleagues in shared professional inquiry.

Table 6.2 frames four principles of Strategic Listening, connected to common leadership pitfalls.

Fortunately for me, I had two contexts in which to influence Abby. I regularly observed her classroom and engaged her in reflective coaching conversations. I also facilitated a biweekly professional learning community (PLC) with Abby and her colleagues in the Humanities Department.

TABLE 6.2   STRATEGIC LISTENING PRINCIPLES AND PITFALLS

Principles for Strategic Listening	Common Leadership Pitfalls
The people closest to the work need a voice in its design.	• Pushing an initiative without getting broad-based input, then watching people resist implementation • Making decisions with limited data or feeble efforts at gathering feedback
Adults engage in learning of their own volition; although the circumstances prompting the learning may come from outside, the decision to learn is the learner's.[a]	• Failing to understand that the decision to learn is always the adult learner's to make • Browbeating or coercing people into a professional learning plan
Adult learners need to engage in critical reflection.	• Telling people what to do or overscripting the learning experience • Taking people's legitimate questions personally • Failing to model the use of critical questions that prompt deep thinking
Adults must have opportunities to innovate, experiment, and apply their learning	• Not allowing people to experiment with new ideas and practices • Fostering a judgmental culture in which people feel that they can't make mistakes

[a] Adapted from Brookfield, S. (2004). *The power of critical theory: Liberating adult learning and teaching.* San Francisco, CA: Jossey-Bass.

As a coach and instructional leader, I helped the team gather and analyze multiple sources of Level 3 literacy data. (See Chapter 1 for a description of the Levels of Data framework.) We identified the students who were struggling the most, administered a comprehensive reading assessment, took detailed observation notes of students engaged in tasks, and interviewed them about their learning. Working with this data, the teachers proposed a literacy focus for the semester and helped design a cycle of inquiry, which I facilitated. As a side note, I baked or bought snacks for each meeting in order to "feed the lizard." It was a joyful and dynamic learning environment.

STRATEGIC LISTENING STANCE 1: AN ORIENTATION TO VISION

An **orientation to vision** means that we listen *for* and *in reference to* a clear picture of success. It helps you program your listening GPS toward a compelling destination: a district vision, an equity framework, a schoolwide instructional focus, a teacher's own goal. Without this picture, you may end up spinning your wheels as the other person wonders, *Where are we going with this conversation?*

As a leadership stance, an orientation to vision achieves a few key things:

A sense of purpose It helps you redirect people out of the weeds into a spacious sense of purpose for their work. The difficulty of school change can suck us down blind avenues and distract us from our core values. By asking a person to articulate his vision of success or link his work to an overarching vision, you construct a purpose-driven platform to revisit in future conversations.

A sense of motivation Just imagining a vision of what's possible releases a hit of dopamine in the body. I vividly recall the moment when a writing mentor asked me, "What would wild success look like for you?" I can see the cup of coffee I was drinking at the time, and hear the casual chatter bouncing off the café walls around me. I felt inspired as I explored the outer edges of what I had previously thought possible, and my brain encoded this positive memory.

A sense of empowerment With this stance, you communicate faith in a person's character and ability to think critically. Too often leaders fall into the same trap that we critique teachers for in the classroom: We carry the cognitive load for adult learners. An orientation to vision is a practical way to shift the load, convey the value of collaboration, and redistribute power. Instead of starting a conversation with *your* vision, elicit the other person's idea of success and then seek alignment.

A bar for excellence Finally, a vision sets a concrete bar for excellence in whatever role the person holds. This bar must feel ambitious and manageable at the same time. When you operate from this stance, you ask people to commit to a specific outcome, then you ask them to consider what changes that will require of them.

Many leaders spend hours crafting and massaging a vision statement to syntactic perfection, but I like mine short, crisp, and clear. A good one passes what the Heath brothers, in their book *Switch,* call "the Champagne Test"—it tells you exactly when to pop a bottle of champagne and celebrate.[3] Rather than overwhelm the adult learner with the magnitude of change, tight visions inspire a real can-do attitude.

To be effective, a vision should also be in our line of sight as much as possible: on meeting agendas, in our notebooks, and plastered on the office or classroom wall as a visible reminder of where we aspire to go. Exhibit 6.1 includes a few sample visions I've coached leaders and organizations to articulate after which you'll find tips and stems for practicing this stance.

EXHIBIT 6.1   SAMPLE VISIONS

A schoolwide vision

"We aspire to build a safe, healthy, and reflective community where children feel valued as they develop resilience and a strong personal and academic identity."

A principal's vision of her leadership

"I want to become more of a facilitator than a director so that change is coming from the staff. To do that, I need to have a clear vision of teaching and learning, promote authentic collaboration among teachers, and invest in coaching conversations with key admin and teacher leaders."

A teacher's instructional vision

"I want to integrate English language development into my math instruction. By the end of the year, I want to see my ELL's consistently using academic vocabulary in discussions of math content."

TIPS FOR USING THIS STANCE

Here are a few ways to practice an orientation to vision:

- Listen for opportunities to connect what people care about (values) with a vision of change.
- Start at the top by exploring people's philosophy and core beliefs about education.
- In your conversations and public speaking, model what a compelling vision looks and sounds like.
- Remember that a good vision can be simple and short.
- Encourage the person to write her vision down once she's comfortable with it.
- Invite her to post it visibly and reference it each time you meet.
- Weave references to vision into your messages and questions each time you meet.

EXHIBIT 6.2   ORIENTATION TO VISION STEMS

What do you see as the purpose of education?

What's your philosophy of education? What do you think your students [or child, in the case of a parent] see as the purpose of education?

What's your vision for this year? What would success look like?

What would be true in [insert time frame] if you achieved your vision?

What's at the border of audacious and feasible within this period of time? What feels at your edge or scary enough that it's worth investing in?

What are your hopes and dreams for [this classroom, this team, this school]?

What's your theory of action? What are the two or three things you need to focus on to get to that destination?

To make progress on this vision, what do you need to do differently? What do you need to learn?

What most excites you about where we're headed as a school or team, and what concerns you?

What do you want to be a part of creating for our community?

What matters most to you about . . .?

Applying Orientation to Vision to My Conversation With Abby

Using an orientation to vision, I helped Abby chart a way forward to reimagining her classroom. She decided to incorporate more small-group instruction and to develop a system "for identifying and addressing skill gaps through the use of exit tickets and other formative assessments." She also identified two "work style" goals: "to reduce my propensity to stress about the details" and to be "open to new ideas instead of feeling stubborn and entrenched." By articulating her own picture of success, she became invested in pursuing it.

STRATEGIC LISTENING STANCE 2: REFLECTIVE INQUIRY

A good question creates cognitive dissonance by unmasking the gap between a person's values and his or her actions.

Reflective inquiry is the bread-and-butter stance of a Listening Leader and an antidote to the quick-fix mentality perpetuated by the test-and-punish era. I often hear educators clamoring for a "tool" or "best practice" that will solve their instructional challenges. Although there are lots of great ones on the market, none will single-handedly improve instruction or produce equitable outcomes. The most critical resource we can provide is the opportunity to grapple with data and tough questions in the presence of a supportive coach, leader, or team.

Reflective inquiry boils down to asking artful questions. A good question creates **cognitive dissonance** by unmasking the gap between a person's values and his or her actions. When you find the right line of inquiry, the person displays telltale nonverbal signs of understanding, such as an alert facial expression or a sudden deep sigh. Or maybe he or she will lean back and just say "Ohhhh . . ." These are rock star moments! You've hit the cognitive jackpot and should feel proud. But be prepared for a less positive reaction as well: defensiveness.

If your question triggers a defensive reaction, don't retract it. Do a mental scan of the core tenets (see Chapter 2)—particularly the areas of social threat (status, fairness, autonomy, etc.)—to diagnose what's happening for the other person. Then practice the Deep Listening stances of mature empathy and affirmation to help the person process his distress. You might ask, "What is coming up for you right now?" or "I notice that you're sitting with some distress. Tell me about the thought or fear that has surfaced." Sit with her through this period of disequilibrium so that she can come out the other side ready to take action.

Reflective inquiry can also help us repurpose our data, treating it not as a source of shame or punishment but as a source of improvement. One consequence of the test-and-punish era is that many leaders have grown accustomed to overrelying on Level 1 "satellite" data to evaluate teacher effectiveness. Assessment expert W. James Popham explains:

> When we use the wrong tests to evaluate instructional quality, many strong teachers are regarded as ineffective and [are] directed by administrators to abandon teaching procedures that actually work well. Conversely, the wrong test scores often fail to identify truly weak teachers. In both these instances, it is the students who are shortchanged.[4]

Although Level 1 test scores or Level 2 data (e.g., annual evaluations) provide some information, they don't deliver the insight we need to support a struggling practitioner to improve. To build people's capacity, we have to gather Level 3 evidence of student learning *and* teacher practice. We need to regularly observe classrooms through a nonevaluative lens, talk with students, observe both teachers and students up close or capture video clips of them at work (with the teacher's permission, of course), and hold one-on-one reflective conversations with teachers. You don't have to be a formal coach to do this; imagine a school district in which leaders at all levels modeled reflective inquiry each time they spoke with teachers about instruction. What a powerful culture would emerge!

Exhibit 6.3 provides 10 types of Level 3 classroom data you can gather and 10 tips for data-driven listening.

Students themselves are another vital and overlooked source of data. Each time I observe a classroom, I sit next to two or three students and pose such questions as "What are you learning?" "Why are you learning it?" "Where are you getting stuck or confused?" Listening carefully, I jot down quick notes of their responses that I later bring to the teacher to ask, "What stands out to you here? Is there any gap between what you're teaching and what they think they're learning?"

Finally, reflective inquiry helps us model with *adult* learners the high levels of cognitive

Listening Leaders understand that if people power lies in the relationship, brainpower lies in the question.

EXHIBIT 6.3   STRATEGIC LISTENING TOOL: LEVERAGING LEVEL 3 DATA

10 Ways to Gather Level 3 Classroom Data	10 Tips for Data-Driven Listening
1. Coplan or review the teacher's unit and lesson plans. (Listen to how he or she *thinks* about curriculum design.)	1. Set a clear purpose for collecting data from the onset, choosing a tool that is connected with the lesson plan.
2. Record and watch short videos of students working on a task or engaged in discussion.	2. Develop a systematic way of collecting data over time; embed specific data-gathering points into the plan.
3. Create a tool to track or script teacher-student interactions. Pay attention to the ratio of positive to negative interactions, disaggregated by race, primary language, and/or gender.	3. Find a way to quantify or describe student and teacher behaviors that show progress.
4. Track the amount and type of teacher talk vs. student talk. Pay attention to the quality of questions posed by the teacher.[a]	4. Ensure that when teachers are planning lessons, they embed some sort of formative assessment.
5. Review sample formative assessments with the teacher; ask the teacher to identify an advanced, at-level, and struggling sample.	5. Don't assume that teachers always understand how to analyze formative assessment data. Model the types of questions you would use to analyze student work.
6. Create a simple tool to tally students' time on task vs. off task.	6. Don't assume that teachers know how to make instructional decisions after analyzing data. Help them plan and practice next steps.
7. Track data on specific elements like wait time, passing back work, proximity, transitions, and clarity of directions.	7. Use questions to probe a teacher's underlying assumptions and push for specific data to support interpretations.
8. Use rubrics to map student performance against specific criteria (i.e., a group-work rubric).	8. Collect different types of classroom data to get a robust picture of student learning.
9. Do a quick sketch of the classroom and track with codes and lines the teacher's path of movement in the course of a lesson.	9. Remain open to different possibilities for what constitutes data. (For example, visual representations or spoken word/hip hop renditions can be a powerful way to express complex content.)
10. Script the teacher's questions during the lesson. Coach the teacher to sort his or her questions into a cognitive rigor framework, such as Webb's Depth of Knowledge.	10. Be cautious with the words "engagement" and "on task." These are not synonyms, and it's easy to interpret student compliance as cognitive engagement when it is not.

Note. These ideas are adapted from brainstorming sessions with the extraordinary team of instructional coaches in East San Jose, California, with whom I have worked extensively.

ᵃ My colleague Staci Ross-Morrison, coprincipal of Oakland Technical High School, encourages teachers to use the "age minus two" rule for teacher talk. Teachers take the average age of their students and subtract two to arrive at a maximum number of minutes for direct instruction, which must be broken up with opportunities for information processing: discussion, small-group work, or other forms of active learning.

engagement that we want them to model with their students. We can't expect teachers to facilitate deeper learning—to deliver rich content in dynamic ways that promote application and transfer of knowledge—unless we provide deeper learning experiences for teachers.[5] This stance will help you close the gap between your stated instructional values and the values you actually *model* as you engage with adult learners. Listening Leaders understand that if people power lies in the relationship, brainpower lies in the question.

Reflective inquiry is a powerful stance for leaders of all levels: coaches, teachers, principals and assistant principals, counselors, and central-office staff. It equips us to effectively challenge beliefs and mindsets and help the practitioner prepare to take more thoughtful, data-based, and equity-driven action. Exhibit 6.4 applies this stance to the process of challenging unconscious bias, and Exhibit 6.5 provides reflective inquiry stems.

Applying Reflective Inquiry to My Conversation With Abby

Our conversation began with a thin slice of Level 3 "street" data—Daniela's run-on sentence/paragraph. The paragraph rang an alarm bell in Abby's brain; it cued her brain to pay attention, but also made her upset.

I used a few carefully crafted questions to create cognitive dissonance that would lead to new action. First I asked, "Why?" Why make Daniela take the class

EXHIBIT 6.4   CHALLENGING UNCONSCIOUS BIAS THROUGH REFLECTIVE INQUIRY

The metaphor of an iceberg is frequently used to explore the less visible dimensions of a problem, those that lie below the water line. This versatile metaphor helps us think about using reflective inquiry to challenge implicit biases that live in the subconscious recesses of the brain.

(Continued)

Imagine an iceberg in the ocean, with only its tip visible (see Figure 6.1). That tip represents the *patterns* and *practices* we observe as we move about our schools; for example, in a school with many Latino students, Advanced Placement courses have a disproportionate number of White and Asian students in them, or a teacher repeatedly sends her African American female students to the office for perceived "defiance." Just below the water line float *perceptions*—the filters people employ to interpret the world and, in schools, to

FIGURE 6.1   STRATEGIC LISTENING CLOSES THE GAP BETWEEN STATED BELIEFS AND ACTUAL PRACTICES

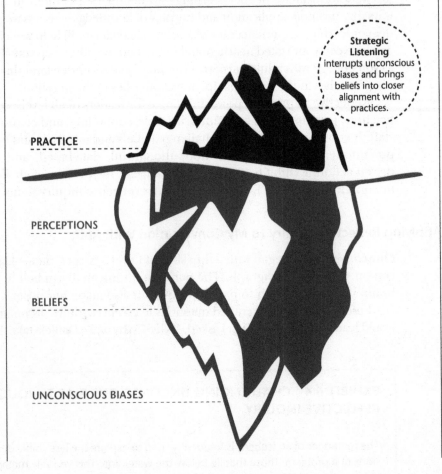

Strategic Listening interrupts unconscious biases and brings beliefs into closer alignment with practices.

PRACTICE

PERCEPTIONS

BELIEFS

UNCONSCIOUS BIASES

evaluate student behavior. The teacher views her African American girls' ways of communicating as "disruptive" and "disrespectful." Below perceptions hover *beliefs,* the opinions one holds about how things are and should be. When you talk to this teacher, she may state a belief like, "Students shouldn't shout out answers in the middle of the lesson" or "Students should only get out of their seat with my permission."

Finally, at the ocean floor lie *unconscious biases,* those attitudes that unknowingly influence a person's beliefs, perceptions, and practices. In this case, the teacher may unconsciously view the same behavior differently depending on whether it's a White girl or a Black girl displaying it. When you observe the class, you may notice that a White girl who shouts out an answer is rewarded with a "Nice job," whereas a Black girl who does the same is told, "Don't disrupt class!" How would a Listening Leader address this issue? Reflective inquiry is key. Strategic questions help you elicit and interrupt hidden implicit biases in ways that push a person's thinking while averting an amygdala hijack. The person maintains enough emotional balance to reconsider and potentially change his or her behavior.

Imagine that you mentor a young teacher in a high-poverty school where a majority of students are English language learners (ELL students). Last week, you observed a math lesson in which the teacher was providing direct instruction. Two ELL students, Adrian and Raul, didn't turn in their homework and were consistently off task. The teacher *believes* that he is doing a great job and *perceives* that the problem lies in the students' cultural, linguistic, and home barriers. In previous conversations, he has made comments that trouble you: "They must not have pencils at home" and "Their parents clearly don't care about homework."

You want him to check his own biases and make a real effort to work with these two students. Here are a few reflective inquiry prompts you might try:

- "Let's talk about the lesson. What did you observe with respect to Adrian and Raul's engagement with the math task?"
- "How do you know that either student understood the content? What's your evidence?"
- "I feel like we've built some trust. May I have permission to push you a bit? I hear you making a lot of assumptions about what's true at home for these two students. What are those assumptions based on? What other interpretations are possible that don't apply a negative, or deficit, lens to Adrian and Raul?"
- "Imagine that you were the mom of either student. How would you want their teacher to view them? To talk about them? To support them? What would it sound like to shift your language as if she were in the room with us?"

Consider any other lines of reflective inquiry you might try.

quiz when she so clearly needs help? As Abby chewed on that provocation, I asked her to recall her stated value—to identify and address students' skill gaps—and to consider a different approach with Daniela. After reflecting on the questions I had posed, Abby was finally able to do that. "I never thought about the fact that I can make choices like this," she said.

EXHIBIT 6.5   REFLECTIVE INQUIRY STEMS

What are your hopes and fears about . . .?
What might be getting in the way of . . .?
Tell me how you understand the problem. What evidence supports that interpretation?
If you step back for a moment, what's a different way of seeing this challenge?
How are you thinking about . . .?
What makes this problem feel confusing or different?
When have you had success addressing a similar problem? What can we learn from that?
What has been challenging about this for you in the past?
What has been your experience with . . .?
What if you tried . . .? What might you learn?
What makes you believe that trying this will result in that outcome?

STRATEGIC LISTENING STANCE 3: A BIAS TOWARD ACTION

Our final stance, **bias toward action**, stems from the principle that adults must see the immediate relevance of their learning and have a chance to put it into practice.[6] (In this instance, I use *bias* with a positive connotation.) Stephen Brookfield places **praxis** at the heart of adult learning, which refers to the continuous process of action, reflection, and experimentation.[7] A bias toward action releases people from the tyranny of perfectionism and mobilizes them to try something new, even if they struggle along the way.

In the accountability climate, many educators grew fearful of trying out new practices. Would they fail or be seen as weak teachers? But Listening Leaders view failure as key to growth—and mistakes as data for learning.[8] When you model a bias toward action, you let go of the need to micromanage what happens in a teacher's classroom, you communicate trust, and you encourage a healthy culture of innovation. This stance is the foundation of a routine called safe-to-learn inquiry, which we'll explore in Chapter 11.

A bias toward action communicates that it's okay to fail—that you'll be there to help your colleagues learn and grow. Invite people to experiment with and "try on" new practices, with an expectation that they'll reflect on what they learn in the process. And every chance you get, ask: "What have you noticed?" and "What did you learn?" Exhibit 6.6 contains stems for practicing a bias toward action with colleagues.

EXHIBIT 6.6   BIAS TOWARD ACTION STEMS

Now that we've debriefed the lesson plan, let's take a few minutes to improve it together. What one or two concrete changes would you make?

As a result of this conversation, what new instructional move will you try out tomorrow?

What specific action steps will you take, and when can we debrief?

What's one small, manageable step you can take in this direction this week?

Let's take a few minutes for you to practice the instructional move you've identified . . . How did that feel?

What are you going to prioritize next, and how can I both support you and hold you accountable to your own goal?

What fears or anxieties surface when you think about doing or trying . . .?

What do you need to do to prepare yourself to do or try . . .?

Applying This Stance to My Conversation With Abby

From her moment of epiphany, Abby and I created an actionable experiment. The next day, she worked with Daniela on her paragraph and felt very successful. That success likely released dopamine in her brain, which would have reinforced the importance of investing in this type of targeted student support. By the year's end, Abby had become so committed to targeted literacy instruction that she spearheaded a new reading intervention program for her school.

INTEGRATING THE SIX STANCES

The Six Stances are the Swiss Army knife of a Listening Leader. They are flexible and adaptable in different settings, and they will help you invest in relational capital with stakeholders. They also function as a scaffold for adult learners, enabling you to work with people inside their **zone of proximal development (ZPD)**—the gap between what they can do alone and what they can do with your support.

When practicing Strategic Listening with teachers, I use the term *instructional conversation* to connote any nonevaluative dialogue focused on teaching, learning, and reflection. You can have an instructional conversation anywhere: over a cup of coffee, on a casual walk-and-talk, beside the copy machine, or, as the principal of a sprawling comprehensive high school told me, "in the golf cart!" These informal exchanges are high-leverage ways to build teacher capacity.

A well-planned instructional conversation fluidly incorporates the Six Stances. Let me illustrate how I might apply them in real time. First, I assess the person's emotional state by paying attention to nonverbal cues (revisit Table 5.3, Interpreting Nonverbal Cues). Then I display mature empathy to connect with the person on a human level. Next, I frame the purpose of the conversation in connection to one or more levels of vision: the school's, the team's, or the teacher's own goals (orientation to vision). From there, I elicit or name a specific celebration—some small sign of growth in the teacher's practice. This affirmation move stimulates happy neurochemicals and primes the pump for learning.

The bulk of the conversation draws on reflective inquiry questions that gently probe and push the teacher's thinking—often using a piece of street data as a third point in the conversation. As new insights arise, I exhibit a bias toward action by asking what concrete next step the person will take and when we can check in to discuss how it went. It's important to close as we began: in the human domain of feeling and connection. Here I return to mature empathy and affirmation, asking the teacher, "How did this conversation feel for you?" and "What are you most excited about [or concerned about, depending on the topic and the mood] moving forward?"

Table 6.3 offers a sample protocol for instructional conversations that can be easily adapted for noninstructional settings. You'll find a template of this planning tool in Appendix C.

SEEDS OF TRANSFORMATION

Abby was so successful at making positive changes in her teaching style that she eventually became her school's literacy specialist, and later an instructional coach for her district. After reading a recent blog post I wrote about our work together, Abby sent me this email:

> I finally had a chance to read your blog and recognized myself immediately! This moment is the exact one that I often quote as a pivotal teaching epiphany, which you coached me towards. I remember it so distinctly. I did become more aware of my need to individualize and was able to let

TABLE 6.3   SAMPLE INSTRUCTIONAL CONVERSATION

Steps	Key Stance	Sounds Like . . .
1. Open	Mature empathy	**Connect with warm, affective questions:** "Hey, how are you? How are things going?" "How did your recent [*blank*] go?"
2. Frame	Orientation to vision	**Set a clear intention for the conversation:** "I'm glad we found time to sit down together. In this time, I was hoping to . . ." "I want to anchor us in [your goals, our school's instructional focus, the district's graduate profile, our equity mission, etc.]."
3. Prime	Affirmation	**Positively prime the brain for learning:** "Let's start with a celebration. Tell me about one recent success you've had [in the classroom, in your leadership role, with a particular student, etc.]." "That's great. I also wanted to commend you for . . . [allowing students to struggle through that problem; challenging students to use the academic vocabulary in conversation; asking high-level questions; etc.]."
4. Probe	Reflective inquiry	**Assess by tapping the teacher's thoughts first:** "So tell me: How did *you* feel about the lesson? How do you think it went?" "What's one slice of the lesson that you'd like to reflect on together today?"
5. Focus	Reflective inquiry	**Model a focus on learning:** "Do you have or were you able to look at student work to assess the impact of the lesson?" "Let's take a look at this data I collected: What does it reveal to you?" "Let's talk about that. What student gaps or misconceptions were revealed?"
6. Prepare	Bias toward action	**Identify an actionable issue and next step:** "What's one element of the lesson that you could improve on?" "What's one instructional move you can try out tomorrow to address the gap we've discussed?" "Let's practice that move. Don't worry about getting it 'right'; just take a stab at it and then we'll pause to debrief."
7. Close	Mature empathy/ affirmation	**Assess through nonverbal and verbal cues:** "How did this conversation feel for you?" "How do you feel about working on this issue?"
Postconversation reflection (This is for you as the leader; you could do it in writing, with discussion partner, or as a silent reflection.)		How did it go? What worked and didn't work? What did you learn?

Note. For a printable version of this tool, and a noninstructional template for using the Six Stances, visit shanesafir.com/resources.

go of some things a little bit more easily. Thank you again for teaching me to see things differently.

Strategic Listening plants small seeds of transformation for adult learners. As we'll see in Chapter 9 on complex change, we can't always predict what will grow, but we *can* create good conditions.

KEY TAKEAWAYS

- The Strategic Listening stances help us water for deep roots (Chapter 2) the brains of our adult learners.
- An orientation to vision helps you take the adult learner to the balcony to consider the larger purpose, or "why," for shifting his or her actions. (Strategic Listening Stance 1)
- Reflective inquiry is the bread and butter stance of a Listening Leader. Good questions provoke cognitive dissonance, leverage data as a third point, and help unmask unconscious biases. (Strategic Listening Stance 2)
- A bias toward action promotes innovative thinking, risk-taking, and experimentation—key conditions for instructional improvement. (Strategic Listening Stance 3)

LISTENING LEADER INQUIRY

Question: What if I need to get rid of a bad teacher? Am I still supposed to listen?

My thoughts: This is an important question that I know many leaders grapple with. My short answer is yes. Sometimes you have to coach someone out of her role to do what's best for students. But this is still a human being in front of you, with thoughts, feelings, hopes, and stories, so you want to be humane. Also, the Strategic Listening stances will help that person process the decision. I once coached a principal out of her job after it became clear that she was not the right person for it. But she needed space to grieve and let go (mature empathy helped here), to envision a new future (orientation to vision was key), and to set herself on a new course (I used a bias toward action). Through our conversations, she was able to see a way forward and leave gracefully instead of being pushed out through the back door.

NOTES

1. Slater, L. (2008). Pathways to building leadership capacity. *Educational Management Administration & Leadership, 36*(1), 55–69.

2. Knowles, M. S. (1978). *The adult learner: A neglected species* (2nd ed.). Houston, TX: Gulf Publishing; Brookfield, S. D. (1986). *Understanding and facilitating adult learning.* San Francisco, CA: Jossey-Bass.

3. Heath, C., & Heath, D. (2010). *Switch: How to change things when change is hard.* New York, NY: Broadway Books.

4. Popham, W. J. (2016, April 4). The fatal flaw of educational assessment. *Education Week.* Retrieved from http://www.edweek.org/ew/articles/2016/03/23/the-fatal-flaw-of-educational-assessment.html

5. Deeper learning is a pedagogy that promotes 21st-century skills and helps students apply what they learn in the classroom to new and real-life situations. For more details, visit the William and Flora Hewlett Foundation's website on deeper learning: http://www.hewlett.org/programs/education/deeper-learning/what-deeper-learning.

6. The phrase "bias toward action" is a fundamental principle of design thinking. In its most basic sense, it means to promote action-oriented behavior, rather than to get mired in process and discussion. The d. school at Stanford University is a pioneer in this work.

7. Brookfield, *Understanding and facilitating adult learning.*

8. Dweck, C. (2006). *Mindset: The new psychology of success.* New York, NY: Ballantine Books.

Chapter 7

Listening to Parents

Preview: For schools to become equitable spaces for every student, educators must break down school-family barriers and listen deeply to parents.

This chapter is designed to help you:

- Understand why listening to parents is critical to equitable school transformation.
- Apply the equity channels to common challenges around parent engagement.
- Flip the parent-educator "script" with a few simple rules.
- Learn concrete routines for listening to parents.

> To take on the work of supporting Black and Brown kids in reaching a college education, you need to leverage every resource and every partnership that's available, and parents are the heart of that work. They are the people who love their children. They are the people who will help you take a system that has marginalized and not served their children and transform it. And they're the ones who hold the perspective and the ability to do that.
>
> —AMY CAROZZA, principal, East Oakland, California

WHEN THINGS FALL APART

Jackie is nervous as she prepares to facilitate a meeting between a frustrated teacher and a distressed mother. As a Black woman administrator at a mostly Asian school, Jackie has dealt with her share of cross-cultural miscommunication, but the stakes feel extra high today. The mother—one of a handful of Black parents at the school—has been called in to school every year of her son's 5-year tenure to discuss something he "did wrong" or why he is "behind," or, most recently, why he "should be tested for special education services." Jackie gets it: The mother doesn't trust the school, and why should she? No one has really listened to or built a relationship with her, and it seems to her that the school is doing everything it can to communicate that her child doesn't belong there.

The three women are meeting to address a recent incident: After the child was allegedly running inside the classroom, his teacher took him into the hallway where the child says she yelled at him and left him unattended for several minutes. Jackie knows the mom is "hotter than hot" and wants the teacher fired. The teacher, however, thinks she has done nothing wrong. In her mind, she didn't yell at the student; she simply wanted him to correct his behavior. To add a layer of complexity, the teacher, who is Chinese, has shared with Jackie that it is unacceptable and unusual for a student or parent to question a teacher's authority. Jackie, who operates with a deep respect for equity and cultural sensitivity, has her work cut out for her.

Before entering the room, Jackie takes a deep breath and pauses to acknowledge her own emotions about the situation. She practices self-affirmation to get herself ready to listen: *Don't worry about the emotions coming up. You have a good plan.* She has three goals for the meeting: She wants the teacher to acknowledge that the situation could have been handled differently; she wants the mom to apologize for her role in the current negative dynamic; and she wants the three of them to leave on the same page about next steps. She has even created what we might call a restorative conversation process that includes sharing, listening, and paraphrasing the other person's words.

Plans aside, Jackie maintains two perspectives that are tough to reconcile. On the one hand, the teacher wants the *mother* to take responsibility; she can't believe that a student would challenge her authority, and she lacks the skills to address the behavior effectively. On the other hand, Jackie knows that the mom's guard is up; the mom wants the *teacher* to take responsibility, but isn't aware of how tapped out the teacher is. In Jackie's mind, this educator has hit the limits of her current skill set and doesn't know what to do differently. *How do I manage both women's experiences and needs?* Jackie wonders.

Once the three women are assembled around a table, Jackie frames the meeting's purpose and process. Everybody plays along until they arrive at the details of the incident, and things go sideways. "Can you share why your son felt the way he did?" Jackie asks. The mom takes a risk to disclose her son's history with the school, as well as his reports of feeling disliked and mistreated by his teacher, and Jackie leans in with compassion. Suddenly the teacher jumps in and calls the child's version of things "ridiculous," claiming he is telling a tall tale to "get attention." At this point, Jackie has an intense emotional reaction.

She is hurt and angry, and not sure what to say next. She wants the teacher to think beyond this dismissive characterization, but the conversation seems at an impasse. In the final moments, the mom rises above the fray to share something she's learned in a recent training: "I realize I have to take some responsibility for whatever is going on here. I want to apologize for my role." Jackie is moved and impressed by the mom's graciousness and upset that the teacher never apologizes. The meeting leaves her feeling raw and disappointed. What can she learn from this experience?

NAVIGATING DIFFERENCE WITH PARENTS

Jackie is a close colleague who reflected on this experience as a case study for navigating difference with parents. (I use the term *parent* expansively to include whoever is serving in the parental role for a student—grandparent, older sibling, or other significant adult.) Sometimes listening to parents requires grappling with your own implicit biases; at other times, it's about helping a colleague understand hers. Here, Jackie demonstrated cultural competence through listening and responding with mature empathy, but she also had to support the teacher—and the school as an institution—to reimagine the relationship with the mother. The Deep and Strategic Listening stances are vital tools in such a complex situation.

When striving to build trust and navigate difference with parents, you must consider the equity issues at stake: how **structural racism** and inequity may impact the parent's experience, any **unconscious biases** you or your colleagues may be harboring about the parent, and **cross-cultural issues** that may be at play. With the benefit of Jackie's insight, let's do a close reading of the story to better understand how to listen to parents.

Structural Racism

The channel of structural racism raises our awareness of systemic barriers to parent engagement, particularly for poor, working-class, and immigrant families. Do you recall the birdcage metaphor from Chapter 3? Factors like transportation, housing, grueling work schedules, and access to child care often act as wires on the birdcage, impeding school involvement. If events take place during working hours, for example, many parents can't attend. Researcher D. C. Peña found that parents want the school to announce meetings and events far enough in advance so that they can arrange for time off from work if necessary. Participants in Peña's study voiced appreciation for schools that acknowledge working parents' needs by scheduling activities accordingly.[1]

In her situation, Jackie realized that she needed to help the teacher recognize a subtle, but equally challenging, barrier: what she called historical marginalization. Even though she came from a middle-class Black family, the mother reported feeling marginalized in her own schooling experience, and she never lost that feeling when dealing with her child's education. The school's 5-year history of treating her son as a "problem" created a barrier to trust with which Jackie deeply identified as a Black woman and parent. Speaking of her stance toward her own children's schooling, Jackie shared, "I come in thinking I have to advocate, and I am already halfway defensive."

By tuning in to structural racism with parents, you can mitigate its effects through the use of creative strategies to connect with your most marginalized families. This begins with listening for the deep "funds of knowledge" that each family possesses about their children and communities.[2] It also requires a willingness to resist defensiveness when a parent shows up in your office with a critique or concern. With parents who've experienced *generations* of educational alienation, leaders must practice mature empathy and affirmation first and foremost to earn trust.

Amy Carozza, principal of the extraordinary Coliseum College Prep Academy (CCPA) in East Oakland, California, focuses on making her school's systems transparent and taking time to educate parents about those systems. CCPA serves a low-income community with virtually all students of color and boasts a 91% graduation rate, compared to roughly 60% in the school district at large, and an 84% college eligibility rate. How did Carozza and her team get these results? In large part, through their alliances with families.

Carozza shares, "Parent frequently ask me, 'What can I do?' so I'm always trying to clarify what a supportive parent looks like so that I can tell people explicitly." She uses the example of report cards. In the early years of CCPA, the staff discovered that many parents didn't know how to interpret a grade-point average (GPA). Report cards went home, and families with struggling students didn't really respond. Carozza realized that she couldn't expect parents to "get on their kids for bad grades if we don't have a shared understanding of a GPA." So the school invested in teaching parents how to read a report card and interpret a GPA, and soon parents were stepping up as partners in this endeavor.

Unconscious Bias

In Chapter 3, we discussed the fact that all people carry unconscious biases, and that it's the job of equity-driven educators to figure out what those are and how they manifest. When entering a meeting with a parent, we need to ask ourselves what implicit assumptions we may hold about that person. This is especially true if the parent has alleged that we, a colleague, or the school at large, is treating his or her child unfairly. If we feel ourselves getting defensive, it's time to slow down and practice Deep Listening.

Understanding unconscious bias helps leaders listen to and *believe* parents' stories of their children's schooling experiences, even when those stories are hard to hear. We have to be willing to acknowledge and interrupt implicit bias, however it manifests—from teachers' lowered expectations of students of color to disproportionate referrals, suspensions, and special education placements. My advice here is pretty plain: If a parent tells you that his or her child is being treated unfairly, start by trusting him or her and asking questions. If it's a simple misunderstanding, you'll uncover that. But if it is indeed an instance of unconscious bias, you'll have the data you need to address the issue with relevant parties.

As a Black woman leader, Jackie was already tuned in to the possibility that the teacher was operating with implicit bias toward this African American male student. And when the teacher called the child's story "ridiculous," Jackie knew she needed to confront her.

Cultural Difference

The channel of cultural difference helps us tune in to patterns of cross-cultural communication between parents and educators. Are the school's formal structures designed to be inclusive of the cultural norms and expectations of parents? Do parents have opportunities to voice their concerns and feedback in informal ways?

Let's take a fairly universal school structure, the parent-teacher conference. Research suggests that many parents of color do not like the business-like manner of school staff during conferences, and feel that teachers, in particular, aren't listening carefully enough to them.[3] Dr. Yanghee Kim, professor of education at Kennesaw State University, suggests that many parents of color find that conferences are just too short to allow them to share their concerns and insights about their children.[4] Time constraints have an even greater impact when it comes to language-minority parents.[5] Table 7.1 contrasts two approaches to communicating with families in parent conferences.

TABLE 7.1   TWO COMMUNICATION APPROACHES FOR PARENT CONFERENCES

Closed Communication Style	Open Communication Style
• Conferences are very short. • The conference structure is formulaic: The teacher will get through a list of things about the child without input from parents. • The only available meeting times are during the school day.	• Inform parents that conferences are coming, ask for best available times, or provide multiple options. • Ask parents what they would like to cover ahead of time or at the beginning of the meeting. • Provide options for when parents can follow up to discuss more and/or check on action items • Check in with parents postconference to discuss progress.

In Jackie's case, the cultural dynamics were on surround sound. She saw right away that the Chinese teacher perceived the mother as "aggressive," whereas Jackie perceived her as appropriately direct and assertive. Jackie also understood that the mom had expected the teacher to "handle the situation" and not leave the child in the hallway alone. In Jackie's words, "When you think about what's happening in the classroom, from my perspective and so many Black parents' perspectives, I expect you—the teacher—to figure out what it's gonna take to help him behave." The teacher's inability to "handle it" connoted a lack of competence to the mother.

The teacher, meanwhile, kept saying, "I'm a professional. I've been taught how to teach math. I know how to teach math." Jackie heard the unspoken cultural subtext of this comment: She had learned from her colleagues who were born in China that in Chinese culture, it's very important to respect the teacher as an authority figure, and that teachers don't typically engage in direct conversations with parents; administrators manage those. So this teacher was operating from an entirely different frame of reference, namely that parents should respect teachers and not challenge their expertise.

Recognizing the competing worldviews in the room didn't solve the issue for Jackie, but it did reveal the depth of her challenge. At the end of the meeting, she had a set of questions she wanted to discuss with staff about parent conferences. Table 7.2 contains Jackie's questions for teachers in the left column and sample questions for parents in the right column.

Note: As you work to build teacher-parent partnerships, consider encouraging teachers to share their answers to the self-awareness questions with parents.

TABLE 7.2   CULTURAL PROFICIENCY TOOL FOR LISTENING TO PARENTS

Five Questions for Self-Awareness/Looking in the Mirror	Five Questions to Pose to Parents
1. What cultural norms do I hold, and how do they intersect with or differ from the norms of the parent I'll be meeting? 2. To what extent are my cultural norms aligned with or in tension with the culture of this school? 3. What might be the parent's cultural norms around schooling, teaching and learning, and discipline? 4. If I don't know, what questions can I ask to find out? 5. What thoughts, feelings, and/or fears do I have about this meeting?	1. "What are your expectations of our school with respect to your child?" 2. "What are your expectations of your child's teacher? Have you shared those?" 3. "What does respect look like to you as a parent?" 4. "How do you want to communicate with me and your child's teacher?" 5. "What do you want us to understand about your culture to better support your child?"

FLIPPING THE SCRIPT BETWEEN PARENTS AND EDUCATORS

To transform our schools, we must listen deeply for the stories and aspirations of our families. It's hard to listen to parents if we are stuck in a well-worn script about how "difficult" it is to engage them. To be sure, there are certain conditions that act as barriers, such as low parent trust in the school and frustration on the part of educators about this situation. So what does it take to rewrite this script and push to deeper understanding?

Here are a few simple rules for the Listening Leader:

It's hard to listen to parents if we're stuck in a well-worn script about how "difficult" it is to engage them.

Interrupt negative talk about parents. Set a tone of respectful discourse, and don't tolerate negative talk about parents. Dr. Tyrone Howard points to a "deficit discourse around students, families, and neighborhoods. Like the kids *don't* have this, the kids *don't* value education, *don't* have the motivation. The parents *don't* value their kids' education. The parents are the problem—if we could just get the kids away from the parents or out of the neighborhood. And I hear lots of it."

What if every time you heard a "parents *don't*," you gently challenged it with a "What *do* our parents have to offer?" Ask the speaker to name a specific asset he sees in families. If he can't come up with an answer, practice Strategic Listening and ask him how he could learn more about the valuable assets every family possesses.

View parents as experts. Model an unwavering stance that parents are experts on the topic of their children. Understand that there are at least 50 shades of parenting, and nobody has a lock on this incredibly complex job. Again, cultivate awareness of your own and your colleagues' unconscious biases; if you notice a negative thought arising toward a parent, check and explore it by asking yourself, *What filter am I running as I view this parent? How do I know that's an accurate interpretation?* If a parent feels judgment from you, you will be unable to grow the relational capital necessary to form an alliance.

Carozza suggests that leaders particularly need to do a better job listening to Black mothers of sons, because of "the level of fear they carry." Consider Michael Brown, an unarmed Black teenager shot and killed by White police officer Darren Wilson in the 2014 incident that sparked the Ferguson protests. Testifying before a grand jury, Wilson said of Brown, "*It* looked like a *demon*" (italics added). This single sentence—with the object pronoun "it" and the frightening connotation of a "demon"—exemplifies the chilling effects of unconscious racial bias. Officer Wilson perceived Brown as a menace and made an instant and fatal judgment call. In 2015, young Black men were nine times more likely than other Americans to be killed by police officers.[6]

Because of that stark reality, fear or defensiveness might be a perfectly natural stance for a Black mother to take regarding her son. So coach teachers to listen deeply, practice mature empathy, and understand the roots of these behaviors. If the teacher chooses to react defensively, he or she can easily make things worse.

Listen to understand. Let go of the need to be right, and listen with mature empathy to a parent's experience, hopes, and needs. As Jackie said to me, "Parents have to feel that you care about understanding where they're coming from. If they don't feel like you care, it'll be hard to use that interaction to build any sort of partnership or investment."

One way to listen better is to view every time a parent approaches you as a form of data. Darrick Smith, professor of education at the University of San Francisco and former codirector of June Jordan School for Equity, said to me, "When a parent comes and cusses you out, that's data. But if you call the security and the security deals with the parent, you never get that data." Sometimes a parent's message is a tough pill to swallow; in those moments, our work is to manage our own feelings and respond in ways that affirm the speaker and calm the amygdala. At other times, we need to be able to decipher a parent's core need from various nonverbal and verbal clues.

What's most important is that we stay curious and dig beneath the surface to understand what is really at stake. If a parent shows up angry, is she worried about her child? Is she mistrustful of you or the school due to her previous experiences? If parents don't show up for a meeting, resist the urge to create a story that assumes they're at fault. Call home and find out what happened. If they can't get to school, consider a home visit.

Make explicit agreements with parents. Finally, forge an agreement with parents around what is important and why. At Carozza's school, what matters is preparing students for college, making sure that students are set up to become financially stable, and making sure a student has a choice at age 19 about what to do with his or her life. Carozza seeks commonality with parents around those things and then builds from there. Because of the strength of the school-family partnerships CCPA has formed, the school has almost no suspensions and very few instances of poor behavior.

FIVE WAYS TO LISTEN TO PARENTS

For Carozza, building a parent-inclusive culture boils down to a basic mindset: "How do you *assume* interest, create multiple opportunities for parents to be engaged, and then create support systems that telegraph parents' assumed investment in their children's education . . . because parents *are* invested." Table 7.3 provides an overview of five ways to listen to families and flip the script.

Parent One-On-Ones

In Chapters 5 and 6, we explored the practices of Deep and Strategic Listening with colleagues. The six stances are equally powerful for building relational capital with families—especially those at the margins of your school or system. Informal one-on-ones allow you to learn more about a parent's identity, culture, and values as you model storientation. Dr. Smith, the USF education professor, asks, "How many teachers don't know the

TABLE 7.3   FIVE WAYS TO LISTEN TO PARENTS

1. Parent one-on-ones	Brief, informal exchanges with parents—20 to 30 minutes—in which you practice the Six Stances of a Listening Leader to build relational capital.
2. Home visits	Similar to a one-on-one, but takes place in a student's home—always with the family's full permission. The focus is on the family's goals and knowledge, and the outcome is often to coconstruct a student support plan.
3. Parent surveys	Regular, efficient ways to gather data from a wide range of parents. Surveys are typically anonymous to allow for more candid feedback. You can customize the questions and format to meet the needs of your community.
4. Focus groups	Facilitated gatherings of 6 to 10 parents, focused on a specific topic, in which you pose questions and gather insight from participants.
5. Community walks	An experiential learning session designed and led by parents and students. These walks help educators view a community through the eyes of families. Parents and students make a community map and introduce participants to important people, places, and landmarks.

stories of their communities that they work in, yet they want parent involvement? So that means we're not asking the right questions!"

Here's an invitation: Think about five parents with whom you think you'd benefit from having a closer alliance. Consider people who represent different demographic groups in your school, including underserved or underperforming students, and prime your brain to take a learning stance in these meeting. Now call those parents and say something like, "I am making a commitment to building stronger relationships with families this year, and I would like to invite you in for a 30-minute one-on-one meeting. This will be an opportunity for me to listen and learn from you."

When you sit down with that parent, aspire to use the 90/10 principle (90% listening, 10% talking). Prepare questions that convey care, interest, and the willingness to learn from someone else's perspective. Here are a few starter questions you can try out:

- "Tell me about your child. What does he love to do after school? How does he learn best?"
- "Describe a time when your child was really successful in school. What do you think made that possible?"
- "What are your biggest concerns about your child? What do I need to know to be her advocate?"

It is astonishing how rarely most parents are asked these simple questions.

During the meeting, practice Deep Listening with a focus on nonverbal cues, mature empathy, and affirmation. Use active listening stems to paraphrase what you've heard and ensure that little is lost in translation. This conveys to parents that you are paying attention and value their words. It also requires you to listen for the speaker's *implicit* messages, the human needs and stories that lie beneath the words. Here, again, are active listening phrases to draw on:

- What I hear you saying is . . .
- Am I missing anything?
- In other words . . .
- As I listen to you, I'm hearing . . .
- Is there anything else you feel I should know?

Home Visits

Where one listens is often as important as *how* one listens. So, at times, we need to step outside our offices and classrooms to visit families in their homes. A **home visit** is essentially a one-on-one with a focus on the family's needs and the goal of constructing together a support plan for the student's success.

Home visits are an inexpensive and replicable routine that can ease the cycle of blame between schools and families and increase cultural sensitivity on both sides.

Home visits are an inexpensive and replicable routine that can ease the cycle of blame between schools and families and increase cultural sensitivity on both sides. This strategy was originated in 1998 by parents from a low-income neighborhood in Sacramento, California, who used principles of community organizing to build trust and mutual accountability between educators and parents. Later refined with the support of teacher and community allies, the home visits model has been adopted in 17 other states and is associated with increased student attendance rates, increased student performance, decreased suspension and expulsion rates, and decreased vandalism at schools.[7]

If you want to incorporate home visits, it's important to consider the respective demographics of your staff and your families. Is there a significant racial, cultural, or linguistic divide? If so, home visits may require a level of **cultural brokering** to ensure that the experience doesn't reinforce implicit biases against families. Dr. Tyrone Howard shares,

Oftentimes you may have folks who are not part of certain communities making home visits, and they can see certain kinds of homes or interactions that may reinforce the negative stereotypes that they already have. But cultural brokers are folks who can help teachers understand what they may have seen so it doesn't end up being something different or worse than what they think it is.

 TIP: BUILD HOME VISITS INTO YOUR PROFESSIONAL DEVELOPMENT SCHEDULE

To demonstrate the value of listening to parents, free up a professional development meeting each year, or even each semester, for teachers to do home visits. This can be done in teacher pairs, grade-level teams, alone, or in partnership with an administrator or community liaison.

A cultural broker can be a parent leader or a paraprofessional who is well grounded in the community. You can ask these folks to train teachers on what to expect and how to demonstrate respect in the home—and perhaps even to accompany the teachers on the visits. Think of this as a form of cultural apprenticeship, and be sure to honor this important work by paying both the teachers and the brokers for their time. At June Jordan School for Equity, we allocated a small budget for teachers' extended hours to do home visits with a select group of students.

Remember Jackie's story of cultural incongruity between her Chinese colleague and the African American parent? Looking back, she says she would have loved for the teacher to do a supported home visit with this family to get to know them better, "because the teacher clearly had her dukes up. If she could have gotten to know the family in a more personalized space, it would have humanized them."

Done well, home visits can transform relationships with families and improve student learning. If we leverage one-on-ones and home visits to listen deeply to families on their terms, we can transform the dysfunctional school-parent dynamic that characterizes so many low-performing schools. Appendix D: Additional Resources for Listening to Parents provides additional resources on conducting home visits, and Exhibit 7.1 presents a case study of this practice.

EXHIBIT 7.1   HOME VISIT CASE STUDY

Carmelita Reyes is the principal of Oakland International High School (OIHS). With more than 400 newcomer students from more than 30 countries, OIHS is a West Coast satellite of a cluster of New York City high schools that serve recent immigrants. Reyes began her teaching career at East Oakland's Life Academy of Health and Bioscience, where she used home visits to listen to her students and families. Her calm, optimistic demeanor helped her greatly in this role.

A typical visit might go something like this: "Tell me about your family. Show me your bedroom. Show me the pictures on your walls. Let me see what you're eating for dinner." Through these open, largely unscripted encounters, Reyes sought to position parents and students as the experts, rather than herself as a representative of the school. "I was very much in listening mode," she says.

When asked what she learned from these visits that she could not have learned any other way, Reyes talks about listening with all her senses and being able to observe family dynamics. In one case, she visited the home of a smart student who was persistently earning C's for failing to complete his homework. Frustrated and incredulous, Reyes visited the student's apartment complex, where she met his mom, three siblings, dad, grandmother, aunt, and the aunt's kids—all living happily together.

She concluded that the reason the student couldn't get any homework done was that his home environment was "so much fun"! From that moment on, Reyes insisted that the student stay after school to finish his homework, and because of her home visit, she had earned the trust to successfully make this demand.

Reyes makes it a point to carve out time for all of her teachers to do home visits. Grade-level teams decide which students to focus on, and teachers receive basic training and engage in role-playing exercises to build their confidence and cultural competence.

Parent Surveys

Surveys allow you to cast a wide and efficient net to gather parents' ideas and perspectives. Most school districts have a prototypical survey that schools are mandated to administer. But what if you took a different approach to parent surveys? What if you designed a customized survey to listen to *your* parents on emerging issues in *your* community and to inform *your* decision making? In addition to collecting a large quantity of data, anonymous surveys offer the opportunity for parents to be completely honest.

A well-designed survey can help you assess and address the current state of parent engagement, with a focus on six key conditions:

1. Empowering families with information to support their children's learning at home
2. Creating channels of communication between home and school
3. Offering an array of opportunities for families to participate in school planning, leadership, and volunteering
4. Connecting families to in-school and community support mechanisms and resources
5. Setting high expectations for students, providing high-quality instruction, and meeting students' individual learning needs
6. Providing a welcoming school climate

Once you complete your survey, it is critical that your team reflect on the data, consider how to respond, and determine the best way to share this information with parents. It is easy to fall into the trap of sharing results via a newsletter or email, but consider the cultural expectations of your community. Emails and newsletters are one strategy for conveying information, but phone calls and focus groups might be in order as well. Those approaches allow you to do more active listening.

It can be particularly helpful to conduct a survey after parent-teacher conferences. Exhibit 7.2 frames four questions you could use to gather data from both teachers and parents.

EXHIBIT 7.2 POSTCONFERENCE SURVEY FOR TEACHERS AND PARENTS

1. What was your experience of that meeting?
2. How do you feel the meeting went?
3. How have things progressed since then?
4. Do you feel closer together in terms of partnership, or further apart?

Focus Groups

If the thought of one-on-one meetings or home visits overwhelms you, or you already administer regular parent surveys, consider hosting focus groups. They're a great next step that elucidates and expands on survey results. Most important, they allow parents to feel involved and part of the school community. It's important to note that the goal of a focus group is not to confirm a preconceived hypothesis but instead to take an inquiry stance as you gather Level 3 "street" data: parents' perceptions, experiences, and understanding around the focal topic. A focus group might explore questions like these:

- How is our school doing with respect to serving African American students?
- How could we do a better job of serving our English language learners?
- What do we need to do to become a more inclusive school environment?
- What are parents' ideas for shaping an effective and equitable discipline policy?
- How could we more creatively engage parents and community members, with all their knowledge, as coteachers in the classrooms?
- What supports should we offer families to prepare students for college?

Let's revisit Jackie's story for a moment. From her perspective as a school leader, the difficult parent meeting made her wonder, *Do other parents feel like this at our school?* This inquiry pointed directly toward the need for focus groups, which, she says, "are so helpful in helping you problem-solve around larger issues. When you find out more people have a certain experience, it motivates you." She recommends organizing focus groups with families that share a similar experience, such as monolingual families, African American families, or parents whose children are in the same program. See Appendix D: Resources for Listening to Parents for tips on implementing focus groups.

Community Walks

I think we've lost this idea of school-community connections, if you will. Now, in many instances, schools operate as these entities independent or disconnected from communities, and I think that's a big error because so much of what school leaders will have to contend with is a direct by-product of what happens in the larger community, whether it's a set of really promising features or a set of challenges. The leaders that have really made inroads with school improvement have made themselves visible in the communities that they are part of.

—DR. TYRONE HOWARD, UCLA professor of education and director of the Black Male Institute

Community walks are one of my favorite ways to listen to parents. Designed and led by students and their families, this routine invites educators to learn about their students in *their* communities and on *their* terms. What are the most important places and landmarks? Who are the spiritual, formal, and informal leaders in the community? Parents and students make a map and host a group of educators for a session of experiential learning.

I credit this routine to Carmelita Reyes, the Oakland principal in this chapter's earlier home visit case study. She stumbled upon the idea while attending a professional development session in which district staff who had graduated from a high school in West Oakland took principals on a "learning walk" of their neighborhood. Seeing the neighborhood through their eyes, Reyes gained a nuanced understanding: "These people took us on a tour of the hood: the post office, the homes they grew up in, the library, where cool spots used to be but had since closed down, where the pollution comes from, the rail yards, the dumps."

Reyes was inspired, and immediately thought about how to duplicate the experience for her teachers. In conversation with her school's parent liaison, she hatched a plan: Organize student- and parent-led walks of the school's different immigrant communities (later named community walks). The first set would target the school's two major language groups: Arabic and Spanish speakers. The second round included any other significantly represented communities, and as the approach gained momentum, groups of teachers began to add more communities to the list.

To ensure that community voices featured prominently in the experience, Reyes and her parent liaison held language-specific parent nights that began with mini lessons on the basics of American education, such as: What is a report card? How do you read it? How does your child graduate from high school? Significantly, Reyes ended each meeting with an invitation for parents to share what staff members needed to know about their particular community and immigrant experience.

The staff collected data from these discussions and repeated the process with students from each major language group. Drawing on these rich data pools, Reyes asked student leaders and host families to design and lead an official OIHS community walk for a group of faculty. Flexible in design, these community walks tended to include a house of worship, key community centers (for example, a halal market in the Yemeni community or the library in Chinatown), and a significant nonprofit organization (students who had arrived as refugees took staff to the International Rescue Committee headquarters). Each walk culminated in a social event, hosted by a family, that typically included a meal and often dancing.

The impact of investing professional development time in community walks was nothing short of transformational. Shortly after the first round of walks, two Yemeni boys got into a terrible fight, and none of their friends intervened to stop it. Reyes didn't hesitate to call the local imam who had participated in the recent walk. The imam came to campus within hours to help facilitate a **restorative circle**—a structured dialogue that allows participants to listen, express themselves, and repair harm that has occurred—with the eight involved boys. According to Reyes, the group discussed "what had happened and what *needed* to happen in the future to maintain a safe school for the community. . . . It was bigger than the fight; it was about the collapse of supportive culture." After the circle, there were no further incidents among these boys; all adhered to the expectations set forth by the imam.

After several years of holding community walks, OIHS now has a collection of such stories. At its core, this strategy empowers families to act as experts with deep knowledge about their community. In Reyes's words, "There's this cultural pride. 'Hey, teachers think our community is important!' There is real validation for these different groups." Appendix D: Additional Resources for Listening to Parents includes a primer for designing and leading Community Walks.

JACKIE'S REFLECTIONS

With a bit of time, Jackie had some powerful insights about her meeting with the teacher and the parent. On the teacher end, she realized that she had underestimated the amount of relational capital she had with this colleague. Although Jackie is always willing to have hard conversations about equity, she realized that you need capital with people to push them. "You've got to have trust, and I misassessed that."

In hindsight, she would have spent more time helping the teacher recognize the assets in her current approach (affirmation) before pushing her to examine her unconscious biases toward the student and parent and eventually shift her practice (reflective inquiry and bias toward action). In preparing for the meeting, she would have tried to understand the teacher's perspective (mature empathy). That would have had the effect, Jackie believes, of encouraging the teacher to do the same with the parent.

On the parent side, Jackie is thrilled to have moved this parent "very far" in a span of weeks. The meeting, she says, "did wonders for the parent. She's coming to school, observing classrooms; she gives me the time of day . . . People get scared of parents, so the interactions aren't quality. You can't be scared! Let's just assume that this woman wants the best for her kids!!! Let's treat her like she deserves this stuff." Likely the mother understood that Jackie had her back in the meeting, which boosted their relational capital and increased the mother's willingness to engage.

Jackie's excitement about engaging the parent is matched by her concern about not having made as much progress with the teacher. Right now, she says, "The teacher doesn't trust me . . . I realize I was not supportive enough. If I can bring a level of empathy in a way that builds trust and generates relational capital, I think we can go somewhere together."

Jackie is an extraordinary leader, not just because she knows her stuff and cares about kids and families, but because she's a learner. She's a listener. She took a trying situation, wrought with emotion, and chose to look at it as an opportunity to grow. We need more leaders like this in our schools. Let's give ourselves permission to try, fall, try again, reflect, and steadily improve our skills in the complex and deeply human project of serving *every* family.

KEY TAKEAWAYS

- The equity channels (structural racism, unconscious bias, and cultural difference) help us gain insight into barriers to parent engagement.
- Listening Leaders flip the script by interrupting negative talk about parents, viewing them as experts, listening to understand, and making explicit agreements.
- Informal one-on-ones and focus groups are powerful ways to collect data and build relational capital with families.
- Parent surveys provide an efficient, adaptable way to gather broad feedback.
- Community walks allow parents to educate school staff about their communities; home visits offer an opportunity to learn about a student in a personalized space.

LISTENING LEADER INQUIRY

Question: I appreciate hearing Jackie's story, but parents and/or teachers don't always rise above the fray to admit where they have responsibility. If the parent and teacher reach an impasse, is it better to end the meeting and try another day or to continue anyway?

My thoughts: I wish I had a one-size-fits-all response to this question, but my answer is really, it depends. If you sense that participants have hit a wall and are beginning to enter fight-or-flight modes, it may well be best to end the meeting and continue later. If you notice a moment of discomfort, but not a full-blown amygdala hijack, I would advise that you name it, model mature empathy toward all parties, and keep pushing forward. That might sound like, "I'm noticing a lot of emotion in the room right now. I want to give each of you a chance to share what's coming up for you: any fears, concerns, or questions." If the participants are willing to do that, you might ask, "Do you feel able to listen to one another and continue, or should we resume this on another day?"

Question: Some of my parents have styles that are not just different from mine but actually offensive to me. How do I build a relationship in a case like that?

My thoughts: This is an opportunity for inquiry through the lens of the equity channels. Is this a case of cultural mismatch? Could it be a case of unconscious bias on your part—where you are holding a latent judgment or assumption about the parent based on dominant cultural messages? I would recommend that you look in the mirror and reflect on your reaction before reaching out to the parent. If you can learn more about your own internal experience, you will be more likely to connect with the parent and build bridges across difference.

That said, there are times when a parent may be acting in ways that are unsafe or that directly contradict the values of your school community; in such cases it's your job to draw a clear boundary with that parent in as respectful a way as you can. Matt Alexander, current codirector of June Jordan School for Equity, offers a useful example: "In one case, I wouldn't let a mom come on campus while she was escalated, but then 10 minutes later she came back in a calmer state and said, 'I'm sorry; I'm working on my anger,' and we were able to move forward constructively."

Question: I have parents who refuse to show up at school or participate in any way. What do I do in such cases?

My thoughts: Can you identify the minimum level of participation and engagement that you feel is a basic parental responsibility—not the ideal, but the level below which you would be concerned? If the parent is not below that line, respect his or her refusal to participate and continue to extend a welcoming invitation. Some parents are literally in survival mode, trying to hold down multiple jobs or deal with physical and mental health challenges that make it nearly impossible for them to participate in the way we might want them to. Don't hold that against them or their child. And make sure they know that when life circumstances change, you would love to have them more involved and won't judge their past absence.

NOTES

1. Peña, D. C. (2000). Parent involvement: Influencing factors and implications. *Journal of Educational Research, 94*(1), 42–54.
2. Moll, L. C., Aman, C., Neff, D., & Gonzalez, N. (1992). Funds of knowledge for teaching: Using a qualitative approach to connect homes and classrooms. *Theory Into Practice, 31,* 132–141.
3. Lindle, J. C. (1989). What do parents want from principals and teachers? *Educational Leadership, 47*(2), 12–14; Smrekar, C., & Cohen-Vogel, L. (2001). The voices of parents: Rethinking the intersection of family and school. *Peabody Journal of Education, 76,* 75–100.
4. Kim, Y. (2009). Minority parental involvement and school barriers: Moving the focus away from deficiencies of parents. *Educational Research Review 4*(2), 80–102.
5. Sohn, S., & Wang, C. (2006). Immigrant parents' involvement in American schools: Perspectives from Korean mothers. *Early Childhood Education Journal 34,* 125–132.
6. The counted: People killed by the police in the US. (2015, June 1). *Guardian.* Retrieved from http://www.theguardian.com/us-news/ng-interactive/2015/jun/01/the-counted-police-killings-us-database
7. Parent Teacher Home Visit Project. (2016). Retrieved from http://www.pthvp.org

Chapter 8

Listening to Students

Matt Alexander*

Preview: For schools to be truly effective and equitable, adults must listen to students.

This chapter is designed to help you:

- Understand why listening to students is critical in any effort to transform schools.
- Consider what makes listening to students difficult, and learn how to overcome those challenges.
- Learn practical strategies to help educators listen more deeply to students, and students listen more deeply to one another.

LISTENING TO STUDENTS TELL THE REAL STORY—EVEN WHEN IT'S HARD TO HEAR

> On a Wednesday afternoon in early 2016, I am sitting in the back row of our weekly staff meeting at June Jordan School for Equity (JJSE), where I am codirector. Rather than leading the day's activities, I am waiting for a group of students from our leadership class to begin a 2-hour session on serving JJSE's undocumented immigrant students.

---

* Chapter 8 is written by guest author Matt Alexander, who worked with Shane Safir as a founder of June Jordan School for Equity and still serves as a teacher and administrator there. Matt has two decades of experience in the San Francisco public schools.

To open the meeting, a poised 11th-grade girl stands up, projects a slide with the school's vision statement, and asks a teacher to read it aloud. When the teacher finishes, the girl repeats one sentence: "We are committed not only to prepare students for college, but to honor the traditions of their communities by teaching students to be leaders who are prepared to work for a more equitable world." She then launches a bold critique: "It is our belief that with respect to serving undocumented immigrant students, JJSE is *failing* to meet this vision."

An uncharacteristic and awkward silence descends upon our chatty staff. A couple of people start to clap, but when no one else picks up on the applause, it quickly dies out. Undeterred, the students push on. They lead the staff in an "agree-disagree" activity to gauge teachers' opinions on statements about the quality of school support for undocumented students—for example, "Undocumented students feel like they can talk to adults about their situation and get help." When some teachers resist having to take a public stand on the statement, a student leader calmly insists that they please use their best judgment to make a choice.

Next, the young leaders present student perception data from a survey taken by over half of the school, and then facilitate a talking circle in which they ask teachers to reflect on the data—specifically on their assertion that undocumented students are not being adequately served. During the circle, several staff members ask detailed technical questions about the legitimacy of the survey, insinuating that perhaps the situation for undocumented students is not as bad as it appears. Other teachers take pains to point out that although we can improve, we are doing better than other schools.

The student leaders are starting to look annoyed, and I myself am struck by the defensiveness of many staff members. We are, after all, a school with a social justice mission, committed to being a safe and welcoming place for all students. And here stand our young people, offering pointed and meaningful data on where we have fallen short. I wonder whether our teachers are feeling threatened around their own status and legitimacy.

By the end of the 2 hours, teachers are beginning to listen to the students and agree that we need to do a better job of serving undocumented students. But the staff's initial resistance to hearing a challenging message from young people—even one framed around our community's shared vision—reminds me of the importance of creating space for student voice. As one of the student leaders later told me, "We need teachers not to be in denial, but to admit the problems—and then we can work together to solve them."

DISCARDING WELL-WORN SCRIPTS

There has to be a serious focus on the voices of students *within a building. I'm really big on asking students: "What do you think will work for you?" I know that some school leaders will say, "That takes up too much time." [But] the work would be easier if students had input in shaping it and if leaders, as well as teachers, trusted the input of students.*

—DIANNE SMITH, professor of urban leadership and policy studies
in education, from an interview with Shane Safir

This story demonstrates a basic truth: Even in schools with a strong sense of community and open lines of communication, students and adults occupy different social roles and inhabit different realities. This is especially true for adolescents, who experience life through a unique developmental lens and often try to differentiate themselves from the adults closest to them. It is doubly true in schools serving poor and working-class children, as educators of all backgrounds hold a different social class position from that of the students they serve.

Despite the best intentions of thoughtful educators, schools are structured in ways that make it hard to hear young people's voices. Students and adults alike are guided by implicit social scripts that can deafen educators to what young people think, feel, and need. I remember the day I noticed a girl named Brenda in the hallway during class—for the third time that morning. We began to play out the same, scripted interaction that we had many times before (Me: "Brenda, go to class!" Her: "Stop bothering me; I'm on my way"), when suddenly my frustration got the better of me. Exasperated, I said, "I don't understand why you're here, walking the halls by yourself all day! If you're not going to attend class, why did you even bother to come to school today?" Brenda stopped in her tracks, looked at me as though I had lost my mind, and said, "What do you mean, why did I come to school? I have to! It's the law!"

In that moment, I began to listen to Brenda. Her refusal to go to class, which I had been treating as defiance or disrespect, was in fact a sign that she felt trapped by a system that compelled her to spend every day in a place she didn't want to be. I softened my tone and said, "Would you like to come to my office so we can talk about this?" She agreed, and I listened to her explain why she hated school, and how going late to class helped delay the boredom. Of course, Brenda's story went deeper, and we didn't come up with an immediate solution—but at least we had discarded the well-worn script of "defiant student and frustrated administrator butting heads in the hallways." Instead, we were having a real conversation.

As all good teachers know, students are full-fledged human beings who behave in unpredictable ways. They may refuse to comply with our rules, and they may disengage from our most carefully crafted lesson plans, preferring to daydream about Disneyland or ogle the cute boy across the room instead of focusing their mind on fractions or foreshadowing.

Sometimes, as students try to navigate the confusing world of adult and peer expectations, they simply tell us what they *think* we want to hear—and we are all too willing to accept their statements at face value. Like adults, young people engage in denial and other forms of self-deception, and have strong reactions based on fear and other emotions. (The core tenets in Chapter 2 apply to students too!) Sometimes what comes out of their mouth is not at all what they mean.

If we want to become effective leaders, we can't disregard what students are thinking and feeling. We must pay careful attention to their tone and body language, and to the subtext of their words.

But if we want to become effective leaders, we can't disregard what students are thinking and feeling. We must pay careful attention to their tone and body language, and to the subtext of their words. Recently I was supervising passing period when I witnessed a ninth-grade girl yell down the hallway at a boy, "I'm gonna beat your ass!" A nearby teacher reprimanded the girl for her language— which I was glad to see—but seemed to miss the fact that the girl was smiling flirtatiously as she made the comment.

I thought to myself that rather than telling this student not to make threats, which was not at all her intention, *Perhaps we need to find this young woman a mentor who could offer guidance on how to express romantic interest in a more elegant manner.* The girl's nonverbal cues had given me a different, and more accurate, interpretation of the situation.

Listen to Students as Intellectuals First

Good teachers have always viewed listening to students as the heart of their practice. My twin sons, Nolan and Ben, had a fantastic seventh-grade humanities teacher, Amina Sheikh, who, Nolan told me, "really made it clear that she valued students' opinions." I asked how he knew this. "Some other teachers, when they ask a question, you know they're looking for a certain answer," Ben explained. "But when Amina asked a question, she was asking us a real *question* . . . She wouldn't directly contradict students' ideas, or gloss over them and move on if she thought they were not the right answer. She would try and build on them and try to get students to think critically about them, and let students come to their own conclusions."

An important point surfaces from this story: As educators, we need to listen to our students *as intellectuals*. New teachers often focus on getting to know things about their students' personal lives, which is important, but the student-teacher relationship is fundamentally an intellectual enterprise. As veteran teacher Robert Roth notes in Kristina Rizga's book about San Francisco's Mission High School, "Students' personal lives, their emotional lives, shouldn't be the center of the conversation or the relationship. We have to allow students to be vulnerable, to provide support, but the essay is due. . . It's about a sustained intellectual dialogue that students can feel."[1]

Listen Deeply, but Don't Enable

Listening deeply does not mean enabling dysfunctional behavior. We are aiming to practice attention to nonverbal cues, mature empathy, and affirmation, not the *pobrecito* syndrome. If a student is feeling victimized or defensive, former JJSE codirector Darrick Smith talks about responding with a "boundaried 'I feel you' statement"—that is, affirming the student's emotional experience but at the same time establishing clear boundaries and expectations. For example, in my conversation with Brenda about her hall-walking, I expressed compassion for her negative feelings about school, but also let her know that lingering in the halls during class time was not an acceptable response. Table 8.1 offers reflective questions for applying the Deep Listening stances with young people.

TABLE 8.1   TOOL FOR PRACTICING DEEP LISTENING WITH STUDENTS

Deep Listening Stance	Questions to Ask Ourselves
Attention to nonverbal cues	• Did the student's tone and body language match his words, or was there a different nonverbal message? • Is there a subtext to what the student is saying? • Is the student responding to another student's nonverbal cues (e.g., a perceived threat because someone was looking at her)? • If there are cultural differences, am I interpreting the student's nonverbal cues correctly?
Mature empathy	• Do I really understand what the student is thinking and feeling? • Are the student and I acting out an implicit social script? • Have I discounted the student's feelings because I think he is acting unreasonably? • Is the student just telling me what I want to hear?
Affirmation	• Am I giving students more positive than critical feedback? (Aim for a 5:1 ratio.) • Am I showing students that I value their opinions and ideas? • Am I validating the student's feelings without being indulgent or enabling (*pobrecito* syndrome)?

The rest of this chapter provides concrete examples of routines and rituals that can facilitate the listening process with and among students.

FIVE WAYS TO LISTEN TO STUDENTS

There are many ways to listen deeply to students. The five suggestions provided here are not a "how-to" guide but rather examples of effective approaches, which may in turn inspire other ideas. As you review them, think about what would work in your own context to help adults truly understand young people's thinking and experiences.

EXHIBIT 8.1   FIVE WAYS TO LISTEN TO STUDENTS

Walk in Their Shoes
- Spend a day **shadowing a student** to immerse yourself in the student experience, gain new insights, and develop ideas for "hacks" to improve school culture and instruction.

Tell Their Stories
- Get students to share their stories so that adults can listen deeply. I'll offer several examples.

Ask Them How You're Doing
- Create processes to allow for student feedback to teachers, including regular **student feedback surveys**, student feedback interviews, or a "What Works Club" where teams of student observers watch classrooms in action.

Give Them a Voice in the Classroom
- Promote student voice through simple rituals like the **one-word check-in** and the more transformative cultural tradition of **talking circles**.

Organize the Classroom Around Their Ideas
- Build an intellectual community in the classroom through **inquiry-based teaching**, which is organized around **essential questions** and uses talk moves to guide students in deep learning.

Walk in Their Shoes

I have made a terrible mistake. I waited fourteen years to do something that I should have done my first year of teaching: shadow a student for a day. It was so eye-opening that I wish I could go back to every class of students I ever had right now and change a

minimum of ten things—the layout, the lesson plan, the checks for understanding.
Most of it!

—Anonymous teacher on Grant Wiggins's blog[2]

One of the best places to start listening to students is by spending a day in their shoes, or shadowing a student. Most educators have heard of the concept—put on your tennis shoes and "be" a student for a day—but how many of us have actually done it? Yes, I know; it's hard to miss a day at our busy jobs, and besides, we interact with students all day: Don't we already know what it's like to be a student? But I have yet to meet an educator who shadowed a student for an entire day and didn't walk away with critical new insights about her work. So if you are a teacher, administrator, or anyone else who works in education, I challenge you to put down this book right now and block out a day to shadow a student. You won't regret it.

As you plan your shadowing experience, you might consult the Shadow a Student Challenge project (shadowastudent.org) developed by the design thinking company IDEO and the School Retool Network in an effort to make schools more innovative and student centered.[3] The website includes detailed guidance on choosing a student, what to pay attention to during the day, and how to take notes. Table 8.2 provides a few practical tips for this process.

An anonymous high school teacher on Grant Wiggins's blog identified three main takeaways from her shadowing day:[4]

• Students sit all day, and sitting is exhausting.
• High school students are sitting passively and listening during approximately 90% of their classes.
• You feel a little bit like a nuisance all day long.

For each of these insights, the teacher identified specific small changes she could make to her classroom routines to improve the student experience. (The Shadow a Student Challenge people call these changes "hacks" in the sense of computer hacking, or making clever modifications to a system that allow you to do new things.)

Like many of us, I knew shadowing was a good idea, but had never actually done it until recently. It was an eye-opening experience that reminded me how easy it is for even the best teachers to fall back on teacher-directed instruction or activities in which students are largely passive. My hack was a commitment to myself that every time I am speaking in front of a group of students, I will set a 10-minute timer on my phone, and when the timer goes off, I will stop speaking and transition to a different

TABLE 8.2   GUIDANCE ON SHADOWING A STUDENT

The Shadow a Student Challenge toolkit provides these guidelines for your shadow day:

How Do I Dress?	What Do I Do?	What Do I Look For?
Ditch the suit and wear comfortable clothes. Or, alternatively, if students at your school wear uniforms, dress that way too to see how that feels.	Meet your student at the bus stop, subway station, or bike rack. Spend the whole day with your student. Attend classes, eat lunch, and hang out by the lockers together.	Approach observation with an open and curious mind. Stay away from generalizations, judgment, evaluation, assumptions, and prescriptions (should/ would/ could). You aren't trying to solve anything today, just observe.

Note. From "Shadow a Student Challenge," by School Retool, 2016, retrieved from http://shadowastudent.org/

activity that requires active student engagement. And every time I do so, I will be thinking of Clarence, the student I shadowed, who leaned over to me in the middle of a 40-minute, whole-class lecture/discussion that seemed relatively engaging and whispered, "See how boring it is to be a student?"

Tell Their Stories

Shadowing a student is a fantastic way to put yourself in your students' shoes and reflect on their daily reality at school. But listening to students also requires that we understand their personal history and their cultural background.

When Denver teacher Kyle Schwartz wanted to know what was really going on in her third-grade students' minds, she gave them sticky notes and asked them to finish the sentence, "I wish my teacher knew . . ." The responses gave her immediate insight into what they were grappling with, from "I wish my teacher knew sometimes my reading log is not signed because my mom is not around a lot" to "I wish my teacher knew I want to go to college."[5] Students had the option of keeping the notes anonymous, or reading them aloud to their classmates.

Schwartz started posting photos of the notes on Twitter using the hashtag #IWishMyTeacherKnew, and teachers around the country began to post their students' responses as well. This is a great example of the power of "storientation," or communicating through stories, which is a fundamental way that human brains understand the world.

A strategy for more in-depth storientation is the **student fishbowl**, in which a group of students (usually 6–10) sit in a circle of chairs in the center of the room and have a discussion, while a larger audience (in this case, usually school staff) sits outside the "fishbowl" and listens to the conversation. A facilitator asks the student participants questions and makes sure that everyone gets a chance to speak. The conversation can explore many different kinds of issues depending on the questions you choose.

EXHIBIT 8.2   SAMPLE FISHBOWL QUESTIONS

The following sample fishbowl questions are from the EdChange Critical Multicultural website:[a]

- What are your favorite things about school?
- What aspects of your school do you feel should be improved?
- What can your teachers do to help you learn better?
- Share a story about when one of your teachers did something that made you feel especially included in the learning process.
- Share a story about when you felt you were especially excluded from your own learning process.
- Who is your favorite teacher? Why?
- What do you feel is the role of school in your life?
- What do you feel should be the major goals of schools?

[a] Gorski, P. (n.d.). Awareness activities: Student fishbowl. EdChange Critical Multicultural Pavilion. Retrieved from http://www.edchange.org/multicultural/activities/fishbowl.html

---

In one fishbowl variation, there is an empty chair left in the circle, and adult observers can temporarily occupy the chair in order to ask the students a new question. In another variation, the fishbowl is followed by a debrief session in which staff can ask follow-up questions to students in small groups. No matter how the process is arranged, it is important to remind adult observers not to invalidate or undermine student perspectives; their role is to remain curious and open minded.

When students don't feel comfortable discussing a topic openly in front of their teachers, consider conducting **audio interviews** with small groups of students and then editing those interviews to play at a staff meeting. At June Jordan School for Equity, my fellow codirector Jessica Huang teams up with a teacher, finds a quiet classroom, and invites half a dozen students to participate. The adults explain that the recording will be played at a staff meeting; they make it clear that participation is voluntary, and they obtain students' permission before asking basic questions, such as: What is it like being a student at our school? What would you like teachers to know about your life? Who is your favorite teacher and why?

Once the students begin to talk, they build on one another's ideas, and minimal facilitation is required. In a recent version of this process, the students spoke for over an hour, after which we edited the audio file to create a 20-minute segment that highlighted the most important themes. We focus the interviews around particular issues or groups of students whose experiences we want the staff to understand, and see it as an opportunity to gather Level 3 "street" data. (See Chapter 1 for a description of the Levels of Data framework.) For example, we once recorded interviews with a group of African American students about what it is like to be a Black student at our school and in the larger community. This focus was especially important in San Francisco, where the Black population has declined by 50% over the past four decades, and remaining Black residents face shocking levels of structural racism in areas ranging from housing and jobs to criminal justice.[6]

One theme that emerged is how racism manifests in low expectations from fellow students as well as teachers—unconscious biases in the classroom. A girl named Monica explained,

> If you're African American, a lot of other students don't think you're really educated. If I'm in class and there are four of us at the table, and I'm the only Black person, they'll ask every other person at the table for help, but not me. I feel like I constantly have to prove myself that I'm not dumb. And then after I do that, they're like, "Oh, she really *is* smart," and they start asking me. I've gotten that from teachers, too. When they talk to [a Filipina classmate], they just explain it a little bit and think she'll get it, but with me, they go step-by-step-by-step.

Monica also gave specific examples of teachers who respected her deeply and held her to high expectations.

To help staff members listen thoughtfully to the audio interviews and discuss what they heard, we made the edited recordings the central "text" of a staff meeting. Exhibit 8.3 shows the agenda.

By using the audio interviews as a text for staff learning, we forced ourselves to consider our own implicit biases. The teachers who had been

---

EXHIBIT 8.3   JJSE STAFF MEETING ON SERVING AFRICAN AMERICAN STUDENTS

Agenda Item

1. Mindfulness & Reading of June Jordan poem
2. Review Agreements & Roles
3. Listen to Audio Recording of Black Student Voices; complete Reflection Sheet with these questions:
   a. How are the Black students in this recording feeling/experiencing things?
   b. What are others (staff and students) doing to make them feel that way?
   c. What is working for our Black students?
   d. What is not working?
4. Small group discussions
5. Whole group: Review of our stance on implicit bias; reflection on racism from [Black teacher]; reflection on racism from [White teacher]
6. Closing personal reflection: Think of a situation where the skin you're in may have impacted your interaction with a Black student or their family.
   a. What biases did you bring to the situation?
   b. How do you think the interaction or situation was interpreted by the student or their family?
   c. What are your next steps and/or personal commitments?
7. Process Check, Appreciations, Announcements

---

explaining instructions "step-by-step" to the African American girl could now see the racist impact of their well-intentioned actions and adjust their practice.

Ask Them How You're Doing

Once you begin to understand your students' stories, enlist their voices to improve instructional practice across the school. Although most good teachers have methods for getting student feedback, it is a rare elementary or secondary school that requires teachers to solicit and use student input on a regular basis.

Asking for student feedback is easy, and we should make it part of our regular routines. As an administrator, I try to model the importance of student feedback when doing informal classroom visits by asking students, "What are you doing today? Why does it matter?" Many teachers I know add a couple of questions at the end of each unit test to ask their students, "What worked for you during this unit? What didn't?"

On a more formal level, I recommend administering **student feedback surveys** at least once a semester. Models are widely available on the Internet; common questions include the following:

- What do you like best about this class? and/or What did you learn in this class?
- What would you like to change about the class?
- What are this teacher's strengths?
- What suggestions do you have to improve his or her teaching?

With younger children, surveys can be adapted into a class activity where students answer questions and share out. Annie Emerson, a Florida kindergarten teacher, reports that a similar feedback process with her 5-year-olds created a "whole new level of trust with my class."[7]

More interesting and potentially more useful than surveys are **feedback interviews**, or focus groups with students, akin to the parent focus groups described in Chapter 7. These are similar to the audio interviews described earlier, but instead of asking students to tell their stories, you ask them for specific feedback on teaching practice. We have found that students are reluctant to criticize teachers out of a sense of deference and respect, and they tend to give more honest critical feedback when the interviewer is a third party (administrator or teacher colleague).

Recently I conducted student feedback interviews for a veteran teacher. In the portion of my summary about being a "warm demander" teacher who creates a safe classroom culture (one of the teaching standards in our JJSE pedagogy), I wrote:

> These students feel that you create a very safe classroom environment. They appreciate your strictness and your proactive approach to making sure "everybody gets along with each other." They feel that you hold them to high expectations, and that you believe in your students and respect them.
>
> Their main critique in this area was that sometimes you can be "too strict" and it's not always clear *why* you are strict about certain things. When I asked for examples, they mentioned tardies ("if you're here but you don't open your binder he marks you tardy") and bathroom passes ("we only get 3 passes for the whole year"). During the discussion of "strictness" they also mentioned that you sometimes get angry easily about little things. One said: "Sometimes it is harsh the way he says it; if he said those exact same words but calmer it would be better."

This feedback was important to the teacher; it motivated him to work on adjusting his tone and providing students with clearer explanations of his behavior. He reflected later that he had given student surveys for years, but had never received such pointed and useful feedback.

At JJSE and several other high schools in San Francisco, we are developing a more comprehensive approach to student feedback through a process called the "What Works Club." Developed by the San Francisco Coalition of Essential Small Schools (SF-CESS) and modeled on the Best Practices Club that existed in the mid-2000s at Lexington High School in Massachusetts,[8] the What Works Club trains a group of students to

- Define culturally responsive teaching practices
- Learn how to give feedback so that it is heard
- Conduct observation cycles of teachers
- Share practices that work with the school community

The idea behind the club is that students are the experts on what works in the classroom, and if we give them a process and the appropriate language to communicate their expertise with teachers, instructional practice will improve. Thus far we are just in the pilot stages of this work, but initial feedback from teachers and students alike is positive.

If you or your colleagues need inspiration about how to ask students for feedback, consult the many books by Kathleen Cushman. In one of her most popular titles, *Fires in the Bathroom,* students give advice to teachers on topics ranging from "Fairness Builds Trust and Respect" to "Helping Kids Stay Motivated" to "Tips on Helping Us Read Difficult Academic Material." Much of Kathleen's work has been in partnership with the organization What Kids Can Do, which maintains a good website with resources. See the Student Feedback Interview Tool in Appendix E.

Give Them a Voice in the Classroom

The routines described earlier allow adults to do a better job of listening to students. But in the best classrooms and schools, students also listen deeply to one another and take ownership of their learning in partnership with adults whom they trust and respect.

Simple classroom rituals can begin to bring student voices out from the shadows. Former JJSE codirector Darrick Smith encouraged teachers to begin each class period with a **one-word check-in**: As you take attendance at the beginning of class, call each student's name and have her say one word describing how she feels. Although this ritual is quick, its impact on class culture is profound: When a student says, "irritated" or "mad," his or her classmates as well as the teacher know to give that person a bit more space on that day. When a student exclaims, "happy!" or "excited!" the emotional tone of the classroom shifts in a positive direction for everyone.

One of the most powerful routines to unleash student voice in the classroom is the **talking circle**. Derived from aboriginal and native traditions, the talking circle creates a humanizing space that lifts barriers between people and allows all participants to speak and listen on an equal footing. At JJSE, as at many community-based schools, all staff are expected to become skilled "circle keepers," or caretakers of the circle process. Appendix E includes Essential Elements of a Talking Circle, which outlines six elements that we believe are essential to the success of a talking circle, and a Talking Circle Planning Tool.

Talking circles can be used with students from kindergarten to college and beyond, for many different purposes. The most basic use of a circle is to create space for participants to build community by sharing feelings and ideas. For example, the circle keeper might ask middle or high school students a question, such as, "If you could be a superhero, what superpower would you have and why?" or "If you could have a face-to-face conversation with anyone in the world, who would it be and why?"

Circles can also provide space for students to practice affirmation with one another. As students mature and build a culture of safety, topics can evolve, moving from low stakes to higher stakes and gradually inviting students to bring their experiences and identities into the classroom. Even a single circle can incorporate multiple discussion rounds that start with fun or silly prompts, and end with opportunities for deeper sharing.

Talking circles can be used with an academic purpose to ensure that all voices are heard on an important topic. Basic prompts can include, "A character I relate to in this book is . . ." or "My favorite way of solving this type of math problem is . . ." For several years now, JJSE math teacher Marcus Hung has been using talking circles to encourage academic discourse. In an article in the journal *Mathematics Teacher*, he notes that his talking circles "led to an increase in the number of individual share-outs by all students, across all student cohorts, thus disrupting existing patterns of stratified classroom talk."[9]

Once a strong community exists in the classroom, a restorative circle can be used to rebuild trust after a specific transgression (e.g., a theft) or to interrupt a problematic pattern (e.g., students engage in frequent and distracting side conversations). Restorative circles are tricky to facilitate, but can be very powerful. One of the most impressive I have observed was a circle that JJSE teacher Giulio Sorro led in response to student complaints about him. He framed the circle in this way: "On Thursday, I got a little frustrated with a couple students. I think I could have done things a little bit better. . . Some people felt I was unfair . . . So I want you to say whether I could have done something different, and then I'll give you my opinion about why I did what I did." By saving his own thoughts for last, Mr. Sorro demonstrated to his students that he really wanted to listen, and modeled humility and vulnerability.

Organize the Classroom Around Their Ideas

Just as the talking circle can strengthen social capital in the classroom, **inquiry-based teaching** can develop and enhance students' intellectual capital. Although there are different definitions of inquiry-based teaching, my favorite comes from Urban Academy Laboratory High School in New York City:

> Inquiry teaching requires the teacher to frame questions in a way which challenges students to examine often conflicting evidence, draw conclusions and support these conclusions in thoughtful discussions with others who, using the same evidence base, reach divergent conclusions.[10]

Research shows that this teaching approach increases student engagement and learning, so it is not surprising that inquiry-based methods have been used since at least the time of Socrates nearly 2,500 years ago.

Unfortunately, in most schools and classrooms, a lot of what happens depends less on what the students really think and more on what the teacher *wants* them to think. In part, this is the result of the increasing standardization of curriculum, and in part it is a reflection of the traditional teacher-led classroom. According to researchers Sarah Michaels and Catherine O'Connor, "The dominant form of teacher-led group talk is still recitation . . . where the teacher initiates a question, a student responds briefly, and the teacher evaluates the student contribution as correct or incorrect."[11] In essence, most classrooms follow what Paolo Freire called the "banking model" of education in which the students are depositories and the teacher makes deposits. The problem with this approach, as Freire explains, is that students learn best by constructing knowledge through "restless, impatient, continuing, hopeful inquiry . . . with the world, and with each other."[12]

To move toward an inquiry-based approach, we must stop giving students answers and start asking more questions, allowing them to wrestle with ideas.

To move toward an inquiry-based approach, we must stop giving students answers and start asking more questions, allowing them to wrestle with ideas. As JJSE math teacher Crystal Proctor puts it, "You actually have to be excited about what your students think."

Urban Academy in New York gives this example of how an inquiry-based lesson differs from a traditional one:

> In a traditional high school American history class, a teacher might ask students to write a report on how Christopher Columbus "discovered" America. Students would be expected to write about Columbus's negotiations with Queen Isabella of Spain, describe the voyages of the Niña, the Pinta and the Santa Maria, and maybe discuss the conflicts Columbus had with the native peoples he encountered. This is a typical "developmental" lesson. In an inquiry lesson, by contrast, students might be asked to argue about how we should remember Columbus today. Some might argue that he was a brave man who set out on a dangerous trip. Others might say he was a racist conqueror who enslaved and killed off a native population. Still others might argue a third, or fourth, or fifth position. There is no "right" answer, and students at Urban are not expected to find one. Instead, they are expected to take a position and argue it using evidence.[13]

In this situation, the question students are exploring is, "How should we remember Columbus today?" Many educators call this an **essential question** because it gets to the heart of an issue or discipline. (See Exhibit 8.4 for criteria.) A great resource for developing these questions is the book *Essential Questions,* by Grant Wiggins and Jay McTighe.

Teachers who facilitate inquiry-based discussions also use what researchers now call *talk moves.* Table 8.3 summarizes four key goals of teachers during a discussion, and associated moves the teacher can make to enhance the classroom conversation.[14]

EXHIBIT 8.4   CRITERIA FOR DEVELOPING ESSENTIAL QUESTIONS

An essential question . . .

1. Is *open ended*; that is, it typically will not have a single, final, and correct answer.
2. Is *thought-provoking and intellectually engaging,* often sparking discussion and debate.
3. Calls for *higher order thinking,* such as analysis, inference, evaluation, and prediction. It cannot be effectively answered by recall alone.
4. Points toward *important, transferable ideas* within (and sometimes across) disciplines.
5. Raises *additional questions* and sparks further inquiry.
6. Requires *support and justification,* not just an answer.
7. *Recurs* over time; that is, the question can and should be revisited again and again.

Note. These criteria are based on the work of Grant Wiggins and Jay McTighe, 2013, in *Essential Questions,* Alexandria, VA: ASCD.

TABLE 8.3   TALK MOVES

Goal	Examples of Talk Moves
Help individual students share, expand, and clarify their own thoughts	• **Time to Think:** partner talk, writing as think time, wait time • **Say More:** "Can you say more about that?" "What do you mean by that?" "Can you give an example?" • **So, Are You Saying . . .?** "So, let me see if I've got what you're saying. Are you saying . . .?" (always leaving space for the original student to agree or disagree and say more)
Help students listen carefully to one another	• **Who Can Rephrase or Repeat?** "Who can repeat what Javon just said or put it into their own words?" (After a partner talk) "What did your partner say?"
Help students deepen their reasoning	• **Asking for Evidence or Reasoning:** "Why do you think that?" "What's your evidence?" "How did you arrive at that conclusion?" "Is there anything in the text that made you think that?" • **Challenge or Counterexample:** "Does it always work that way?" "How does that idea square with Sonia's example?" "What if it had been a copper cube instead?"

Goal	Examples of Talk Moves
Help students engage with others' reasoning	• **Agree/Disagree and Why?:** "Do you agree/disagree? (And why?)" "Are you saying the same thing as Jelya or something different, and if it's different, how is it different?" "What do people think about what Vannia said?" "Does anyone want to respond to that idea?" • **Add On:** "Who can add on to the idea that Jamal is building?" "Can anyone take that suggestion and push it a little further?" • **Explaining What Someone Else Means:** "Who can explain what Aisha means when she says that?" "Who thinks they could explain in their words why Simon came up with that answer?" "Why do you think he said that?"

Note. Additional training materials and resources are available on the Inquiry Project website, http://inquiryproject.terc.edu/.

The idea behind these moves is to minimize the amount of teacher talk and instead to empower students to use their voices and build an intellectual community in the classroom. After videoing a lesson where JJSE humanities teacher Armon Kasmai used talk moves to lead an inquiry-based discussion, we asked two students to explain what his role was. Meghan said,

> I feel like Mr. Kasmai's role was to facilitate us and make sure our opinions were heard—not to make anyone feel like they were wrong, and not to make anyone feel like they were right, but just to make sure our opinions got out there and were understood.

Sasha agreed and added, "I feel like Mr. Kasmai was basically trying to make sure that everybody would say something, and make us feel comfortable saying what we had in our minds."

Bob Moses, the civil rights leader and founder of the Algebra Project, likes to say that in a good classroom, it's clear that the students are not the spectators; they are the ones on the field playing the game. When we really listen to our students, we can create classrooms and schools like this, where students listen deeply to one another as they construct a community of ideas.

LISTENING AND DEMOCRACY

The student-led staff meeting on serving JJSE's undocumented students was a powerful example of students challenging adult perceptions and taking leadership to improve our school. A week after the meeting, I met with some of the student leaders. They were still exasperated over the apparent resistance of some teachers at the meeting and asked me, "Why were they acting like that?!? Why didn't they understand?" Like a good inquiry-based teacher, I turned the question back on the students and asked them, "What do *you* think?" After a long pause, one boy said, "Maybe it's because none of the teachers are undocumented themselves."

In his response, this student captured the essence of why listening is so important: For professional educators, with master's degrees and salaries, it can be very difficult to imagine the lives and experiences of some of our students, no matter how well intentioned we are. If we walk in their shoes by shadowing, tell their stories through fishbowls and interviews, ask them how we are doing by getting their feedback on our work, give them a voice in the classroom through check-ins and talking circles, and organize classrooms around their ideas—then we will be much more likely to know what our students think, and they will be much more likely to tell us what they need.

The goal of listening to students is not just to make our work better—although it will. It is also fundamental to the idea of democracy, the belief that all people have equal rights, responsibilities, and voice.

The goal of listening to students is not just to make our work better—although it will. It is also fundamental to the idea of democracy, the belief that all people have equal rights, responsibilities, and voice. Author and professor Lisa Delpit explains that to educate all children, "We must be convinced of their inherent intellectual capability, humanity, and spiritual character."[15] We must believe that all of our students might one day be our doctor, or the police officer who interacts with our child in a tense moment, or the president who will lead our nation in its most critical hour.

If we share this belief in democracy, then our schools and classrooms will be places where all young people have a voice and are taken seriously as they learn to be tomorrow's leaders. And to make this happen, listening to students must be at the heart of everything we do.

KEY TAKEAWAYS

- Listening to students is challenging, even for well-intentioned educators, because school structures and social-cultural expectations create barriers between adults and students.
- The only way we can hold our students to high expectations, behaviorally and intellectually, is by listening to them.
- The Deep Listening stances can and should be used with students just as with adults.

- There are many practical routines that can help educators listen deeply to students, from student shadowing, to collecting and sharing student stories, to gathering formal feedback from students.
- It is also essential to teach students to listen to one another, through such strategies as talking circles and inquiry-based teaching, which give students a real voice in the classroom.

LISTENING LEADER INQUIRY

Question: I agree that we should listen to students, but when does it go overboard? I don't want to be permissive or enabling. Hasn't teachers' (and parents') authority eroded too much already in our society?

My thoughts: I share your concerns. Some new teachers think that listening to students means abandoning their authority by validating students' worst selves. (For example: "My student said he didn't want to work today, so I listened to him and let him text on his phone all class period instead.") To me, that's not deep listening because we're not hearing what lies beneath a young person's bluster or negative emotions or momentary desires—that is, the true sound of his best self. Sometimes the greatest gift we can give young people is to hold a firm boundary for them when they are incapable of holding it for themselves. In such a case, the student may feel as though we didn't listen to her in the moment, and that's OK. At JJSE, we use the "warm demander" teacher framework to help describe the kind of authority a teacher should have. Listening is a key piece of being a warm demander, and so is holding students to high expectations even when they are struggling with self-discipline or doubting their own ability.

Question: How do I get students who tend to be more introverted or quiet to speak, so that I may listen?

My thoughts: That is a great question. I have found that the strategies described in this chapter work well with most young people, but very shy and introverted students may be reluctant to open up even when they feel safe. I have tried one-on-one meetings with quiet students, with some success. (See Chapter 7 for general guidelines for a one-on-one.) Sometimes a quiet student has a friend who is more outgoing, and in those cases I have consulted with the friend about how to encourage the introverted one to speak up more. When I was teaching, a technique that I found effective with shy students was reciprocal journaling: I would ask students to write responses to questions during class, and I would read the journals in the evening and write back. Finally, as someone who was shy myself when I was younger, I also know that quiet people sometimes just need to be allowed to be quiet, as long as they know they can speak up if they need to.

NOTES

1. Rizga, K. (2015). *Mission High*. New York, NY: Nation Books, p. 59.
2. Wiggins, G. (2014, October 10). A veteran teacher turned coach shadows 2 students for 2 days—a sobering lesson learned. *Granted, and . . .* Retrieved from https://grantwiggins.wordpress.com/2014/10/10/a-veteran-teacher-turned-coach-shadows-2-students-for-2-days-a-sobering-lesson-learned/
3. School Retool. (2016). Shadow a Student Challenge. Retrieved from http://shadowastudent.org/. For more on the design thinking process, you can find IDEO's free educator toolkit at designthinkingforeducators.com.
4. Wiggins, A veteran teacher.
5. Gumbrecht, J. (2015, April 20). "#IWishMyTeacherKnew shares students' heartbreak, hopes." CNN. Retrieved from http://www.cnn.com/2015/04/17/living/i-wish-my-teacher-knew-kyle-schwartz-schools-feat/
6. Alexander, A. (2016, January 6). How Mario Woods stands in for vanishing black San Francisco. *Atlantic*. Retrieved from http://www.theatlantic.com/politics/archive/2016/01/how-mario-woods-stands-in-for-vanishing-black-san-francisco/458763/
7. NEA Foundation. (2013, May). Students speak: Teachers in Lee County, FL embrace student feedback to improve instruction. (NEA Foundation Issue Brief Number 8). Retrieved from http://www.neafoundation.org/public/uploads/1369072304%20NEAF_IssueBrief8_May2013.pdf
8. What Kids Can Do. (n.d.). Reflections on what works: A group of teenage classroom observers raises the bar for teachers. Retrieved from http://www.whatkidscando.org/archives/featurestories/bestpractices.html
9. Hung, M. (2015, November). Talking circles promote equitable discourse. *Mathematics Teacher, 109*(4). Retrieved from http://www.nctm.org/Publications/Mathematics-Teacher/2015/Vol109/Issue4/Talking-Circles-Promote-Equitable-Discourse/
10. Urban Academy. (n.d.). Inquiry-based teaching. Retrieved from http://www.urbanacademy.org/new-page-35/
11. Michaels, S., & O'Connor, C. (2015). Conceptualizing talk moves as tools: Professional development approaches for academically productive discussions. In L. B. Resnick, C. Asterhan, & S. N. Clarke (Eds.), *Socializing intelligence through talk and dialogue* (pp. 333–347). Washington DC: American Educational Research Association. Retrieved from http://www.ngsx.org/files/5414/2463/8487/MichaelsOConnor_Talk_Moves_as_Tools_Resnick_Volume.pdf
12. Freire, P. (2000). *Pedagogy of the oppressed*. New York, NY: Continuum, p. 72. (Original work published 1970)
13. Urban Academy, Inquiry-based teaching.
14. Michaels, S., & O'Connor, C. (2012). Talk science primer. TERC. Retrieved from http://inquiryproject.terc.edu/shared/pd/TalkScience_Primer.pdf
15. Delpit, L. (2012). *Multiplication is for white people*. New York, NY: New Press, p. 49.

Part 3

COMPLEX CHANGE

Chapter 9

Influencing Complex Change

Preview: By listening deeply to our colleagues, families, and students, we uncover a moral imperative for change. Next we learn to influence, rather than control, the change process.

This chapter is designed to help you:

- Understand the properties and features of a complex living system.
- Diagnose the types of challenges you face as a leader.
- Influence complex change by pursuing a few key steps.

THE LISTENING LEADER'S LANDSCAPE

In August 2010, I flew to the Middle East, a region I had never set foot in, to spend a sabbatical year teaching Jordanian and Palestinian high school students in Amman, Jordan. I had been working as an instructional and leadership coach for several years, and the opportunity to return to the classroom appealed to me. My partner and I also wanted to travel and live abroad before our older child started kindergarten; little did we know the complex landscape that awaited us. Within the year, the Arab Spring erupted in Egypt, and the now-entrenched Syrian crisis began. It was a wonderful and trying 10 months for which we had no road map.

In Figure 9.1, my 4-year-old daughter is hiking through the Dana Nature Reserve in central Jordan a few weeks after our arrival. The air was hot and dry as we followed a poorly marked trail looping back to "head-quarters," a woven tent where hot mint tea was offered to sweaty hikers.

FIGURE 9.1   AUTHOR'S DAUGHTER HIKING IN CENTRAL JORDAN, AUGUST 2010

Photo by the author

Each time I saw a cairn—one of the stacks of rocks beside her—I felt relieved and grateful: We were still on the trail. Adapting to a new climate, culture, and reality had been difficult, and each cairn reminded me to pause and take in the experience rather than march mindlessly toward a destination.

I offer you this metaphor for the work that lies ahead. In the landscape of school transformation, there are no predictable rules or neatly mani-cured paths. We have to find our way forward, step-by-step, with courage and listening. Think of your role as stacking cairns along a path to gently guide your team. Cairn-builders have a vision of what's possible and a plan, but they are not tour guides leading passive hikers by the hand. Likewise, Listening Leaders mark out a promising direction while resisting the urge to prescribe every step or micromanage the journey.

First, the levels of data, core tenets, and equity channels shine light on our current landscape. Next, Deep and Strategic Listening help us popu-late the landscape with people . . . community members with whom we grow relational capital. Over time, and with each conversation, we build the capacity of our team to reimagine the landscape entirely—to create an equitable learning environment for every student. The question, then, is, How do we organize the work above the green line (recall the circles of structures, patterns, and processes from Chapter 4) to produce dramatically different outcomes for students?

> *Cairn.* The Gaelic term for a human-made pile of stones, carefully stacked and left behind as a memorial, landmark, or trail sign. The image of a cairn, which adorns the cover of this book, has always spoken to me—its delicacy and strength; its sense of balance and building *upon* rather than knocking down; the generosity in the act of leaving something behind for others. I love that cairns (by many names) have been used throughout history across continents and cultures—from Ireland to Somalia to Hawaii, South Korea, and South America—to shape a path through uncharted territory.

As a leader, you're in charge, but you're not in control.

There's an underlying premise and paradox woven into this chapter: As a leader, you're in charge, but you're not in control. Great leaders, like great teachers and parents, understand that at the end of the day, people must find their own way forward. They attempt to influence rather than control, offering just enough parameters before stepping back and allowing powerful work to emerge. This approach requires what we can consider a balcony orientation and a dance-floor sensibility: It means holding the big picture in mind while moving with grace and intention through every interaction that shapes your culture. But first, we need to unlearn some problematic habits and mindsets.

 MAKE IT MINDFUL

Ask yourself these questions:

- What has been my approach to change leadership until now? Do I tend to be task oriented (the Manager) or top-down (the Driver)? Do I avoid conflict and hope that everyone will get along (the Peacekeeper)?
- How did I learn my current approach: from a mentor, a leadership training program, or perhaps my family of origin? How has or hasn't it served me?
- Are there beliefs I need to revisit? Possibly let go? Embrace?

LEADERSHIP IN A LIVING SYSTEM

The pressures of the test-and-punish era led many leaders to pursue structural or cosmetic fixes for their toughest challenges: We purchased new curricula, invested in student interventions, and "rolled out" professional development (PD) initiatives with little attention to human dynamics. Over time, many educators became weary and seemingly resistant to change.

In this climate, dysfunctional "microclimates" proliferate within school buildings. These will likely include staff talking in hushed tones about **nondiscussables**, topics that are important enough to merit frequent conversations, but so burdened with anxiety and fear that they are discussed only in the parking lot, near the water cooler, or at happy hour.[1] Often this means that equity conversations that should be engaged *publicly* go underground (recall Chapter 3).

The whole situation originates with a faulty view of schools as machine-like entities in which change is linear, measurable, and predictable. A machine has clear lines of cause and effect and distinct compartments, or silos. Pull a lever, and the conveyor belt moves. Call a team a PLC, and its members will dutifully comply. As I mentioned in Chapter 3, public schools were built in the Industrial Age to resemble machines that can be broken down into discrete parts: seven periods, master schedules, disciplinary codes, and elaborate organizational charts. Follow this logic to its end point, and you'll find leaders who believe that a detailed strategic plan, implemented through top-down management, will generate results.

Here's the uncomfortable truth: School transformation doesn't follow a mechanistic logic. Whether you lead a school, a team, or a district, you sit at the helm of what is often called a **complex, adaptive system (CAS), or living system**. This system is *complex* because people interact with each other in "dynamic, evolving, and unpredictable ways,"[2] and it is *adaptive* because human behavior constantly shifts and self-organizes in response to events—both at the micro and macro levels.[3]

Here's another truth: Every complex system sits within the sociopolitical context of inequity. The National Equity Project has added a circle to Wheatley's Six Circle Model (described in Chapter 4); this new circle encompasses the others and is labeled *systemic oppression* (see Figure 9.2). According to feminist author bell hooks, oppression means the absence of choices.[4]

FIGURE 9.2   SEVEN CIRCLE MODEL

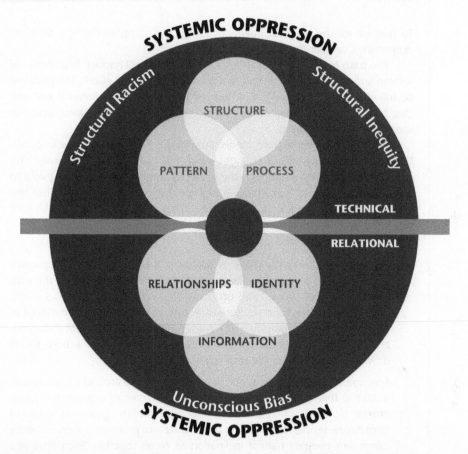

Adapted from the Seven Circle Model, which was developed by the National Equity Project

If we are truly committed to reaching the students furthest from opportunity, we must reimagine our approach and infuse choice and voice at every level of the system: for students, families, and staff.

When we try to control the change process, we strip people of the very thing that liberates them from oppression: the right to choose. If we are committed to reaching the students furthest from opportunity, we must reimagine our approach and infuse choice and voice at every level of the system: for students, families, and staff. Exhibit 9.1 unpacks some basic properties of complex change.

EXHIBIT 9.1   THE KEY PROPERTIES OF COMPLEX CHANGE

To prepare for the ups and downs of navigating complex change, study its properties. Consider the following:

The path is full of detours. Expect that change will happen in a nonlinear fashion and only rarely according to the laws of cause and effect. The path will be full of detours, and you'll find yourself taking two steps forward and one step back. Don't feel defeated by this! Accept that you cannot always predict the impact of your actions.

Initial conditions matter. Understand that a very small change in conditions can lead to significant changes down the road. (Conversely, sweeping policies may have little impact on the ground.) Leverage your listening skills to stay attuned to what's happening in any given moment; we'll delve into this more in the pages that follow. Ask yourself, *What reality are we sitting with right now? Not tomorrow, but right now.*

Patterns emerge and guide you.

Patterns replicate across levels. A **fractal** is a pattern that self-replicates across different scales, like a Russian doll. In organizations, fractals show up in the behaviors, values, and processes that repeat across various levels. For example, a classroom culture of lecture-style instruction is mirrored in site and district meetings in which leaders talk *at* instead of *with* stakeholders. Find and study these patterns and consider how your actions trickle down to other levels of the organization.

Leverage self-organizing behavior. People will organize around the issues that matter to them, a pattern that can have a negative or a generative force. Provide gentle direction for self-organizing. Establish "guardrails"—what I term "a few simple rules" later in the chapter—to promote coherence while harnessing people's natural inclination to come together. Each time you launch a project, you might say, "Here are the parameters and expectations. I trust you, and I'll be here to support, listen, and offer feedback."

New, unexpected patterns will emerge. As people and teams interact in dynamic ways, you'll see patterns and ideas arise that you could not have predicted. This is mostly good news! Again, listen for, draw out, and make visible the exciting work that emerges.

As you notice these properties, take a mindful moment to note, for example, "We've clearly hit a nonlinear twist in the change process" or "Wow, people are self-organizing in some powerful ways right now!" This self-talk is especially crucial for leaders who like to run a tight ship and are uncomfortable with uncertainty. Accepting the natural fluctuations of complex change will allow you to take a deep breath, loosen your grip, and listen for opportunities to influence rather than control.

DIAGNOSE YOUR PROBLEMS AND CHALLENGES

Understanding complex change is the first cairn on the path to equitable school transformation. Next, we need to accurately diagnose the challenges we face so that we don't apply a Band-Aid to a gaping wound. This requires that we develop **situational awareness**, or the ability to discern between two sets of problems: those that are complicated and/or technical, and those that are complex and adaptive.

Complicated problems, or **technical problems**, are important and often multifaceted, but they have known solutions that can be identified with a standard toolkit—for example, goals, benchmarks, and work plans with discrete steps. Think of designing a master schedule or training people in the content of the Common Core Standards. We can address each of these with technical expertise, by adjusting structures and processes above the green line.

Complex challenges, sometimes called **adaptive challenges**, have no known solution. They live in the gap between people's values and their current reality, and can only be addressed through changes in priorities, behaviors, and loyalties.[5] To influence complex change, we must fundamentally shift the paradigm we hold about reality. Consider a teacher who is confident that lecturing students is the best way to teach math. He views himself as a content expert and students as consumers, and he is frustrated by the district's new math curriculum requiring that students collaborate in small groups. If we take a technical approach to this situation, such as by writing the teacher up for refusing to implement the curriculum, he will feel threatened and default to fight, flight, or tend-and-befriend behaviors.

In situations like this, we need what I would call a bifocal lens, a view that focuses on both complexity and equity. A Listening Leader would take time to understand how the teacher views himself and his core identity. He or she would leverage Deep Listening to help the teacher tolerate the losses inherent in changing his established practices, and Strategic Listening to challenge the teacher's mindset and help him develop new competencies. Finally, the leader would organize professional learning opportunities that make it safe for the teacher to take risks and try out new practices.

The big idea here is that when we're dealing with complex problems, technical solutions are not just inadequate; they have a strong likelihood of reproducing the status quo. Table 9.1 provides criteria for diagnosing the challenges you face.

Let's reexamine earlier stories in the book through the lens of complex versus complicated challenges. Remember Jason, the district

TABLE 9.1   DIAGNOSING THE CHALLENGES YOU FACE

	Complicated Problems (Also Called Technical Problems)	Complex Challenges (Also Called Adaptive Challenges)
Definition	• These are multifaceted problems that require technical expertise and know-how to solve. • Solutions do exist. • You have a high probability of success in addressing these problems.	• These are problems of great complexity for which we can't identify a clear solution in advance. • They require social processes like listening and dialogue. • You have to stand in the space of possibility because laws of probability don't apply.
Decision making	• Decision making drives toward a quantitative goal. • The process is as follows: collect data; analyze data; respond with a strategy. • Strategy is often a prescriptive course of action (e.g., the No Child Left Behind Act).	• Decision making is nonlinear and driven by shared vision and principles. • The process is as follows: probe and engage in inquiry; create opportunities for dialogue; guide, facilitate, and influence. • Strategy depends on collaborative inquiry to arrive at possible solutions.
Approach	• Find a range of practices that work. • Write a detailed strategic plan.	• Experiment with and build on emerging practices that work. • Coconstruct a "skinny plan."
Examples	• How can we train teachers to use the pacing guides so that we meet our district literacy goals? • How can we add additional Advanced Placement courses to our master schedule?	• How can we build teachers' capacity to engage English language learners and special education students in meaningful and complex content? • How can we ensure that every child—regardless of race, language, or zip code—has access to a college-preparatory curriculum?

Note. Table cocreated with Victor Cary of the National Equity Project, 2016.

supervisor in Chapter 2 who wanted Estella to discipline her teacher? Jason viewed the teacher's failure to count answer sheets as a technical problem that Estella should solve with discipline. Estella, by contrast, viewed it as an adaptive challenge; she wanted to maintain the teacher's loyalty and their budding relationship while addressing the simpler *technical* problem of the missing materials.

In Chapter 3, Joy and Wendy grappled with an adaptive equity challenge—how to respond to an incident of cultural insensitivity and racial bias. Looking back, Joy felt that her first attempt to educate the staff was too technical and directive; she hadn't created a safe environment for people to learn and grow together. Wendy, by contrast, tried to address a

complex situation with the reactive gesture of giving flowers to her boss. Had the two women understood this moment as a complex challenge, they could have modeled an inquiry stance by sharing their respective experiences, thoughts, feelings, and questions with their colleagues.

Chapter 5 began with my own leadership blunder: I drew on technical expertise to design a cross-content PD model that seemed great at face value. However, I quickly found myself staring down a complex challenge. My staff felt overwhelmed by the demands of our young school and needed time to master their own content before working with other departments. Imposing a plan from above bred passivity and resentment.

This process of distinguishing complicated problems from complex challenges is key. The actions you take will be predicated on that initial diagnosis, but your paramount move remains listening. Moving a complex system is less about crafting a detailed plan and more about listening well enough to assemble the right cairns. Next, we'll examine what those "right" cairns look like.

SIX STEPS TO INFLUENCE COMPLEX CHANGE

There are six steps to shaping a path forward, which I will illustrate with examples from the founding years of June Jordan School for Equity (JJSE), where I was coprincipal. These steps will help you stack cairns that offer just enough direction without shutting down a sense of exploration and discovery. Table 9.2 previews the steps.

Step 1. Tell the Current-State Story

If I had an hour to solve a problem, I'd spend 55 minutes thinking about the problem and five minutes thinking about solutions.

—ALBERT EINSTEIN

We begin by collecting data to tell the current-state story of your team or organization. A well-rounded story includes different types of data: Level 1 "satellite" measures like test scores, attendance, and course passage and graduation rates; Level 2 "map" measures like reading Lexile levels, algebra readiness scores, and student perception surveys; and Level 3 "street" data that you can gather only through listening and observation. Of all of these, Level 3 data is the most important source for understanding the current reality, or at least what people *perceive* as real.

TABLE 9.2   SIX STEPS TO INFLUENCE COMPLEX CHANGE

Step	Guiding Questions
1. Tell the current-state story.	• What data (Levels 1, 2, and 3) do you need to understand the current reality? • What evidence can you collect of conditions below the green line? • If you listen carefully, what micronarrative patterns stand out?
2. Name an equity imperative.	• What pressing equity challenges emerge from the current-state story? • What is your community's call to action? • What is its North Star, or vision of success?
3. Identify a few simple rules.	• What guiding principles will help you and your team stay true to its intentions and values? • What tensions might get in the way?
4. Create a "skinny plan."	• What's your good-enough vision of progress? • What will tell your team to pop a bottle of bubbly and celebrate? • What are your must-dos, and what are you willing NOT to do to make progress?
5. Establish a few clear metrics.	• How will you know you've made progress? • What Level 1, 2, and 3 data will you collect?
6. Distribute leadership; build capacity.	• How will you build a model and structure for distributed leadership? • Who will lead which pieces of the work, and how will you build their capacity?

Level 3 data is the most important source for understanding the current reality, or at least what people perceive as real.

Street-level data includes the stories we hear when we really listen. Often these aren't fully developed stories, but more like anecdotes or snippets of stories that I'll refer to as **micronarratives.**[6] Remember that organizations have core memories. Micronarratives form the raw material of those memories, and as they replicate across the organization, they begin to shape what people perceive as reality. These stories float about inside every organization; you need only turn up the volume and focus your brain on hearing and interpreting them.

Imagine that you lead a middle school with a troubling equity gap around discipline: Black boys are disproportionately sent out of class and to the office with referrals. On closer examination, you find that three teachers write the vast majority of these referrals. This Level 1 data has surfaced an equity challenge, but now you need to investigate the story beneath the numbers. How do the students who are sent out of class talk and *feel* about their experience? How do the teachers rationalize their actions? Listen carefully for these micronarratives.

After you've analyzed key Level 1 and 2 data, listen below the green line for story patterns around

Identity How do stakeholders talk about organizational identity—who are we, and who we have been?

Relationship How do people talk about relationships across the organization—student to student, student to teacher, teacher to parent, leader to teacher—and across teams?

Information How does information flow in the organization? Do people have access to the information they need?

JJSE emerged from the current-state story of southeast San Francisco, which our founding team pieced together through multiple data sources. Figure 9.3 illustrates one piece of the story, Level 1 data revealing a stark literacy gap across the city. To investigate the story below the green line, we

FIGURE 9.3   THE CURRENT-STATE LITERACY STORY BEHIND JJSE

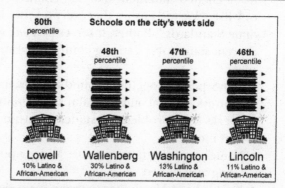
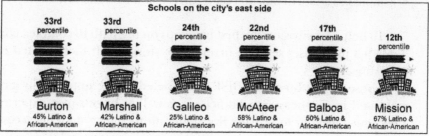

11th grade reading scores

at SF high schools

Are large traditional high schools working for our children?

Schools on the city's west side

Lowell	Wallenberg	Washington	Lincoln
80th percentile	48th percentile	47th percentile	46th percentile
10% Latino & African-American	30% Latino & African-American	13% Latino & African-American	11% Latino & African-American

Schools on the city's east side

Burton	Marshall	Galileo	McAteer	Balboa	Mission
33rd percentile	33rd percentile	24th percentile	22nd percentile	17th percentile	12th percentile
45% Latino & African-American	42% Latino & African-American	25% Latino & African-American	58% Latino & African-American	50% Latino & African-American	67% Latino & African-American

This chart includes all San Francisco public high schools that enroll over 500 students.   *Small Schools for Equity 2001* held home visits with over 200 families and collected micronarratives by asking parents, "What have been your experiences in neighborhood schools?" "What are your hopes and dreams for your child?" "Describe an ideal high school that you would love to send your child to." By integrating these various data, we were able to make a compelling case for a new high school and stack our first cairn.

Appendix F includes a Telling the Current-State Story Tool for writing your school or organization's current-state story.

Step 2. Name an Equity Imperative

The current-state story pulls back the curtain on inequity, which will generate strong emotions and reactions from various stakeholders. This is when you need a clear and compelling "why," or what I call an *equity imperative*. It's also when you need to practice Deep Listening to validate people's visceral reactions to the data, even if you do not agree with those reactions. There is an art to affirming people feelings with Deep Listening while at the same time pushing them forward with Strategic Listening that drives toward a vision of equity.

An **equity imperative** is like the Declaration of Independence—a moral standard toward which your team, school, or system will strive. It is not a clichéd statement like "All children will learn," nor a transactional one like, "We will ensure that every teacher implements the Common Core State Standards." Rather, it serves as a *call to action* that emerges from the current-state story. A strong equity imperative:

• Draws people together around a focused change agenda
• Conveys a moral and ethical responsibility to disrupt the status quo
• Speaks to a problem of student learning or access, refusing to sugarcoat inequity
• Names an intention to serve and empower constituents who are not being well served
• Establishes a North Star to reach for, a vision of transformation

To help you envision the first two steps on the path to complex change, Table 9.3 juxtaposes several current-state stories with their related equity imperatives.

Those of us who started JJSE were fueled by the opportunity gaps we witnessed in southeast San Francisco, as well as by our own experiences. I became a teacher to provide first-generation college students access to a

TABLE 9.3   SAMPLE CURRENT-STATE STORIES AND EQUITY IMPERATIVES

Current-State Story	Equity Imperative
School Level: Our current state-story reveals a rigidly tracked school in which English-speaking students progress toward college while English language learners flatline in ELD or remedial courses. In listening sessions and surveys, our ELL parents and students express a lack of hope for the future.	We commit to detracking our school and providing every ELL student with access to a college-preparatory curriculum. In aspiring to build our ELL students' confidence and hope, we will run focus groups with them twice each year and prioritize home visits with our most struggling ELL students. **North Star:** We will reduce the college readiness gap between ELL students and English-speaking students to less than 10%.
School Level: Our current-state story is that White, middle-class families engage in school structures while Black and Latino families feel marginalized and unwelcome. This pattern tracks to our reading data, which reveals a 15% gap between White students who are proficient by third grade and Black and Latino students who are proficient by third grade.	We commit to transforming our school culture so that families of color feel welcome and participate in equal numbers to White families. We will research and implement creative ways to engage our most marginalized families and rigorously track parent engagement. We will also focus all instructional improvement efforts on reading acceleration for struggling readers. **North Star:** We will eliminate the racial literacy gap by the end of third grade.
District Level: Our current state is a bifurcated school system in which affluent families attend high-performing "hills schools," while schools in high-poverty communities struggle to access basic resources. Student performance data mirrors this resource and opportunity gap.	We have an imperative to share resources more equitably across our district. We will develop an enrollment policy that provides access to high-performing schools for *every* student while we strive to redistribute resources in ways that benefit students furthest from opportunity. **North Star:** We will adopt an equity policy to ensure that every student gains entry into one of their top two school choices and that every school retains quality teachers.

rich intellectual world. This goal matured into an equity *imperative* after I lost a brilliant young scholar named Sameerah. A senior in my American Democracy class, Sameerah possessed a piercing intellect and natural leadership skills; I appointed her president pro tem of our Mock Congress. She had a 4.0 GPA, interned at an elderly home, and wanted to become a geriatric doctor.

One week, Sameerah didn't show up to class for five days in a row. When she returned, I pulled her aside and learned that she and her mother, who was dying of AIDS, had become homeless. She hadn't had access to a shower all week and was too embarrassed to come to school.

The mother and daughter eventually found housing, and Sameerah went on to finish my fall course with flying colors, but by the spring, I had lost track of her. At graduation, I scrolled the program for her name and couldn't find it. She had disappeared. That night, I committed myself to building a school where Sameerah and other brilliant young people would not disappear.

JJSE's founding team set our compass toward a North Star to educate and empower a new, multiracial generation of leaders through a dynamic and personalized learning environment. We oriented our work toward three cairns that still adorn the walls of the school: Community, Social Justice, and Independent Thinkers. Equity imperatives matter. They spring from an honest assessment of your current state and the courage to set your compass in a bold direction. Who is your Sameerah? Whose stories do you carry close? Why do you drive into the parking lot each morning, and what equity imperative will emerge if you listen deeply?

Step 3. Identify a Few Simple Rules

In the summer of 2015, my family spent a few weeks in Hanalei, Kauai. Entering the town of Hanalei from the south, one encounters a historical, single-lane bridge that bears a lot of North Shore traffic. This could be a disaster, but I was fascinated by how smoothly the negotiation of cars went. As we approached the bridge, I saw a sign messaging a single rule that governs the behavior of hundreds of drivers each day: "Local courtesy is 5–7 cars" (Figure 9.4)

This story exemplifies my favorite mantra for influencing complex change: *A few simple rules guide complex behavior.* If your equity imperative is the Declaration of Independence, your simple rules are the Constitution: overarching, foundational principles according to which you'll govern. A strong set of principles provides organizational coherence, fosters collective identity, and drives purposeful decisions about resources and initiatives.

After you capture and tell the current-state story, consider hosting a staff or leadership team retreat to home in on an equity imperative and guiding principles—the nucleus of collective identity. Ask your team, "What simple rules can we create to guide all of our actions and decisions and help us stay true to our equity imperative?" Allow people to brainstorm at first, but ultimately aim for a short list of no more than five or six principles. If you can get the team to agree, you have built your next cairn.

Table 9.4 illustrates the five simple rules our founding team created, each of which can be traced to a design feature. These framed everything

FIGURE 9.4 SIGN ON THE APPROACH TO HANALEI BRIDGE, HANALEI, KAUAI

Photo by the author

we did as a school, and they live on today. Simple rules are the banks of the river that allow water to flow powerfully and productively, and they can be leveraged at any unit of change, from the classroom to the district. Exhibit 9.2 offers a district example of simple rules.

Step 4. Create a "Skinny Plan"

With a few simple rules acting as cairns, you're ready to design a course of action. Instead of a detailed strategic plan, you need a planning tool that's nimble and responsive to the dynamic conditions on the ground. Enter the "skinny plan," which invites the team to articulate a good-enough vision of progress and prioritize a short list of strategies.

When crafting a skinny plan, the mindset is elimination—less (stuff to think about and do) equals more (impact). Organizational theorist Michael Porter writes, "The essence of strategy is choosing what not to

TABLE 9.4 SIMPLE RULES AND DESIGN FEATURES FOR JUNE JORDAN SCHOOL FOR EQUITY

Guiding Principles	Core Design Feature
Nurturing adult-student relationships in a safe, personalized learning environment	**Advisory** system: Every certificated adult acts as an academic and social-emotional support person for roughly 20 students.
Challenging academics with strong support structures	**Performance assessment system:** Tenth and twelfth graders collect, polish, and defend their best work before a committee of teachers, parents, and peers. **Discussion-based classrooms:** Teachers cultivate an inquiry pedagogy that focuses on rigorous academic discussion in which students defend their ideas with evidence. **College access:** The school houses a state-of-the-art college access program for first-generation students, and college-prep seminars and university courses for credit.
Expert teachers who continually refine their craft	**Teacher development:** Significant time is devoted to collaboration and professional learning, during which students engage in internships or service learning.
Powerful connections with parents and families	**Creative approaches to family engagement:** The staff uses home visits, a parent organizing committee, and a school-funded parent liaison to maximize parent engagement.
Real accountability through democratic decision-making and multiple measures of success	**Codirectorship:** JJSE has a unique coprincipal model that exhibits the value of shared leadership. **Consensus-based decision making:** All major decisions that will impact staff are made through discussion and consensus.

EXHIBIT 9.2   A FEW SIMPLE RULES FOR A DISTRICT

For those of you who work in a central office, I offer an example of simple rules at that scale. Consider the adaptive challenge of implementing the Common Core State Standards (CCSS), reflecting on the implementation phase, and refining next steps.

- Rule 1: Our first year of Common Core implementation will be about learning, not performing.
- Rule 2: We will use culturally responsive teaching as our primary lens for implementing the standards.
- Rule 3: We will design hands-on PD that supports teachers to experiment with planning Common Core units, and engage in short inquiry cycles.
- Rule 4: We will deploy ourselves to sites to coach school leaders in designing this PD.
- Rule 5: We will build the capacity of teacher leaders to facilitate collaborative inquiry.

do."[7] A skinny plan will help you clear the rubble of past change initiatives and focus on the basic ingredients of school transformation—the learning of students and adults. A skinny plan can be crafted at any level of the system, including, for example, a district, a middle school network, a whole school, a school culture, an instructional program, or a specific team.

Exhibit 9.3 provides a tool for facilitating this process.

In the spring of JJSE's second year, our leadership team analyzed Level 3 classroom data and identified the following issue: Our students needed more practice having high-level academic discussions. Because we knew they needed this skill set for college, we decided to create a skinny plan focused on building teachers' capacity to facilitate discussions. This aligned with two of our simple rules: "challenging academics with strong support structures" and "expert teachers who continually refine their craft."

EXHIBIT 9.3   SKINNY PLAN TOOL

Our Current-State Story as a School/Organization:	Our Equity Imperative:

Our Simple Rules/Guiding Principles:

Skinny Plan:

1. **What's our "good-enough" vision of success for this year?** (Note: I find it helpful to include a concrete date here, like "What would success look like on June 1, 2018?")
2. **What are our "must-dos"?** (Start with an open brainstorm; then review each proposed item by asking, "Could we achieve our vision without doing this?" If the answer is yes, cross it off mercilessly!)
3. **What are we *NOT* willing to do to make progress?** (Write up a formal list of what you're NOT going to do this year and celebrate the courage to name those things.)
4. **Who will lead each big piece of the work, and what support will they need?**

Zeroing in on this instructional area helped us prioritize the work for the following year. We set our sight on three must-dos:

- Devote professional learning time to modeling and practicing inquiry-based discussions.
- Invest in high-quality training on how to lead inquiry-based discussions. (We brought in master teachers from a mentor school, Urban Academy in New York City, to train us.)
- Develop and study one another's discussion lessons within curriculum teams.

The staff made great strides in the course of a year, as evident in classroom observations and the level of discourse in collaboration meetings. And because we stuck with this focus for the next couple of years, people got progressively better at facilitating discussions. By the time I left the school, I would enter most rooms to find students engaged in debate, rigorous group work, hands-on labs, or Socratic discussions.

Step 5. Establish a Few Clear Metrics

The next step in influencing complex change is to become extremely clear about how you will measure success. What types of evidence will you gather to assess progress on the equity imperative? How will you evaluate the skinny plan? Most site plans revolve around goals like, "We will increase test scores by 10%" or "We will decrease suspensions by 5%." Although these measures provide a balcony view of progress, they fall short of illuminating the deeper dimensions of transformation: Are students are ready for college? Are they intellectually engaged? Do they have an academic identity and a sense of personal and cultural pride?

We need more robust metrics. Consider the following questions for a more holistic approach to measuring success:

1. *Deliverable.* Did we do it? Yes or no. (The above-the-green-line aspects of the work can often be measured this simply.)
2. *Development.* Has there been *some* movement? What's our evidence?
3. *Transformation.* Has something significant changed that will never be the same?[8]

Table 9.5 provides a framework for evaluation that incorporates the Six Circle Model and the Levels of Data framework.

TABLE 9.5   A HOLISTIC TOOL FOR MEASURING SUCCESS

	Development	Transformation
Above the Green Line (Patterns, Structures, Processes)	What evidence do we have of changes in patterns, structures, or processes?	Has a system or structure changed so fundamentally that our organization will never be the same?
Below the Green Line (Information, Relationships, Identity)	What evidence and artifacts do we have that point to improved trust, relational capital, or collective capacity to lead the work?	Have our identity, relationships, or ways of sharing information transformed in an indelible way?
Level 1 examples	We've increased graduation rates for low-income students of color by 10%. We've adjusted our master schedule to provide common planning periods for content (or grade-level) teams.	Our graduation rates for low-income students of color are now consistently on par with graduation rates for White, middle-class students.
Level 2 examples	The percentage of third graders reading on grade level increased by 15% this year. We've increased teacher retention by 20% this year.	There is no longer a correlation in our data between reading/Lexile levels and a child's zip code, race, or socioeconomic status. In an end-of-year survey, every teacher reported that he or she is returning and feels a "high level of satisfaction" with his or her working conditions.
Level 3 examples	In guided reading assessments, we found that half of our struggling readers now read with grade-level fluency and demonstrate strong comprehension.	In guided reading assessments, we found that 100% of our struggling readers have mastered fluency and comprehension and express excitement about reading.

At JJSE, we regularly looked at course passage rates, disaggregated by race, socioeconomic status, and special education. Eventually, we transformed our grading policy to an A, B, C, no-credit model to encourage students to make up D and F grades. We also paid attention to attendance data, behavior referrals, and suspensions to assess the functionality of student support systems, and as the school evolved, graduation rates and college access rates became focal metrics.

To map our progress below the green line, we conducted surveys with students, staff, and parents. We also structured into the professional culture opportunities to analyze student work. Every year, students compiled portfolios of their best work in the core content areas. Tenth and twelfth graders had to defend two of their strongest artifacts before a committee of teachers, staff, and peers in order to move on and graduate. This process, coupled with monthly student work protocols, provided continuous access to street-level evidence of learning and built another cairn on the path of complex change

Step 6. Distribute Leadership; Build Capacity

Finally, we need models of **distributed leadership** in which a cadre of teacher leaders deeply understand the work and help develop their peers. In such a model, administrators spread responsibility for instructional improvement across a high-functioning team of talented educators. Team members distribute their expertise to facilitate collaboration, run their classrooms as "laboratories" for peer learning, and informally coach their colleagues on a day-to-day basis. A strong schoolwide leadership team promotes sustainability and coherence across the organization.

As compelling as this may sound, we are more likely to see the alternatives represented in Figure 9.5. In Waiting for Super(wo)man, the principal

FIGURE 9.5   INSTRUCTIONAL LEADERSHIP TEAM MODELS

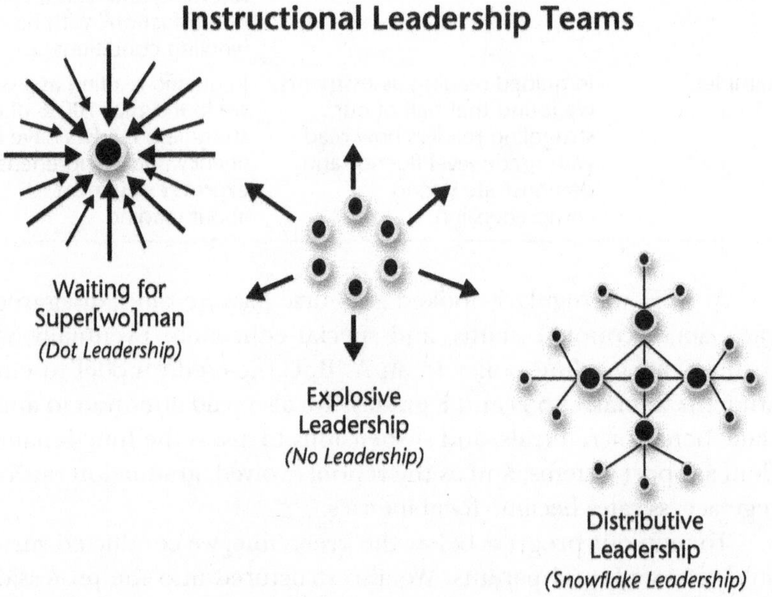

Instructional Leadership Teams

Waiting for
Super[wo]man
(Dot Leadership)

Explosive
Leadership
(No Leadership)

Distributive
Leadership
(Snowflake Leadership)

Inspired by the work of Marshall Ganz, senior lecturer in public policy at the Harvard Kennedy School of Government and APs take responsibility for all instructional leadership duties and become quickly overwhelmed. A leadership team exists to rubber-stamp the principal's decisions, and instructional improvement efforts are so fragmented that teachers tend to close their doors and stick with what they know best. According to a 2015 Bain study, 96% of principals said they were responsible for the performance and growth of the teachers in their buildings, and 82% said they were the primary person responsible.[9] This is not a sustainable scenario, and it's why most schools see little instructional improvement from year to year.

On the flip side, we have schools or systems with a decentralized model in which everyone moves in their own direction, the Explosive Leadership model. Lacking a shared focus or vision, the organization feels fragmented, and people either bury their heads in the sand or self-organize into competing factions. In these organizations, teachers lack not only support to improve but also clarity about what matters.

To influence complex change, we need to emulate the snowflake model of *distributed leadership*. We know that the principal cannot possibly visit every single classroom and provide quality feedback. This model allows positional leaders to spend the majority of their time developing *other* leaders to help implement the work, and thus creates a structure for building collective capacity across the organization. In the snowflake model, the lines in between each dot, or leader, represent trust and relationships—the glue that holds an organization together. This approach demands that leaders pay attention to conditions above the green line (e.g., team structures), and below the green line (e.g., trust).

Here are some of the visible features I would look for in a distributed leadership model:

A representational structure Each person on the central leadership team is charged with leading another team. The positional leader thinks carefully about who will be on the central team, recruiting emerging leaders with energy and passion. I have heard that eight people is the optimal size for a leadership team.

Clear roles and responsibilities Each team has clearly defined, publicly shared roles and responsibilities. Team leaders have clear lines of responsibility for significant and meaningful work; for example, the math department lead acts as the instructional leader around math work at the school, not the woman who orders textbooks.

Interdependence The leadership team functions as a professional learning community, with processes that promote peer-to-peer learning and interdependence. For example, leadership team meetings might include feedback protocols in which team members bring a dilemma or a piece of work to share on a rotating basis. Site administrators view this group of leaders as their classroom and invest in the day-to-day coaching of members. (See Chapter 11 for one-on-one routines with team members.)

Collaborative culture The culture of the team is dynamic and highly interactive, and dissenting perspectives are welcomed rather than feared. Team members deeply understand and feel ownership of the core work. They help construct the equity imperative, the simple rules, an instructional focus, and a skinny plan as well as drive decisions on professional learning and/or policy.

Consistency The leadership team meets regularly and consistently, ideally at least twice a month for at least 90 minutes each time. Once the team is built, members actively participate for at least a year. That expectation creates stability, which is the only way to build collective capacity.

JJSE's founding team believed in the power of distributed leadership and welcomed staff to initiate projects. One founding teacher based the design of our performance assessment system on her experience teaching in the Bronx. Another built the aforementioned partnership with the New York school where he had done his student teaching. JJSE's college access program was the brainchild of a second-year hire, and two founding teachers pioneered an Aztec dancing course for our 3-week "classroom without walls" program. Among the many benefits of shared leadership, we lost only one teacher in our first 3 years.

We also built formal distributed leadership structures, including an academic equity committee, a school culture committee, and a central leadership team. Members of those teams facilitated teacher collaboration in smaller teams. Our guiding principle of democratic decision making meant that we made most decisions together as a staff.

Here's a key assumption behind distributed leadership: A room full of leaders may come up with a better idea than you could have come up with on your own. To leverage distributed leadership, you have to trust the process and be comfortable enough in your own skin to take feedback and input.

SHAPING THE PATH

Life can only be understood backwards; but it must be lived forwards.

—KIERKEGAARD

The big idea of this chapter is essentially this: Your job as a leader is to *influence* the process of school transformation, not control it. This is about navigating the uncertain path by leveraging your growing listening skills and your ability to read satellite, map, and street data. It's about tolerating the sometimes galling fact you are both in control and not in control at the same time. It's about those stones you place, one atop the other, to mark the way, but ultimately it's about having faith in other people to walk with integrity.

What are we afraid of? For 15 years, and in some ways since the invention of public schools, we have suffered under an industrial model that essentially ignored the human element of education. If you follow the six steps in this chapter, you will be able to influence change and empower the people you lead to tackle complex equity challenges with courage and a spirit of inquiry. But remember this: The ways in which you show up every day—your awareness of the brain and of equity, your practice of Deep and Strategic Listening—are the foundation of the work.

French writer Rene Daumal states,

> When you strike off on your own, leave some trace of your passing which will guide you coming back: one stone set on another, some grass flattened by a blow of your stick. . . This applies to anyone who wishes to leave some mark of his passage in the world. Be ready to answer . . . for the trail you leave behind you.[10]

You are key to healing the past and transforming the future. Listening will make it possible for people to manifest a new future together. Our final chapters offer concrete routines for growing a listening culture.

KEY TAKEAWAYS

- As a leader, you're in charge, but you're not in control. Work to influence complex change.
- Schools and districts are dynamic, living systems in which people interact in unpredictable ways, and behavior constantly shifts in response to events.

- We must learn to distinguish between complex challenges and complicated, technical problems. Each requires different leadership moves and change processes.
- There are actionable steps you can follow to shape a path to school transformation.

LISTENING LEADER INQUIRY

Question: I love the idea of a skinny plan and a focused strategy, but my district is so not on this page. Every year, I'm asked to create detailed strategic plans and juggle 10 new district initiatives. Any advice?

My thoughts: You are not alone. Consider revisiting the section of Chapter 1 on maintaining integrity in the face of pressure. Sometimes we have to learn how to say no to the latest district initiative. Other times we have to fly under the radar long enough to earn increased respect and autonomy. It sounds as though your district leadership could benefit from exposure to the ideas in this chapter and to coaching. At the end of the day, you have to define your circle of influence and do your best to push at its edges. Find allies in the central office with whom you can strategize.

Question: I am worried that if I address what is below the green line, we won't have enough time to accomplish the important work above the green line. As a new school, we really need to build structures and routines to support our work. What is the right balance of focus between above and below the green line?

My thoughts: Wonderful question! Remember that Wheatley and her colleagues who crafted the Six Circle Model say that all six circles are equally important and interdependent. If you only focus on below the green line, you'll end up with strong relationships and no sense of structure or coherence. If you only focus on above the green line, you'll end up with a technocratic culture in which people feel disconnected or dehumanized. The trick is to infuse both aspects into all of the work. Chapter 10 provides a framework for designing meetings and other spaces for listening and dialogue that balance above- and below-the-green-line concerns.

NOTES

1. Barth, R. S. (2002). The culture builder. *Educational Leadership, 59*(8), 6–11.
2. Auspos, P., & Cabaj, M. (2014). *Complexity and community change: Managing adaptively to improve effectiveness.* Washington, DC: Aspen Institute, p. 2.
3. Miller, J. E., & Page, S. E. (2007). *Complex adaptive systems: An introduction to computational models of social life.* Princeton, NJ: Princeton University Press.
4. hooks, b. (2000). *Feminist theory: From margin to center.* London, England: Pluto Press, p. 5.
5. Heifetz, R. A., Linsky, M., & Grashow, A. (2009). *The practice of adaptive leadership: Tools and tactics for changing your organization and the world.* Cambridge, MA: Harvard Business Review Press.
6. Snowden, D. (2009). Micro-narratives for knowledge management. YouTube. Retrieved from https://www.youtube.com/watch?v=A5FcEaYoysw
7. Porter, M. (1996, November). What is strategy? *Harvard Business Review*, p. 70.
8. The language of "developmental" and "transformational" change is inspired by the EvaluLEAD framework, developed by an organization called See Change, to which I was exposed when I worked at the National Equity Project.
9. Bierly, C., Doyle, B., & Smith, S. (2016, January 14). Transforming schools: How distributed leadership can create more high-performing schools. Bain & Company. Retrieved from http://www.bain.com/publications/articles/transforming-schools.aspx
10. Daumal, R. (1974). *Mount analogue: A novel of symbolically authentic non-Euclidean adventures in mountaineering.* Baltimore, MD: Penguin Metaphysical Library, p. 116.

Chapter 10

Leveraging Listening Routines

Preview: Now that you have learned to influence complex change, it's time to consider the day-to-day routines that will foster a humanizing culture of learning and collaboration.

This chapter is designed to help you:

- Learn to diagnose and manage the group dynamic of your team or staff.
- Design adult learning experiences that align with your values.
- Explore powerful routines that promote listening, trust, and meaningful dialogue.
- Use hands-on tools to create agendas that change the culture and the conversation.

A STAFF MEETING WITH 100% ENGAGEMENT

The staff of June Jordan School for Equity (JJSE) sit in a circle, chatting casually as they await the start of their meeting. Soft light filters in from nearby MacLaren Park as teacher leader Lenore Kenny flips off the lights and invites people into a mindfulness practice.

"Start to settle down in your chairs. Put your feet flat on the floor, and make sure there's nothing in your hands. Take a deep breath in, and let it out slowly. Notice where there's tension in your body. Begin to take whatever happened in your day and set it aside, like boxes on a conveyor belt." The room breathes in, breathes out. A few minutes later, Lenore closes the practice and turns the light back on.

Codirector Jessica Huang stands up to explain the meeting's purpose: "Today we are going to talk about the role of gender in society and how it affects all of us, staff and students. Next week, we'll be led by a group of students to continue this conversation, and after that, you'll facilitate similar conversations with your Advisory class. Think about this: Who do you *want* to be, taking into account the prescriptive gender roles of society?"

Huang's codirector Matt Alexander takes the metaphorical baton: "We're going to listen to an audio clip called Free to Be You and Me. How many of you have heard of this?" Younger staff members stare back blankly while the over-40 crowd nods. "Oh, this is so sad," Alexander teases as laughter ripples across the room. "The younger generation just doesn't understand." The group dynamic is fluid and engaging.

Matt shares a personal story: "I was born in 1970, and this album came out in 1972. Marlo Thomas, Alan Alda, and Diana Ross did songs and audio skits about feminism and gender equality. And my mom made me listen to it over and over again to where I *loved* it. I was completely obsessed with it! My own education around gender and gender roles began with this." Matt cues a clip called "Boy Meets Girl," about two babies having a conversation right after they're born. Voiced over by adult actors, the babies mistake each other for the opposite gender in a hilarious volley of stereotypes about what constitutes a boy or girl.

When the clip ends, Jessica invites people to find a partner for an "active listening dyad: Turn to someone near you and sit knee to knee. After you've shared, the other person will repeat back what they *think* you said. Try to keep eye contact, and think about how it feels to look at somebody and not respond while your knees are touching." People giggle again; laughter is a key feature of this culture. Huang repeats the guiding question: "Who do you *want* to be, given the prescriptive gender roles of society?"

For the next few minutes, people lean in toward one another to listen intently. Afterwards, Huang asks the staff how the exchange felt. One teacher shares, "I really enjoyed listening to my partner restate what I had said. I felt acknowledged." Huang scans the room and mirrors back what she sees: "I notice a lot of head-bobbing. Who else felt like it was validating to hear what somebody else thought you said?" She skillfully links this experience to the challenge of communicating with students: "Kids feel validated too if you repeat back what they've said—even if you don't agree with it. It's really affirming to hear your words restated."

In the second half of the meeting, Huang, Alexander, Kenny, and two other female colleagues circle their chairs in the middle of the room to perform a live skit. First Kenny establishes the setting: "We've been in a district meeting, and we're now in the parking lot talking about gender issues at school. The conversation takes a sudden turn to personal stories." Now in role-play mode, Huang says, "Hi guys, I know it's really late, but

I think we need to have this conversation because it impacts all of us." Each woman proceeds to share a real-life story illustrating the vulnerability women can experience simply walking down the street.

Alexander, the only man in the circle, takes a deep breath before responding: "Wow, on an intellectual level, I know this stuff happens all the time, but it's crazy hearing it from such powerful women. You're all so strong that I can't imagine anyone messing with you guys like that! It's just reminded me of what you have to deal with as women all the time, no matter who you are or how strong you are." The scene closes.

The energy in the room has shifted to a quieter place of mature empathy. Kenny tells the staff that this conversation had really happened, and the women had been struck by Matt's open and heartfelt reaction to their stories. She identifies the importance of listening across difference as a way to create emotionally safe spaces for everyone in the community. Alexander chimes in: "I realize I have the privilege to *not* imagine things like this happening because I've never experienced them." A hard conversation is in motion, and no signs of fight or flight are visible.

Next Huang announces a "gender split"—men and women (as self-identified) will move into separate rooms to view clips about the *opposite* gender from two films produced by Jennifer Siebel Newsom.[1] She reminds the staff that this is a dress rehearsal for discussions they will lead next week with male and female students. I follow the women to a nearby classroom in time to hear Huang offer this prompt: "How can we help male students, and staff, remove the mask of masculinity that Siebel Newsom describes to become whoever they want to be?"

All eyes are glued to the screen, not a cell phone or computer in sight. The group dynamic is focused and alert, with 100% engagement. What will emerge from these exercises?

GROWN-UPS NEED ROUTINES TOO

Meetings are the building blocks of a listening culture. Without thoughtful routines, a meeting is just an empty vessel—a place where staff gathers without much meaning or purpose. If we structure our meetings around powerful routines, however, we have the potential to change the conversation among our colleagues and interrupt the status quo.

Think about how much time educators spend together in various configurations: staff meetings, grade-level or department meetings, leadership team meetings, district trainings, professional development, parent

If we structure our meetings around powerful routines, however, we have the potential to change the conversation among our colleagues and interrupt the status quo.

conferences, and more. Think, too, about how often the agendas for those meetings are left to the last minute, expectations for clear communication are thrown to the way-side, and planning becomes an afterthought. This seems to be particularly true right at the time when communities may need thoughtful meetings the most—when people are experiencing trauma or stress. When emotional needs go unmet, meetings can become a breeding ground for anxiety and dysfunction, which inhibit productivity.

To leverage the transformative potential of these gatherings, leaders must design them with as much care as the best teacher puts into lesson design. A great meeting or adult learning experience follows a story arc that is linked to the Strategic Listening stances from Chapter 6. We choose a theme and begin, as Huang did, with a compelling introductory activity that communicates the "why" (orientation to vision). We then invite people to participate in interactive activities that help them grapple with important ideas or practices and build to a learning climax— some sort of breakthrough, insight, or reframing of the problem. Finally, we close by allowing people to integrate their learning (reflective inquiry) and identify possible next steps (bias toward action). Table 10.1 summarizes this arc.

Learning to structure meetings around engaging and humanizing routines will also make planning more sustainable for *you* as a leader. Hold this in mind as we discuss how to gauge the mood and receptivity of your team.

TABLE 10.1   STRATEGIC LISTENING STANCES

Orientation to Vision (Stance 1)	Reflective Inquiry (Stance 2)	Bias Toward Action (Stance 3)
Begin with a compelling introductory activity, or hook, that communicates the "why."	Allow people to make meaning together and integrate their learning.	Identify concrete next steps.
Invite people to participate in activities that help them to arrive at some sort of insight or reframing of the problem.		

FIRST, TAKE YOUR TEAM'S TEMPERATURE

The dynamic of the group is grounded in the life of emotion and feeling. [A crucial role of the facilitator is] managing the dynamic directly at the affective level.

—JOHN HERON[2]

Every team has its own culture. I would characterize JJSE's as open, participatory, and leader-ful. Team members enter into hard conversations with open hearts and minds, and are willing to explore personal values and identity. Staff meetings are led by a combination of formal and informal leaders, and agendas incorporate multiple learning modes. All signs point to a healthy group dynamic—a high-performing culture in which people feel safe enough to push the envelope, and one another.

If this is not yet your team, don't despair! Many groups get stuck in unproductive dynamics for a variety of reasons: low trust, lack of shared language (especially around equity), fatigue over new initiatives, and more. The good news is that you have tremendous ability to promote listening and meaningful dialogue. Before we explore specific routines, I want to discuss an important topic: how to read the **group dynamic**, that subtle blend of mental, emotional, and physical energy in a room at any given moment.

If you are leading a meeting, how do you know when something feels "off"? What nonverbal and verbal signals tell you to adjust your facilitation moves? How do you manage your own emotional triggers? Even in a strong adult culture, the group dynamic can turn on a dime, and it's helpful to have explicit language for managing these moments. See Figure 10.1 as a guide to diagnosing four group dynamics that act like rising temperatures on a thermometer, and to understanding effective facilitation strategies for each case.

96 Degrees: Emotional Repression

When a group is at 96 degrees, participants' behavior seems constrained by an invisible set of implicit norms; for example, it's understood that "we don't speak up here or we'll meet with retaliation from the higher-ups." People display little to no emotion, participation is low, and nonverbal cues signal a lack of ease and relaxation (e.g., hunched shoulders, limited eye contact, opaque facial expressions, crossed arms).

FIGURE 10.1   CHALLENGING GROUP DYNAMIC: WHAT'S THE TEMPERATURE?

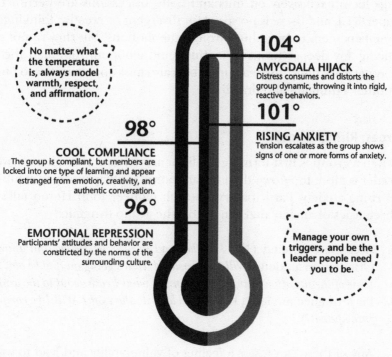

No matter what the temperature is, always model warmth, respect, and affirmation.

104°

AMYGDALA HIJACK
Distress consumes and distorts the group dynamic, throwing it into rigid, reactive behaviors.

101°

RISING ANXIETY
Tension escalates as the group shows signs of one or more forms of anxiety.

98°

COOL COMPLIANCE
The group is compliant, but members are locked into one type of learning and appear estranged from emotion, creativity, and authentic conversation.

96°

EMOTIONAL REPRESSION
Participants' attitudes and behavior are constricted by the norms of the surrounding culture.

Manage your own triggers, and be the leader people need you to be.

	96°	98°	101°	104°
POSSIBLE INDICATORS	• A few people dominate the discussion. • There is minimal participation, and few questions are asked. • There is limited eye contact and closed body language: arms crossed, sitting back in chair, hunched over. • Patterns of participation reveal racial and/or gender disparities.	• Participants comply with leader requests. • Facial expressions are largely neutral. • There is an appearance of "doing work" vs. learning or collaboration. • Only clarifying questions are asked.	• Furrowed brows, tense shoulders, and frowns point toward rising distress. • There are frequent side conversations, whispering, or passing notes. • Participants yawn or get up frequently to grab water or take a "break." • Room is uncomfortably quiet.	• Participant walks out of meeting. • People announce a refusal to participate. • Angry or accusatory comments indicate a tipping point in anxiety. • May see shortness of breath or shallow breathing in some people.
FACILITATION MOVES	• Help the group establish agreements. • Ask for a volunteer process observer to collect and share participation data. • Engage the group in setting an improvement goal for participation. • Encourage questions. • Model distress-free authority in the face of hard questions.	• State your intention for the group to engage in open, meaningful dialogue. • Build in movement activities. • Actively use the experiential learning cycle to promote whole–person learning. • Vary your modalities and types of learning.	• Raise awareness of the anxiety in the room or issues being avoided. • Ask people to journal and talk in groups about their fears and feelings. • Respect that every individual chooses when and how to take risks. • Use structured protocols to lower the affective filter (Chapter 2) and increase well-being.	• Name the tension in the room. • Model mature empathy stems. • Hold space for emotion and dialogue (i.e., dyad, fishbowl, etc.). • Give people explicit permission to be candid and vulnerable. • Stage a debate in which two people or teams publicly argue both sides of a contested issue; debrief together.

98 Degrees: Cool Compliance

At 98 degrees, the group appears to be functional, but works in a very technical or transactional way, with an above-the-green-line orientation. Meetings focus exclusively on nuts and bolts, discussions are perfunctory or superficial, and there is no space for divergent or creative thinking. Team members seem to be going through the motions, but they're not experiencing any deeper forms of learning and emotion. Although the group may get work done, the team members also miss opportunities to push one another's thinking and practice.

101 Degrees: Rising Anxiety

When a group is first forming or its membership is changing, or when its leader is more top-down than collaborative, participants may exhibit signs of rising anxiety. Participatory research pioneer John Heron talks about three types of anxiety that can distort the group dynamic:[3]

1. Acceptance anxiety (*Will I be liked and wanted, or rejected and unwanted?*)
2. Orientation anxiety (*Will I understand what's going on and be able to make sense of the situation so that I can connect what I care about to the work?*)
3. Performance anxiety (*Will I be able to do the work? Will I be competent or incompetent?*).

Any of these can foster a feeling of vulnerability and lead to wary and distrustful behavior. When individual anxieties permeate the group dynamic, you are likely to see tend-and-befriend behaviors like whispering, exchanging knowing glances across the room, or gatherings in the parking lot after the meeting. Remember that these are brain-driven coping mechanisms, not personal attacks on you.

104 Degrees: Amygdala Hijack!

At 104 degrees, anxiety levels reach a tipping point, and the group enters fight, flight, or tend-and-befriend survival mode. Participants begin to display rigid, reactive behaviors—refusing to participate, lobbing explosive comments, or even walking out of the meeting. In a classic tend-and-befriend response, other members may also leave to comfort the person who has walked out, or stay behind to rally around the one who is feeling victimized. (That's what happened with Joy and Wendy's colleagues in Chapter 3.)

I recently coached a teacher leader whose attempt to facilitate data-driven dialogue with an underperforming English Department went up in flames. He brought the department data that revealed two patterns: poor student perception of their teachers and a persistent performance gap between Latino and White students. Can you guess what happened? Teachers were deeply triggered, and the meeting slid into a hyperdefensive dynamic. Participants actually said, "I'm not afraid of you. You can't fire me," "You're trying to steer us to where *you* want us to go," and "It's these kids and where they live … They're just low, and it's hard to change them."

First, a moment of mature empathy for this leader whose equity agenda became unhinged! But surely he is not alone. I invite you to consider that a well-designed meeting works in part because it shifts the group dynamic into one of four *positive* forms that I will unpack later in the chapter.

Managing the group dynamic is one of a Listening Leader's most important tasks. It's also hard work that requires a clear diagnosis of what is happening in the room and a responsive set of facilitation moves. In Exhibit 10.1, I share a few high-leverage strategies that I have honed over time and that can help you pivot out of difficult moments. Appendix G also includes a tool for applying each of the Six Stances of a Listening Leader in a challenging meeting.

EXHIBIT 10.1   BRAIN-FRIENDLY FACILITATION MOVES

Even with the best agenda, the group dynamic can take a sudden turn, requiring us to facilitate on our feet. The moves in the table here are designed to help you pivot out of difficult meeting moments without alienating the group. Sometimes the room gets so "hot" that it's no longer healthy to continue the conversation. The listed moves allow you to transition with grace so that the issues can be taken up later in a more productive manner.

All that said, a little heat in the room isn't always a bad thing. It is especially important not to allow tone policing. If a person of color, for example, speaks up about a microaggression she has experienced, be sure that other folks in the room don't focus on how "upset" or "agitated" the speaker seems. In that situation, you might redirect by saying, "We need to focus on listening to our colleague's experience and not questioning her or the emotion she is carrying. Racism *is* raw and emotional, not a theoretical construct."

(Continued)

EXHIBIT 10.1   (CONTINUED)

Key Move	Sounds Like . . .
Name to neutralize	• "It seems like there's a lot of passion on this issue." • "It sounds like you have a unique viewpoint on this." • "At this point, it's clear and it's *okay* that we have different perspectives on the issue."
Affirm	• "Thank you. I appreciate your taking a risk to speak your truth." • "I love that we are a team where people can disagree." • "I appreciate that this team welcomes dissent and stays at the table through a hard conversation."
Inquire	• "What do other people think about this issue?" • "What are other ways to approach this problem?" • "What other data do we need to think deeply about this?"
Redirect	• "Thanks for your energy and passion around this. We do need to move on, and I hope we can continue the conversation." • "That's such an important point. Let's find a time to give it the attention it deserves." • "I would love to take that up with you in our next one-on-one. Thank you for raising that concern."

 MAKE IT MINDFUL

Think about a challenging meeting that you facilitated—one that left you with a pit in your stomach. What behaviors did the group exhibit? What was the temperature of the group dynamic? How did you respond, and what would you do differently?

NEXT, DESIGN HUMANIZING ROUTINES

As a principal, I often planned meetings that dove headfirst into what I perceived to be "the real work"—data analysis, curriculum planning, or whatever was on tap. I've since learned the importance of warming up the room so that people feel relaxed and connected enough to do whatever "the work" is. I now strive to design humanizing routines that honor the whole *person*, just as great lessons honor the whole child. Please find in Appendix G the handy one-page reference, Quick Design Tips for Meetings.

When planning a meeting or professional learning session, I start by identifying two different types of outcomes.[4] **Technical outcomes** live above the green line and point toward concrete deliverables, actions, or content. I ask myself, *What do I want participants to learn, do, or produce?* For example, "We'll learn three new strategies for teaching academic vocabulary," "We'll clarify team roles and responsibilities," or "We'll draft grade-level team skinny plans for the fall." **Relational outcomes**, by contrast, have to do with the *experience* I want people to have (below the green line). For these, I simply ask myself, *How do I hope people will feel both during and after the meeting?* As a side note: I often choose not to share the relational outcomes with participants; I write them really to remind myself of my facilitative intentions.

Guided by these holistic outcomes, I use the **experiential learning cycle** to craft an agenda incorporating four different types of routines that encompass both the technical and the relational: the affective, the imaginal, the conceptual, and the practical.[5] Table 10.2 explains each

TABLE 10.2   THE EXPERIENTIAL LEARNING CYCLE

Cycle	Short Description	Sample Routines
Affective routines	Connect participants to the feeling dimension of learning and to one another; allow for the release of pent-up emotion.	• Turn and talk • Constructivist Listening dyads • Reflection on a quote • Community circles
Imaginal routines	Tap into participants' preexisting knowledge, intuition, and/or creativity; invite multiple ways of seeing an issue. Often involves movement and multisensory inputs.	• Brainstorming or visualization activities • Response to music, poetry, images, or video clips • Movement activities, such as quote mixers or four corners
Conceptual routines	Involve learning, discussing, and reflecting on important content or ideas.	• Book study • Text-based discussions • Data-based inquiry • Presentation of new instructional practices
Practical routines	Involve learning by doing, producing, or practicing.	• Curriculum planning • Writing a skinny plan • Creating a budget • Role-playing a new skill • Engaging in collaborative planning and protocols • Differentiating instruction, lesson planning

Note. Adapted from *The Complete Facilitator's Handbook,* by J. Heron, 1999, Philadelphia, PA: Kogan Page.

type of routine. This framework can be used to plan any type of meeting or professional development, but it's not to be confused with an ongoing schoolwide inquiry cycle, which I'll discuss in Chapter 11. Think of it as a mini cycle that leads you to design humanizing adult learning experiences.

 MAKE IT MINDFUL

- Think of a meeting that you facilitated or participated in that went really well. Which of the routines—affective, imaginal, conceptual, or practical—did you incorporate? Which went particularly well, and why?
- Think of a meeting that didn't go so well. Which types of routines were embedded? Which were missing? Consider setting a stretch goal around one or two of the points in the cycle.

Affective Routines: Start with the Heart

Affective routines promote listening, reflection, and empathy across difference. By inviting people to release emotion and connect with one another, they also marshal the group's energy in a healthy direction. As a rule, I open and close every gathering with some sort of affective routine. If I don't make time for these transitions, I find myself managing an unproductive group dynamic as people struggle to suppress their emotions.

Affective routines promote listening, reflection, and empathy across difference. By inviting people to release emotion and connect with one another, they also marshal the group's energy in a healthy direction.

The JJSE leaders used two affective routines to start their meeting—mindfulness and an active listening exercise—which altogether took about 15 minutes. You can follow suit or choose to open your meeting with a no-frills turn and talk, such as "Share a recent success in your classroom," "What do you need from the team to bring your best thinking forward today?" or "What's the best thing that's happened to you lately?" These simple moves warm up the room and link team members across the islands of daily experience. Here are a few more examples.

Constructivist Listening. Constructivist Listening (CL) is an umbrella term for a set of routines developed by the National Coalition for Equity in Education and popularized by the National Equity Project.[6] In a Constructivist Listening protocol, each person enjoys equal, uninterrupted time to speak and, one hopes, to construct new insight. The listener's job is to offer focused attention and support for the speaker. Because of its structure, CL offers a way to practice the Deep Listening stances in Chapter 5; for example, the listener can affirm and express empathy for the speaker through nonverbal cues. There is an important idea undergirding this routine: Given time to reflect, people have the ability to solve their own problems. See Ways to Facilitate Constructivist Listening in Appendix G.

Agreements. Community agreements are explicit ways of working together that a team adopts through consensus. They're not *rules* imposed from above; nor are they *norms*, which are the unofficial ways a group does business (e.g., teachers grade papers during meetings, or meetings always start 10 minutes late). Agreements only work if the team generates and genuinely *agrees* on a few simple rules for group behavior.

There are two different types of agreements: operational and interpersonal. Table 10.3 provides examples.

When forming agreements with your team, be clear about your purpose. I often talk about the need for adults to model a healthy culture for the watchful eyes of students. Sometimes, I acknowledge how hard it is to

TABLE 10.3   TWO TYPES OF SAMPLE AGREEMENTS

Operational Agreements (above the green line)	Interpersonal Agreements (below the green line)
We commit to	We commit to
1. Stepping up, stepping back; monitoring our patterns of participation	1. Listening to what has heart and meaning
2. Assigning and rotating meetings roles (recorder, timekeeper, participation tracker, process observer[a])	2. Showing up, being visible, and empowering others through example
3. Using texts for urgent messages; responding to emails within 48 hours	3. Speaking our truth without blame or judgment
4. Sending out meeting notes within 24 hours	4. Being open to different outcomes, noticing discomfort and staying curious

Note. The Interpersonal Agreements column is adapted from Angeles Arrien's four rules, in *The Fourfold Way*, 1993, New York, NY: HarperCollins.
[a] The process observer role entails taking notes on the group dynamic throughout the meeting and giving a brief report at the end. The process observer could use the group dynamic temperature check as a framework or use the agreements themselves. The idea is to listen for and jot down evidence of the agreements in action.

confront equity issues without consensus around how we will communicate when the conversation gets hard. Once you've established the "why," have people recall an experience of being on a thriving and a dysfunctional team. Ways to Facilitate Agreements in Appendix G includes a graphic organizer and tips on facilitating agreements.

Appreciations Many teams end their meetings with appreciations, a few minutes during which people can express gratitude for each other. This ritual ends the gathering on a positive affective note. Encourage folks to be specific in their comments and stay tuned to equity here: If you notice that a particular person isn't getting much recognition, it's nice to appreciate him or her publicly in some way.

My favorite version of appreciations comes from Principal Audrey Amos at John Muir Elementary School in Berkeley, California, whom I had the good fortune to coach for two years. Amos has an overflowing basket of shells in her office that she brings to every staff meeting. In the last five minutes, team members have an opportunity to present a seashell to a colleague along with a verbal appreciation. This simple metaphor brings magic to what can feel like a tedious ritual. I've watched Seashells many times and am always moved by the ways in which it binds the group together.

Imaginal Routines: Get Your Team to Dream

Imaginal routines invite your team up to the balcony to view what *could be* rather than what *is*. They do this by incorporating visualization and brainstorming activities, tapping into multiples senses, and integrating movement and other nontraditional learning modes.

If these ideas sound far outside your repertoire, a word of assurance: Imaginal routines can be quite straightforward. Have people discuss a compelling TED Talk. Give team members a collection of quotes from a relevant article or author—one quote per paper and one paper per person—and have them stand up to meet, greet, and discuss the ideas with a rotating cast of partners. I usually facilitate three rotations and ask people to switch quotes each time. Play a song that your students are listening to, and ask people to interpret the lyrics from the perspective of a student.

Jessica Huang and Matt Alexander, the JJSE codirectors, wove two imaginal activities into their meeting. First, Alexander shared the 1970s audio clip to provide a historical context for the theme of gender. Second, they and their colleagues performed a skit to model how to respectfully engage in hard conversations about this issue. There are endless ways to promote imagination! Here are a few more.

Four Corners Four Corners is a movement-based activity that can crack open dialogue and new ways of perceiving an issue. Think of a topic about which you want to push people's thinking, and craft four related scenarios, or statements. Post large number signs around the room (1, 2, 3, 4) to represent each scenario. Then, during the meeting, invite people to choose one scenario that resonates with them, move to the corresponding corner, and discuss their thoughts with whoever else landed there.

I recently led a seminar for a large group of school administrators and coaches. To activate participants' schema, I prompted them to

Think about a time when…

1. You missed or avoided an opportunity to have a courageous conversation.
2. You set a compelling vision for the work, but realized later that your team wasn't on board.
3. You complied with a mandate that went against your core beliefs and values.
4. Your sense of urgency prevented you from taking time to listen to someone.

This imaginal routine ended up having an *affective* benefit: As participants shared their experiences, they clearly felt some catharsis. The room buzzed as people laughed, patted each other's backs, and sighed in recognition of how incredibly difficult it is to lead with integrity in a high-stakes, high-pressure climate. As a bridge to the content I wanted to share, Four Corners primed them to learn with greater purpose and investment.

Kiva Process. Derived from Native American traditions, the Kiva Process opens up dialogue on an issue of importance to the community. Structured as a panel discussion interspersed with small-group conversations, this routine allows you to bring new voices and perspectives into the public domain and capture the collective wisdom of the group.

A while back, I facilitated a middle school staff retreat in which teachers and administrators were wrestling with their approach to student discipline. The absence of clear systems had created an "us vs. them" dynamic, and the group was locked in a 96 degree group dynamic of emotional repression. (Recall Figure 10.1 from earlier in this chapter.) People could barely restrain their frustration. Recognizing the need for honest dialogue, I decided to facilitate a Kiva panel with four teachers who represented different but equally strong positions on the topic.

These four brave souls had a chance to publicly respond to several prompts, punctuated by breaks for small groups of listeners to discuss what they had heard. Here are the prompts:

- Share your experience and feelings on how the school approached discipline last year.
- How could the school promote a restorative justice approach that balances a high level of order with a high level of support for students?
- What other ideas do you have to strengthen our school culture?

The panelists sat nervously before their colleagues. As they spoke, listeners jotted down words and phrases before turning in to discuss what they had written, and their own views, in small groups. By the end, the staff felt relieved by the degree of frank truth-telling that emerged from this process, and managed to land on some creative solutions. Ways to Facilitate a Kiva Process in Appendix G presents a series of steps for organizing a Kiva Process.

TED Talks. TED Talks are another great resource for getting people to think and dream together. Once you find a talk that fits your purposes, it's as simple as plug, play, and prompt. Share the talk or a 5-minute excerpt. Design your questions and let people dive in to discussion in pairs, trios, or small groups. To cross-fertilize insights, take time to debrief small-group dialogue with a whole-group discussion. In Appendix G you will find Top 10 TED Talks and Corresponding Prompts, a tool to facilitate such discussions.

Conceptual Routines: Learn to Discern What Matters

Affective and imaginal routines till the below-the-green-line soil of identity, relationship, and information. Now it is time for conceptual routines, which engage participants in learning and reflecting on key ideas. Depending on your equity imperative and skinny plan, your conceptual routines might focus on literacy, math, culturally responsive teaching, or social-emotional development. What's most important is that you *learn to discern* what content your team needs to explore, and what can be set aside for now. Remember, when watering the brain for deep roots, less is more, and a narrow focus yields deeper learning.

Just like in a classroom, there are many fun ways to introduce concepts: Socratic Seminars, debates, literature circles, or even project-based learning. One year, JJSE's staff created portfolios of their work including student artifacts, lesson plans, and personal reflections. Whatever routines you design, model the instructional practices you want to see in classrooms. If your school is focused on academic discussion, have teachers try out text-based protocols and academic language frames like "I would argue" or "I agree with So-and-So because…" The idea here is for adult learners to *experience* the type of rigorous learning you hope will transpire in the classroom.

Because social justice is a pillar of JJSE's vision, the leadership prioritizes discussions of social issues like race and gender to prepare adults to facilitate student discussion around these same topics. In the opening vignette, the leaders used contemporary texts—the films *Miss Representation* and *The Mask We Live*—to spark a rich conversation. What follows are a few examples of conceptual routines that can help you deepen the dialogue around what really matters.

 MAKE IT MINDFUL

- What content is most important for your team or staff to explore this year?
- How will you model an orientation to vision and explain *why* that matters?

Text-based protocols. A text-based protocol is a step-by-step process that allows you to engage a group, big or small, in meaningful discussion. In this usage, a "text" can mean an image, a quotation, a video, or a song as well as the more traditional reading. The National School Reform Faculty website houses a number of my favorite examples, including the Three Levels of Text, the Four A's, and Save the Last Word for Me (http://www .nsrfharmony.org/free-resources/protocols/text).

If you have a long article and limited time, consider using a jigsaw routine—a best practice in English language development instruction named to evoke a jigsaw puzzle. To prepare for this routine, split your chosen text into several sections and assign an "expert group" to each one. Once expert groups have had a chance to meet, discuss their piece, and pull out the main ideas, create mixed groups with one person representing each section of the text.

At the end of any text-based discussion, I always invite whole-group reflection, asking "What stood out from the readings?" and "How can this text help us rethink our work?"

Data-based inquiry. Conceptual routines also include analyzing data and monitoring progress on our skinny plans and shared metrics for success. In Chapter 11, I'll describe a big-picture routine called "safe-to-learn inquiry," but on a smaller scale, you can build in regular opportunities for data-driven dialogue, structured around four phases:

Prediction What are our assumptions and expectations around the data?

Observation What trends and patterns does the data actually reveal?

Inference What conclusions can we draw, or what hypotheses can we generate?

Action What will we do or try next?

By slowing the process down and leading your team through each phase, you will produce meaningful dialogue around the root causes of student performance gaps. As you decide which data to bring to the team, keep in mind the Levels of Data framework from Chapter 1. Strive to regularly analyze all three types of data, but especially Level 3 "street" data. Consider using this same inquiry process in parent meetings and the classroom to introduce inquiry and rigor.

Data can trigger powerful emotions in a group. Before initiating any form of data-based inquiry, consider facilitating a Constructivist Listening dyad with a prompt like "Share an experience of looking at data that was helpful to you as a teacher. What did you learn, and what was the impact on your practice?" If you sense a lot of anxiety in the room, you might use a prompt like "What are your fears and concerns about looking at this data?" In Appendix G, Guidelines for Data-Based Inquiry also provides sample guidelines for looking at data that you can share with your team in advance.

Sorts. Sorts are one of my favorite ways to model critical thinking and water for deep roots the brains of adult learners. This hands-on routine has team members prioritize and/or categorize a variety of ideas, all of which are related to a key framework or question. You can provide the categories in advance or have the group come up with their own. A sort might be something like giving a fourth-grade team the standards for their grade level and asking them this: "Given what we know about our students, which standards are most important to teach this year, which are nice-to-teach but not essential, and which should we *not* teach this year? Create three buckets, and be prepared to explain your choices."

Here's another example: Imagine you're trying to get your leadership team to come to consensus on an instructional focus for the year. People brainstorm a number of possible directions and place each idea on a giant Post-it note. Next ask the team to sort the options from "least likely" to "most likely" to "help us improve student outcomes." If there are competing perspectives, all the better! Stage a real-time debate to elicit the rationale behind each option, then take a straw poll to see which arguments were most persuasive. Sorts like this force people to justify their thinking and discriminate between the least and the most important ideas.

To create a more tactile learning experience, preprint the sorting examples on slips of paper or cards.

Practical Routines: Retrain the Brain

Finally, practical routines give your team the time and authority to plan, practice, and implement new ideas. When shifting into practical mode, be mindful to frame the work as low stakes and experimental, in an effort to calm the amygdala and avert performance anxiety. These routines can be as fine-grain as lesson planning or examining a single piece of student work, or as large-grain as developing a budget or redesigning the master schedule. Grain size aside, what matters is this: building in the time necessary for adult learners to *apply* their learning into action.

Here again, **protocols** are your friend. A protocol supplies a step-by-step framework for group discussion that promotes equitable participation and makes it safe for people to ask probing questions of one other. Protocols also provide busy educators with an excuse to pause, reflect, and listen instead of giving a knee-jerk response. Finally, they maximize the precious resource of time in schools. Here are a few practical routines and protocols.

Consultancy protocol. A consultancy protocol allows someone to bring a dilemma and learn from the collective thinking of colleagues. It begins with the presenter providing the context for his or her dilemma and a question for discussion; after this, listeners typically have time to ask clarifying and probing questions before the group enters into a conversation while the presenter listens and takes notes. Ideally, a well-guided consultancy helps the presenter gain fresh insight on their issue, and even a new way to approach it.

Helping Trios, a structure in which three people provide feedback on each other's work, is the simplest format for consultancy and gives every team member a chance to get feedback within a 30- to 45-minute window. Appendix G includes the Helping Trios Protocol.

"I Like, I Wonder". This routine offers quick feedback to teams who present a proposal on issues ranging from curriculum and pedagogy to professional learning or communication systems. It works best if people are divided into working groups in which they tackle different issues, or different angles on a single issue. For example, imagine that focus groups with parents have revealed that monolingual families don't attend school events because of language barriers and work schedules. You present this challenge to the leadership team, divide the team into four groups, and have groups develop proposals to address the issue.

When the groups arrive at a natural pause in their thinking, have each present to another group, explaining their current thinking and any questions or roadblocks they've bumped into. Then time the listening for 5 minutes of "I Like" statements and 5 minutes of "I Wonder" statements. Urge people to offer concrete, specific feedback—both "warm," or affirming, and "cool," or constructive. This routine normalizes feedback as a low-stakes and supportive practice.

Looking at student work. There are many versions of student work protocols, all of which converge around two goals: to ground teachers' instructional decisions in real-time, formative data and to develop their reflective capacity. However you mix and match available protocols, follow these guidelines to ensure a rigorous discussion:

- Encourage presenting teachers to choose a puzzling piece of student work about which they have real questions.
- Encourage presenters to choose work from an assignment with some degree of complexity—preferably not a rote task or recall-style quiz.
- Move the group through the four stages of data-based inquiry: prediction, description, interpretation, then action.
- Model a Bias Toward Action: "What will you try out based on this discussion?"

There's a premise behind the flow from the affective to the practical: Human beings feel their way toward thoughtful action, not the other way around. This approach addresses the three neighborhoods of the brain:

There's a premise behind the flow from the affective to the practical: Human beings feel their way toward thoughtful action, not the other way around.

the limbic system, or emotional brain; the neocortex, or thinking brain; and the lizard brain, or brain stem. Picturing those regions helps me remember to start every gathering with an affective routine—however brief. Even though it's tempting to drop people right into a task, the Listening Leader capitalizes on feeling and imagination to animate the work. In Appendix G, you'll find a sample Agenda Template to help you integrate and connect the four types of routines.

REVISITING THE ENGAGED STAFF MEETING

Now that we've delved into successful meetings and routines, let's revisit the engaged staff meeting that opened this chapter. The team had split based on their gender, and when the men and women return from viewing their respective film clips, the mood is quiet yet alert. Teacher leader Lenore Kenny has the staff organize itself into mixed-gender groups to discuss their learning. Before asking each group to share an insight, codirector Jessica Huang models mature empathy: "We've been talking about how to make these conversations a regular part of our culture, and I want to name how emotional and deep it is to talk about identity."

A male teacher talks about how *different* student-teacher conversations can look and feel depending on the teacher's gender: "Female teachers often have to work toward the respect that I just implicitly receive." Another teacher tells a story from his group about a difficult interaction between a female teacher and a male student who didn't want to give up his cell phone. The teacher, Renee, gave the student two options: "You can give it to me or to the security guard." But the student offered to give it to Mr. K, another male teacher. Renee challenged him, saying, "You know, it looks really sexist when you do that. Maybe you trust Mr. K more than you trust me, but you have to realize that when you agree to give your phone to him and not me, it *looks* pretty sexist." The student paused and then handed her the phone.

At this point, the room erupts in approval; people clap, issue an emphatic "Yes!" and laugh out loud. Through a beautifully crafted process, the group has hit a breakthrough moment (See Figure 10.2, the positive group dynamic thermometer). Renee's micronarrative has demonstrated how to effectively challenge a student around unconscious gender bias, which unleashes a sense of discovery and empowerment.

To close the meeting, the leaders use three affective routines.

A Shredding Ritual

Each staff member receives a blank purple strip of paper and a blank pink strip . On the purple, they answer the question: "What is one way that you have participated in gender inequality?" Once they're done, Kenny invites each person to symbolically shred their purple paper. On the pink strip, people respond to this prompt: "What is one change you could make to reinforce your commitment to gender equality in our school?"

A Process Observation

A designated teacher has been observing the meeting through the lens of four staff agreements: "assume positive intent; speak your truth; appreciate the contributions of others; notice patterns of participation." In closing, he presents evidence of how the group performed around these agreements. He specifically celebrates the fact that the meeting structures allowed a lot of different people to speak and participate.

Appreciations

Finally, Huang opens the room to appreciations. Each time someone shares gratitude for a colleague, the room brims with snaps, claps, and affirming vocalizations. This final routine binds the group dynamic and ends the meeting on a high note. Figure 10.2 outlines four positive forms of group dynamic, each of which the JJSE meeting hit on at one moment or another.

This type of meeting can happen anywhere. It requires focus, creativity, and insight on our part as leaders, and it requires humanizing routines. We must understand that a meeting is never just a meeting; it's the town square of human dynamics—the place where people gather to act out their anxieties and fears, and hopefully to find joy and rejuvenation in their connections. Imagine a world where 100% of your team is engaged in learning, doing, and *being* together. This world is possible.

FIGURE 10.2   PRODUCTIVE GROUP DYNAMIC: WHAT'S THE TEMPERATURE?

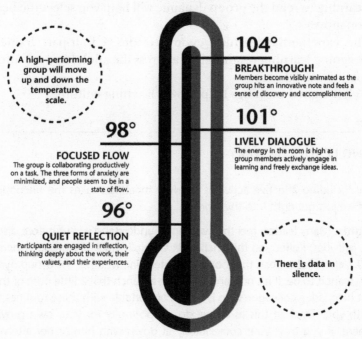

A high–performing group will move up and down the temperature scale.

104°
BREAKTHROUGH!
Members become visibly animated as the group hits an innovative note and feels a sense of discovery and accomplishment.

101°
LIVELY DIALOGUE
The energy in the room is high as group members actively engage in learning and freely exchange ideas.

98°
FOCUSED FLOW
The group is collaborating productively on a task. The three forms of anxiety are minimized, and people seem to be in a state of flow.

96°
QUIET REFLECTION
Participants are engaged in reflection, thinking deeply about the work, their values, and their experiences.

There is data in silence.

	96°	98°	101°	104°
POSSIBLE INDICATORS	• Room feels calm, yet alert. • Participants write, think, or listen to a partner. • There are no technology distractions, no side conversations. • Facial expressions are contemplative.	• Every group member is actively engaged in the task at hand. • Leader or facilitator assumes a guide–by–the side role. • Facial expressions and body language appear at ease and unself-conscious. • Team members ask one another for support.	• Participants lean in toward one another to listen intently. • There are no technology distractions, no side conversations. • Smiling, laughter, nodding, etc. signal high engagement and emotional safety. • Room feels abuzz with energy.	• There is a sudden elevation in volume or tone, or a ripple of laughter across the room. • People lean forward or stand up in excitement. • A wide range of group members speak to how promising the idea or the work feels. • A participant comment is met with vocalizations, head nodding, or "thank you!" • People start scribbling down their thoughts and reactions.
FACILITATION MOVES	• Engage people in journal writing. • Use Constructivist Listening structures (e.g., dyads). • Invite people into a walk–and–talk on a reflective prompt. *Emphasis on affective routines*	• Review team agreements to promote group safety. • Facilitate safe-to-learn inquiry cycles. • Remind the group of the "good–enough vision." • Chart and celebrate progress. • Affirm people's hard work and effort. • Build in breaks and movement. • Create moments for simple, iterative feedback (e.g., "I Like, I Wonder"). *Emphasis on practical routines*	• Use varied discussion structures to maximize engagement (Socratic Seminars, pair-share, text protocols). • Stage debates to tease out competing sides of an issue. • Facilitate a Kiva Process to promote public dialogue and inquiry on a key dilemma. *Emphasis on conceptual routines*	• Celebrate the breakthrough! • Use metacognitive prompts like, "What happened, and what can we learn from this moment?" • Facilitate a protocol like Success Analysis (nsrfharmony.org) to leverage the learning opportunity. • Coach the group to draft a skinny plan that builds off of the breakthrough. • Model a bias toward action: Ask people to name a few next steps they can commit to. *Emphasis on imaginal and practical routines*

KEY TAKEAWAYS

- Every team has a distinct culture.
- Learning to read the group dynamic will help you select the best facilitation moves.
- The experiential learning cycle provides a four-part framework for designing learning routines that address the adult learner's affective and cognitive needs.
- Well-designed meetings help grow a listening culture.

LISTENING LEADER INQUIRY

Question: Including affective activities in every meeting makes me uncomfortable. Why can't we just get right into the work?

My thoughts: Many leaders feel this way, and I understand it. But before dispensing with such activities, I offer you this challenge: Carefully track the group dynamic. Use Figures 10.1 and 10.2 to read the room and determine whether the group dynamic is where you want it to be. If it's not, and you have a hunch that a little dose of the affective might help, ask a colleague who is more comfortable with these routines to cofacilitate with you. Think of this as a "we do" opportunity for your own growth and development. If you trust your cofacilitator, sit down with him or her afterwards to debrief the experience; share how it felt, when you noticed your own discomfort, and, most important, what shifts you observed in the group.

Question: Is it important for every member of our team to speak in every meeting? I don't want to force people (if they have nothing to share) to talk just so that I can listen.

My thoughts: I used to hold myself accountable to 100% verbal participation in a meeting, but I've since changed that stance. After one leadership retreat I led, a quiet participant thanked me for not "calling her out" when she chose not to speak publicly. She disclosed that she had been deeply involved in the retreat, but that she tends to think about things more often than verbalize them. I have come to understand that many people, particularly introverts, process their thoughts and feelings like this, which sometimes maps to cultural difference as well. I now use nonverbal cues alongside verbal ones to assess whether an individual is engaged.

Question: I love the ways you have broken down the structure of our meeting, but we have only 60 minutes of time together each week and can rarely get through everything. Is there a way to structure a 1-hour meeting so that we can have affective conversations but still get the work done?

My thoughts: Great question! Think of the experiential learning cycle like a flexible pie chart whose pieces can grow or contract depending on the context. For a 60-minute working meeting, you might spend 5 minutes doing a circle check-in and 10 minutes engaging a relevant short reading before jumping into the practical work. Or you might choose to spend an entire meeting on the conceptual domain, reading and discussing an anchoring text, to set you up for practical work. I remember my son's pediatrician telling us it was fine if he didn't eat vegetables at every meal, as long as he ate them over the course of a week. Think of the cycle this way and strive to balance the components over time. For the record, though, when planning longer PD sessions, I do aim to incorporate all four types of routines.

NOTES

1. Newsom, J. S. (2011). *Miss representation* [Motion picture]. San Francisco, CA: Girls' Club Entertainment. This film explores the underrepresentation of women in positions of power and influence across society; Newsom, J. S. (2015). *The mask you live in* [Motion picture]. New York, NY: Virgil Films and Entertainment. This film follows boys and young men as they navigate cultural norms of masculinity.
2. Heron, J. (1999). *The complete facilitator's handbook*. Philadelphia, PA: Kogan Page, pp. 64–65.
3. Ibid.
4. This concept is inspired by the work of Steve Zuieback, who uses the language of rational and experiential outcomes in his book *Leadership Practices for Challenging Times* (Ukiah, CA: Synectics, 2012).
5. Heron, *Complete facilitator's handbook*.
6. Weissglass, J. (1990). Constructivist listening for empowerment and change. *Educational Forum 54*, 351–370.

Chapter 11

Growing a Listening Culture

Preview: You've built relational capital, shaped a path toward equity, and incorporated humanizing routines. How do you grow and sustain a collaborative, equity-driven culture?

This chapter is designed to help you:

- Reimagine your role as a host of ongoing, meaningful dialogue among stakeholders.
- Locate your organizational culture in the seasons of development.
- Learn transformational routines that form the architecture of a listening culture.
- Begin to map out your year as a Listening Leader.

A HIGH SCHOOL NETWORK IN TRANSITION

Much-needed rain drenches the parched California landscape as 15 urban school leaders file into an overnight, district-sponsored retreat—the first in 8 years. The persistent drought that has faded green hills to a thirsty brown appears to be ending. A metaphorical drought has befallen these leaders in recent years, sapping their creative and emotional energy. Locked in cycles of reorganization and initiative fatigue, many feel like widgets in a district machine with unclear rules and fragmented parts.

Entering the meeting space, participants find a sensory-rich environment: tables with brightly colored cloths, walls adorned with inspiring quotes and images, baskets of materials and snacks, and music playing in the background. Patrick, the recently appointed network superintendent and a former site leader, opens the convening: "I am so happy to welcome you here for 2 days of learning, planning, and team development. We chose this beautiful spot to invest in you and in our network."

He cuts to the heart of the group's equity imperative: "In our district, if 100 students start the ninth grade together, 67 will graduate high school, 46 will start college, 10 will graduate college within 5 years. We can and must transform this reality, together." Rather than blame and shame the leaders, he calls out the lack of trust across the system and the need for deeper relationships, a collective vision, and shared best practices.

Next Patrick organizes participants into small groups to reflect on their schools' current realities. Each leader has time to present a current-state story that incorporates Level 1 "satellite" data, such as graduation rates, course passage data, and college readiness statistics; Level 2 "map" data from local reading and math assessments and student surveys; and Level 3 "street" data that the leaders have collected by listening to and observing staff, students, and parents. Afterwards, each group nominates a representative to a fishbowl discussion—a circle of six chairs in the middle of the room, with other leaders sitting outside the circle to listen in.

Patrick appeals to participants to speak openly and without fear on these questions:

- What is our history and story as a high school network?
- What barriers and constraining patterns must we overcome to transform our schools?
- What do you need from the district to lead this work?

The fishbowl speakers go deep. They name the district's lack of understanding of their programs as a major challenge. They speak of "continuing change and turnover from one dysfunctional system to another." They speak of the structural inequity that disproportionately places students with special needs and those exiting the juvenile justice system in the three highest poverty schools. They speak of teacher turnover, vacancies, and schools with middle-class populations that "mask some of that failure . . . mask the population at the bottom." Finally, they speak of the need to shift educator beliefs: "We can build systems, we can create structures, but we have to shift the belief systems of some of our adults." They speak truth to power, and power—the district leadership—listens.

After breaking bread over dinner, the group returns to the meeting room to create and share core memory maps—visual depictions of life experiences that have shaped each leader's identity and values. Returning to the intimacy of small groups, they disclose stories of hardship and hope that most have never shared in a professional setting. As an observer, I stand back and watch as people lean in toward one another and listen with great intensity. I watch the awakening of compassion and mutual understanding as colleagues, many of whom barely knew one another, begin to form a community.

 MAKE IT MINDFUL

How did the network superintendent create an environment in which participants were willing to share their experiences and perspectives? What specific strategies did you see him use?

FROM HERO TO HOST

Authors Margaret Wheatley and Debbie Frieze describe the traditional model of "heroic leadership" as one in which the leader has the authority, charisma, and expertise to save the day. But they argue that instead of heroes, we need **leaders-as-hosts**—leaders who create the conditions for people to come together positively and productively to uncover local solutions.[1]

In *Visible Learning*, an analysis of over 800 studies of the factors that impact student performance, researcher John Hattie names "collective teacher efficacy" as a critical condition. He found that teachers' ability to work together in a purposeful fashion has a whopping 1.57 effect size (.4 is the "hinge point" above which any intervention is considered to have a positive effect on learning).[2] How do we get a group of diverse educators or leaders—with competing needs and priorities—to become collectively efficacious? We do it by listening to them, hosting them, lifting up their stories, and creating opportunities for relationship building and deep dialogue.

In our opening vignette, Patrick, the network superintendent, acted as a host. (By way of disclosure, I coach this leader and helped him design the retreat.) So just what does a host *do*?

How do we get a group of diverse educators or leaders—with competing needs and priorities—to become collectively efficacious? We do it by listening to them, hosting them, lifting up their stories, and creating opportunities for relationship building and deep dialogue.

A Host Sets the Table for Dinner

This means devoting time and attention to creating a "container" for learning—from the tone you set to the physical arrangement of the learning environment to the sense of purpose you invoke when you open a convening. My colleague Victor Cary of the National Equity Project likes to say, "Experience has a structure. Change the structure, and you change the experience." As a host, you have the power to change the structure and, by extension, to transform people's experiences. Experiences are the fabric of culture.

Recall the staging of the retreat. The room was saturated with brain-friendly stimuli: colorful tablecloths and wall quotes for the eye, music for the ear, snacks for the taste buds, and supplies for idle hands. These subtle touches feed the lizard brain and reward the limbic brain, priming people to relax into the learning environment. Meetings begin to feel joyful and alive rather than tedious and operational. The network leader and I took great pains to create a space that felt welcoming, alive, and culturally different from your run-of-the-mill meeting.

As you "set the table" for your team, surprise people! Liberate your office and meeting rooms from an institutional, sit-and-get feel, and have people face one another to promote dialogue. Build frequent movement into the learning. Provide chocolates or other fun snacks. Setting the table also implies that you plan every convening with intentionality, as we discussed in Chapter 10, starting with your technical and relational outcomes. Table 11.1 includes the technical and relational outcomes from the high school network retreat.

A Host Tunes in to the Group Dynamic

As we discussed in Chapter 10, the group dynamic comprises those positive and negative forces and dispositions that surface within any group.[3] Throughout the retreat, Patrick and I kept close tabs on the participants' facial expressions, their body language, who was sitting and talking to whom, and who wasn't talking at all. In one early activity, we asked people to organize into groups representing the types of students *they* were in high

TABLE 11.1   OUTCOMES FOR THE LEADERSHIP RETREAT

Technical Outcomes Leaders Will . . .	Relational Outcomes Leaders Will . . .
• Engage in a root-cause analysis of their school's current state. • Get a clear vision of success for 2016–17. • Develop a theory of action and core strategies. • Make progress on site plans.	• Build a stronger sense of team across the network. • Experience critical feedback in a safe, supportive environment. • Uncover an equity imperative for their schools. • Embrace a spirit of innovation and experimentation.

school. Most participants were laughing as they met up with their fellow "overachievers," "artists," or "athletes." However, the activity activated a social threat for several folks, including a woman who had been an underserved student with special needs. As hosts, we had a responsibility not only to notice this dynamic but also to check in one-on-one with her and others who were left feeling vulnerable.

A Host Welcomes Guests and Models Grace Under Pressure

Consider a leader you admire who moves through her work with emotional grace—warmth, openness, and a lack of distress in her interactions with others. What does she say and do to convey goodwill and generosity? How does she hold her body and face as she talks to people?

As you tune in to the group dynamic, consciously use nonverbal cues that express inclusion, affirmation, and hope. Smile, take time to greet people, offer a warm handshake or a hug. If you know someone is having a hard time outside of work, ask how he or she is doing. Remember this principle of Deep Listening: "Power lies in the relationship." Use the two W's—"welcome" and "we"—to evoke a sense of community and draw the brain's ego-self away from "I." The network superintendent employed these words and a tone of respect and appreciation as he opened the retreat.

A Host "Holds Space" for Meaningful Conversations

In Chapter 9, we explored how Listening Leaders help people reconcile the gap between their values and the culture or environment in which they work. In that process, it is critical that leaders learn how to facilitate the deeper conversations that allow people to address the complex challenges they face.[4] This requires a versatile range of moves, some of which I mentioned in Chapter 10. Keep in mind that the Six Stances of a Listening

Leader (outlined in Chapters 5 and 6) offer a great foundation, including sentence stems and questions that you can draw on to facilitate substantive dialogue.

A Host Models Storientation

Recall that storientation entails careful attention to story as a vehicle for social and organizational change. In Chapter 2, we studied the privileged status that stories hold in the brain. Stories help people deal with the moral question of fear, which is a fundamental part of any change process. As former community organizer and Harvard University lecturer Marshall Ganz explains, stories do "emotional work" within a community, helping people grapple with such human dilemmas as "How do I live with empathy as opposed to alienation? How do I live with a sense of my own value as opposed to a feeling of deficiency? How do I live in a spirit of hope instead of fear?"[5]

Listening Leaders are curators who collect, arrange, and highlight stories as a way to affirm our shared humanity and make the impossible seem possible. As you prepare to host, embrace storientation by creating opportunities for people to share and exchange personal narratives. Help

Listening Leaders are curators who collect, arrange, and highlight stories as a way to affirm our shared humanity and make the impossible seem possible.

your team construct a *collective* narrative, rooted in shared values and aspirations. Finally, begin to create a *future-state* narrative of hope and possibility. Patrick used language like "Imagine what is possible if we continue to work together. Imagine if every one of our students gains access to a personalized, intellectually stimulating pathway to learning."

THE FOUR SEASONS OF A LISTENING CULTURE

Growing a listening culture is the ultimate complex challenge and the key to sustaining equitable school transformation. Inspired by the work of John Heron, I like to think of this cultural process through the metaphor of the four seasons. In winter, trust is low, anxiety is high, and the group may become stuck in one or more of the negative dynamics depicted in Chapter 10. In spring, trust is building, anxiety decreases, and the leader applies strategies like those in this book to slowly shift the culture.

By summer, the group has coalesced around its mission, or equity imperative; trust is in full bloom; and anxiety has evolved into a positive force for growth and change. People seem open to each other as they take risks, collaborate, and share emerging practices. The organization is increasingly leader-ful as team members innovate and drive projects that arise from the group's creative thinking. Finally, in autumn, team members prepare to harvest the fruits of their labor, taking time to celebrate success and reflect. Rituals of affirmation and reflection are very important in this season.[6]

Prior to the retreat in the opening vignette, I had observed the principals in their normal "habitat" of a district meeting. Listening in on their

---

 MAKE IT MINDFUL

Which season do you believe your team or staff is in? What's your evidence? Nonverbal cues can be a great source of data for this assessment. See the Seasonal Rubric of Group Behaviors in Appendix H for a season-by-season rubric of group behaviors.

---

conversations, I realized that this group was locked in a long, stormy winter. My diagnosis: business-as-usual meetings had perpetuated a dysfunctional culture of passivity and an "us" (site leadership) vs. "them" (district leadership) dynamic. The group needed an intervention.

I brought my observation notes (Level 3 street data) to the network superintendent and encouraged him to consider hosting a retreat—and luckily, he agreed. Our goal was to model a listening culture and move the team from winter into spring. Table 11.2 previews five routines I'll unpack to help you grow a listening culture.

"SET THE TABLE" WITH ANNUAL RETREATS

Why is being listened to healing? Listening creates relationship. Our natural state is to be together (though we keep moving away from each other)—we haven't lost the need to be in relationship. Everybody has a story, and everybody wants to tell it in order to connect.

—MARGARET WHEATLEY[7]

TABLE 11.2   KEY ROUTINES FOR GROWING A LISTENING CULTURE

Routine	Brief Description
Annual or biannual retreats	Off-site, often residential gatherings that enable you to set the tone, renew the vision, and develop a collaborative culture
Listening Campaigns	An organized effort to build relationships and gather data from a pre-identified group of stakeholders via listening sessions
Learning Leader Chats	An efficient way to gather Level 3 street data at scale; allows the leader to listen to *groups* of stakeholders from each key site or team once or twice a year
Team one-on-ones	A regular, nonevaluative meeting between leader and team member, geared toward the team member's development
Safe-to-learn inquiry cycles	Small-scale experiments that empower the adult learner to identify a problem of student learning and pilot a quick cycle of experimentation, data gathering, and adjusting practices

If I could convince you to make one high-leverage budget decision, it would be to allocate funds to implement off-site team retreats at least once a year, preferably twice, and ideally overnight. You'll be astounded by the level of creative thinking unleashed by a simple change in venue. Yes, people have families to care for. Yes, they may complain about being away from home (and personally, I would never mandate someone to attend). Yes, you may need to pay your staff extended hours or a stipend to attend. It's worth it on all counts. When educators feel cared for and invested in, the sacred cows of the status quo cease to moo and people open to change.

You can host a retreat for an entire staff, a leadership team, or a collection of teams. One school I support hosts an August and January all-staff retreat, followed by an April leadership team planning retreat. A well-planned retreat will help you hone an equity imperative, identify a few simple rules or guiding principles, and craft a skinny plan. Here a few activities to consider as you plan your retreat.

Core Memory Maps

Always begin with story. After watching the 2015 Pixar film *Inside Out,* I created a retreat activity I call "core memory maps" that models storientation and provides a safe platform for participants to share their identity. The film features a young girl named Riley, whose important recollections, or "core memories," are depicted as radiating golden spheres that power "personality islands"—key aspects of her identity. I introduce this concept with a brief clip from the film before asking participants to think of life experiences that have shaped who they are as educators or leaders, and to identify *specific* values or stances that grew out of each experience.

I always draw my own core memory map on chart paper to model strategic vulnerability—an appropriate level of risk and disclosure that makes it safe for others to share. Sometimes I share how my experience working for a civil rights attorney inside the Rhode Island youth prison system engendered a lifelong commitment to racial justice. Other times I share how my experience of attending a highly tracked high school was the genesis of my commitment to equity and access for every student. I often invite a colleague with a different identity profile from me to model his or her core memory map. After seeing examples, participants construct their own visual to share in small groups.

Figure 11.1 provides a sample structure for how a core memory map could look. Now that I have led this activity many times, I also share examples from previous participants.

This activity works like magic every time. People travel safely below the green line through an opportunity for **self-authorship**: telling one's own

FIGURE 11.1   SAMPLE VISUAL FOR CORE MEMORY MAPS

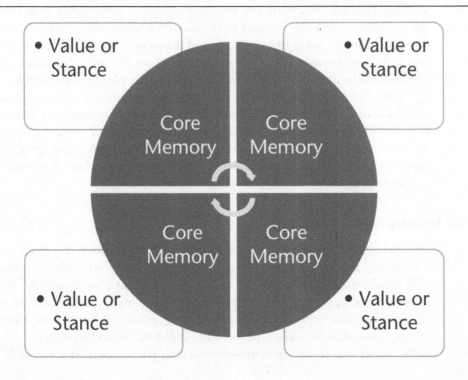

story on one's own terms. Each time I've led a group through this process, I've seen relational trust bloom and implicit biases get checked as participants discover shared humanity.

Fishbowl Discussion: Equity Imperative

Retreats present an opportunity to establish or renew an equity imperative—your clear and compelling "why." Consider using a fishbowl structure—a small discussion circle around which the rest of the group sits and listens—to crack open a new public narrative. (Figure 11.2 depicts the fishbowl structure with a few best practices.)

FIGURE 11.2   FISHBOWL STRUCTURE AND BEST PRACTICES

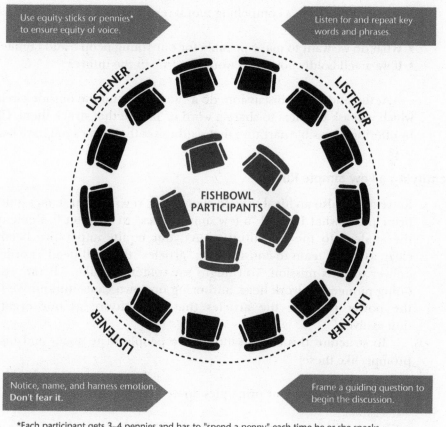

Use equity sticks or pennies* to ensure equity of voice.

Listen for and repeat key words and phrases.

LISTENER

LISTENER

FISHBOWL PARTICIPANTS

LISTENER

LISTENER

Notice, name, and harness emotion. **Don't fear it.**

Frame a guiding question to begin the discussion.

*Each participant gets 3–4 pennies and has to "spend a penny" each time he or she speaks.

A fishbowl can be a powerful strategy for shifting the discourse about your current data and results. In traditional staff meetings, educators are often asked to analyze data as a technical exercise, devoid of the emotion that it evokes. Over time, the data ceases to pack a punch, and people grow desensitized or even defensive in its presence. By contrast, a fishbowl invites onto center stage emotion, passion, and a courageous conversation about the current reality.

Before facilitating this activity, have *all* participants analyze and discuss multiple sources of data that illuminate equity challenges, just as the leaders in Patrick's network did. From there, tap a range of voices, but no more than six to eight people, to participate in the fishbowl discussion. I often leave an empty chair in the "bowl" and encourage listeners to jump in and add a comment or question at any point. Gently guide the discussion with questions like these:

- Whom do we have a compelling moral responsibility to serve differently or better?
- What do we want to make possible for our young people and families?
- If we acted boldly now, what would be true in the future?

At the end of the discussion, do a "wave" around the outside circle in which you ask listeners to share a word or phrase that struck them. Close by offering a possible narrative that synthesizes the themes you have heard.

Identifying a Few Simple Rules

Retreats are also an ideal time to charter (or revisit) your team's guiding principles—what I called "a few simple rules" in Chapter 9. Remember the analogy to the Constitution? As your equity imperative becomes clear, ask your team to consider the "articles" they will need in order to deliver on this mission. You might say something like, "Team, we are doing pioneering work here, authoring our own Constitution. We have the power to write the articles that will endure as our organization evolves."

To structure this conversation, have people write about and discuss prompts like these:

- What simple "rules" or principles do we need to govern our actions and decisions?
- What shared values will keep us closely tethered to our equity imperative?
- What cairns will we build to keep us on the path to our vision?

Remember the Chapter 9 metaphor of building cairns—those stacks of rocks that guide walkers along a path? You might even bring rocks to the meeting to inspire your team. Assign a guiding principle to each person, and invite people to stack the rocks up as a way of visualizing the mission. See Tips for Creating Simple Rules in Appendix H.

Skinny Plans

Lastly, retreats should include time for boots-on-the-ground planning. Whether your focus is instruction, school culture, or big-picture strategy, the skinny plan is your friend. Revisit Chapter 9 to reacquaint yourself with the components and guiding questions for crafting a skinny plan.

LISTENING CAMPAIGNS

To gather data on the current-state story, conduct a **Listening Campaign**— a focused effort to identify concerns and priorities through a series of structured one-on-one or small-group meetings with key stakeholders. This routine can be incorporated at any time of year, but is often most effective before the school year begins. Listening Campaigns generate rich, qualitative, Level 3 street data with which to shape your equity imperative, hone an initiative that arises out of common concerns, or expose a gap between current state and future state. See Appendix H for a Listening Campaign Tool that outlines essential steps and questions to pose.

If you ask a question that generates a one-word answer, prompt the speaker again with, "What are some examples?" or "Can you share a concrete time when you saw this happening?" The data is in the details, not the generalities. And know that it's fine to go off script during a listening session; you're a human being after all, not a robot.

Finally, decide how you will synthesize and share the data you collect. I always ask permission to take computer notes, let people know I'll be writing an anonymous report, and reassure them that their comments will be held in confidence and included anonymously if at all. I invite them to flag any remarks that they want to make off the record. Once I've conducted all sessions, I review the notes and pull out trends, combing in particular for micronarratives that repeat across the data. My goal is not to represent every point of view or story in the data, but to illuminate patterns. Through this process, I sort the data into a simple report organized around a few core themes and populated with direct quotes. I try to highlight both strengths and challenges.

LEARNING LEADER CHATS

If you lead a large school or an entire system, **Learning Leader Chats** are a great alternative to Listening Campaigns. Inspired by FDR's famously named Fireside Chats, I developed this routine to support system leaders to listen at scale by regularly rotating through key sites or teams. It's important that the chats honor the voluntary principle of adult learning, meaning that stakeholders choose whether to attend or not.

Here's how it can look in action. Chris Funk is the superintendent of the East Side Union High School District (ESUHSD) in San Jose, California, with 24,000 students and over 1,000 teachers. He took up the mantle after a revolving door of superintendents had all but guaranteed a cynical, low-trust culture. A Listening Leader by nature, Funk wanted to change stakeholders' perceptions of the district. As his coach and collaborator, I helped him design a structure for Learning Leader Chats; twice a year, he hosts listening session at each site and with any central-office team whose members express interest. Initially, these took place after school, but Funk now commits a full day to each site.

Funk views this routine as a way to flip the accountability paradigm from top-down to increasingly bottom-up. In his words,

> My goal from these chats is to learn from staff in the trenches what is working well and what can be improved, or what we need to *stop* doing as an organization. My expectation is that all levels of the organization will review the notes and take the opportunity to enter into dialogue that will effectively and efficiently address the concerns that have been raised.

Ultimately, Funk believes that Learning Leader Chats have built and will continue to build trust throughout the organization.

The chats enable the district's top executive to set a powerfully responsive tone. Funk opened one chat that I observed with these words:

> I'm here to listen, to learn, to clarify if I can. If there's some low-hanging fruit that I can take care of, I will. If there are more systemic things that I can take back and work on, I'll do that. . . There's no topic that we can't discuss. If there's something that I can't answer, I'll try to find an answer for you. But this is really for me to learn what's working and not working here and throughout the district.

The chats also provide Funk with real-time feedback on progress and barriers in the field. At one site, he learned that employees didn't know how to apply for maternity leave. Incredulous, he reviewed the district website and couldn't locate any information on this topic. Within a week, he had commissioned a staff person to create a graphic illustrating the process. At another site, teachers were frustrated because buildings and grounds staff had pruned trees and left behind a huge pile of trimmings that began to decay. The next day, Funk sent staff out to retrieve the pile. On an instructional note, Funk collected lots of micronarrative data on a controversial district-wide math initiative. With new insight, he helped his executive team design a much-improved process to rethink the initiative, garner teacher buy-in, and pilot new curricula.

I asked Funk how he felt about his first series of Learning Leader Chats. Here is his candid answer:

> It required me to face the potential discomfort of getting harsh criticism or negative comments from staff members who may not have bought into my vision for our schools. There is no question that if a superintendent is pushing the organization forward and not settling for the status quo, mistakes will be made and feathers will be ruffled.

Three rounds of chats later, Funk reflects that "every single session was a great dialogue, filled with tough but fair questions and extremely positive; all stakeholders were very respectful."

Remember this: Small moves can yield a big impact. When a positional leader takes time to listen and engage in dialogue without a preconceived agenda, people feel that they matter, and cultural knots begin to loosen. Exhibit 11.1 provides data from Funk's chats.

EXHIBIT 11.1   DATA FROM LEARNING LEADER CHATS

After each chat, Funk administers a participant survey—a Level 2 data source. Here are a few data points from a recent one:

- 98.7% said that the chat "met" or "exceeded" their expectations.
- 97.33% said they felt able to ask the superintendent all of their questions.
- 98.7% said that the content of the conversation with the superintendent was "meaningful" or "very meaningful."
- 97.4% said that the chat was worth their time.

Open responses revealed an appreciation for the superintendent's willingness to listen. One participant wrote, "Thank you so much for coming. This is a great idea. Hopefully site administration will see the merit in it and do the same." Another chimed in, "I appreciate that the superintendent wanted to hear about problems and not just talk "at" us."

TEAM ONE-ON-ONES

A **one-on-one** is a regular, nonevaluative meeting between a leader and a team member, geared toward the team member's growth and development. To promote distributed leadership and keep your finger on the cultural pulse, hold regular one-on-one meetings. If you lead a sprawling school or organization, narrow your list to no more than 10 key people with whom you commit to meet every week or two. Your roster might include department chairs, grade-level leads, team facilitators, or informal influencers with deep social networks. In an ideal world, every staff person would have *someone* he or she sits down with regularly. To achieve this goal, train your core group to hold one-on-ones with their team members.

As you customize this routine, be explicit with stakeholders about your purpose. You might have multiple purposes for facilitating one-on-ones, including listening, offering support, reviewing work plans, or discussing a classroom observation. These can change from meeting to meeting, but having a sense of *why* you are meeting with a person is important. Here is an excerpt from assistant principal Emily Rigotti's letter to her staff framing the purpose of one-on-ones:

> I've decided to start meeting individually with you (and everyone else on the team) on a weekly basis. We'll call these meetings "one-on-ones." I think this is a great way for us to maintain good, open communication, and continue to build our relationship. We'll be meeting for 30 minutes once a week, at a prescheduled (and usually unchanged) time. It will be a private conversation—just you and me. We'll meet at my desk; if you have concerns about privacy, we'll talk about those once we get going.
>
> The primary focus of this meeting is going to be YOU. . . You may be thinking, "Can I trust her?" Well, I hope so. I can tell you, if you want to complain, I'm willing to listen. If I'm messing up, I'm ready to hear it. I expect you to deliver it fairly and professionally, and I'll be willing to have a dialogue with you. This will also give me a chance to share feedback and coaching with you on things you're trying to improve on. I encourage you to be as open as you can be, and over time I bet we both will get more comfortable. Exhibit 11.2 frames tips for this routine, and Exhibit 11.3 includes possible one-on-one questions.

EXHIBIT 11.2   TIPS FOR TEAM ONE-ON-ONES

Here are a few simple rules for leveraging this routine:

- Don't ever cancel a one-on-one unless it's an emergency. It conveys a lack of value in the person and the process.
- Try to hold at least 30 minutes for each meeting, and aspire to spend roughly 90 percent of the time listening and posing questions, and 10 percent talking.
- Always begin with a human check-in: "How are you? How have things been going?"
- Demonstrate openness to input from the team member by asking, "What feels most important to *you* that we address today?" Minimize logistical talk, and focus on substantive issues.
- Model the Six Stances (revisit Chapters 5 and 6).
- Take notes on next steps, and follow up in your next one-on-one.

If done with fidelity—at least biweekly, if not weekly—this simple listening routine will keep communication channels open and flowing as you build a culture of distributed leadership. It's important to let go of being the expert and to pursue the good ideas you hear. Be humble enough to say, "Wow, this colleague knows more than I do about this topic," and invite him or her to facilitate a learning experience for the team.

EXHIBIT 11.3   NINE REFLECTIVE QUESTIONS FOR TEAM MEMBER ONE-ON-ONES

1. Tell me about your week. What's it been like?
2. Tell me about a success from the past week or two.
3. What are you feeling most confident and excited about?
4. Tell me about something you struggled with recently. What's keeping you up at night?
5. If you had the chance to do it again, how would you approach this challenge differently?
6. What's a current hope or goal you're holding in your work?
7. What's your plan or next step to get there?
8. How can I support you?
9. What suggestions do you have for me?

SAFE-TO-LEARN INQUIRY

Safe-to-learn inquiry cycles are a powerful way to promote self-directed adult learning. Instead of trying to "intervene" our way to better results, safe-to-learn inquiry helps educators build their capacity to solve complex instructional challenges by engaging in rapid cycles of **prototyping, or piloting**. The practitioner begins by looking at data, asking questions, pinpointing a problem of learning, and forming a hypothesis. Next, he or she prepares to take action through small-scale experiments, punctuated by opportunities to pause, gather data, and study results.

This professional learning routine cuts across all content areas, grades, and roles. For example, an algebra teacher might begin with Level 3 street data from an in-class math assessment which reveals that a small group of students are still struggling with fractions. An elementary teacher might examine data from running records showing that a third of the class can't retell a story in an organized fashion. A principal might study data from classroom learning walks to find that a majority of teachers still spend most of the class period lecturing from the front of the room.

In a well-facilitated safe-to-learn inquiry process, the practitioner moves from *What happened?* to questions like *Why am I getting these results? How do I understand these results? What do I need to do or try differently?* This is a very empowering process for adult learners, in stark contrast to top-down planning cycles that are driven by Level 1 satellite data. Rooted in street data, safe-to-learn inquiry draws on people's existing knowledge and skills while pushing them to innovate and take risks. The process embodies a bias toward action and elevates the role of failure and struggle in learning. Table 11.3 compares this routine with traditional planning.

Two important elements characterize this process. First, teachers try something new and then reflect on their learning with colleagues. In this way, they begin to build a community of local knowledge and experience with validity unmatched by outside research. Second, whether the practice each teacher tried was helpful or not, they all gain courage from each other's willingness to try out new and uncomfortable practices. My colleague Joe Feldman, CEO of Crescendo Education Group, facilitates safe-to-learn inquiry cycles with high school teachers focused on grading. As he puts it, "You stand on each others' shoulders, and it builds stronger collegial relationships because we're all trying to figure this messy stuff out."

TABLE 11.3.   SAFE-TO-LEARN INQUIRY VS. TRADITIONAL PLANNING

Example of Safe-to-Learn Experiments	Traditional Planning Approach
Short cycles of learning (4–6 weeks max)	Long cycles of planning (semester or year)
Narrow focus: e.g., improving our literacy instruction in grades K–2. Shrink the change.	Broad focus: e.g., organizing a schoolwide response to data from Smarter Balanced Assessment Consortium, (SBAC) tests.
Driven by a range of teacher hypotheses:	Driven by illusion of certainty:
Teacher 1: "I think that adding 30 minutes to each day's guided reading instruction will improve students' success in other content areas." Teacher 2: "I think that emphasizing decoding for a targeted group of low-performing students will improve their success in other content areas."	"We will improve reading levels by having all teachers K–2 double the length of the literacy block."
Iterative: Practitioners reflect and adjust along the way.	Fixed: Practitioners stick to a plan no matter what.
"Whoa, we've realized that the problem isn't the reading block instruction. It's that we're not incorporating literacy when we're teaching other content. Let's develop some strategies to teach reading within our math and science curriculum."	"We said we'd double the literacy block, and we have to stay the course for the rest of the year"

Safe-to-learn inquiry isn't always easy. It requires an emotional and cognitive shift on the part of leaders; we have to let go of the reins and allow people to plunge into unknown waters. We have to believe in the merit of "fail fast, fail frequently" as a vehicle for learning. Educators have been conditioned to avoid failure in the high-stakes testing era. We can't just tell people that it's safe to fail. We have to *model* this belief.

If a colleague is feeling down about a lesson that didn't go well, model affirmation and a bias toward action by saying, "It's okay! Let's think of some adjustments you can make tomorrow and then check in on how it went." As teachers take risks and experiment, celebrate successes and failures in equal measure. I love leadership author Ronald Heifetz's routine in which leaders ask team members to reflect on their "best failure" from the week.

Also, if you're an administrator, model the value of inquiry by engaging in your own cycles with fellow leaders. Be sure to share and reflect on your own learning in staff or team meetings. Appendix H includes a tool called Facilitation and Design Tips for Safe-to-Learn Inquiry

TRANSFORMING A CULTURE

To create a healthier system, connect it to more of itself. Living systems contain their own solutions. When they are suffering in any way—from divisive relationships, from lack of information, from declining performance—the solution is always to bring the system together so that it can learn more about itself from itself. . . It is crucial to remember that in organizations we are working with webs of relations, not with machines.

—MARGARET WHEATLEY[8]

Hosted by the network superintendent, the high school leadership retreat was the opening act in a process of school transformation that continues today. Facing dismal outcomes and a persistent pattern of failure, Patrick knew that he had to change the conversation and relationships among site leaders. This necessitated taking people away from the daily grind and designing a radically different environment and experience. Instead of telling leaders what to do, he listened to them. Instead of prescribing a solution, he created the conditions for site leaders to determine a course of action. Instead of being a hero, he became a host.

Participating leaders affirmed these choices as moves toward a responsive, listening culture. The following are some of the feedback comments Patrick received on an anonymous survey:

- "The best PD we have had as a network since I've been a principal. The retreat was focused on our immediate work, well-facilitated, differentiated enough to meet everyone's needs, and built community. No one was doing other work, reading emails, or exhibiting off-task behaviors. Not because there were 'rules' against this but because what we were doing was important, interesting and relevant."
- "It allowed time unpack multiple layers of the work. I think I got a sense of how the dots connect!"
- "The retreat was very hands on with many social-emotional learning activities. It was great seeing what other schools were doing; it gave us many ideas. Sitting down with colleagues without school distractions and in a great environment helped. Love having support from the district team and finally great leadership and facilitation."

Wherever you sit in the school system, you have the power to design experiences that will shift the discourse and transform your team culture. I've offered you a set of routines that you can adapt and map out across a school year (see Listening Leader Year at a Glance in Appendix H).

Together, these routines form the blueprint of a listening culture—one in which solutions emerge locally, through dialogue and the collective intelligence of your team. In building an annual calendar like this you can tackle crucial questions, such as, How do we get a diverse group of educators or leaders—with competing needs, identities, and priorities—to unify around a vision? How do we grow and sustain a listening culture?

KEY TAKEAWAYS

- To cultivate collective teacher efficacy, become a host who holds space for meaningful dialogue.
- Assess the evolution of a listening culture through the seasonal rubric of group behaviors (see Appendix H)
- To accelerate the growth of a listening culture, host annual or biannual team retreats.
- Leverage the power of Listening Campaigns, Learning Leader Chats, and one-on-ones to build trust and keep your finger on the organizational pulse.
- Facilitate safe-to-learn inquiry cycles to promote self-directed adult learning.

LISTENING LEADER INQUIRY

Question: I love the idea of retreats, but we can't afford that. What can I do instead?

My thoughts: I appreciate this question. Money shouldn't act as a barrier to the kind of deep cultural development work represented in this chapter. If you've scrubbed your budget and just can't find the funds, I would suggest reserving an affordable local spot like a community center or church hall. Many nonprofit organizations are willing to offer discounts to schools. The most important thing is to get people away from their regular place of work in order to lower their anxiety and liberate their imaginations.

Question: My colleagues seem so afraid of losing status by admitting their mistakes. How do I reassure them that failure is okay?

My thoughts: Fear of failure can be paralyzing, for adults and students alike. With a heavy emphasis on sanctions, the test-and-punish era created a culture of fear in many schools and districts from which we are still healing. Here are a few antidotes to this situation:

- Model making and admitting mistakes. Do this publically and with humility so that people see you as a learner too.

(Continued)

- Practice mature empathy by acknowledging people's fears. You might say, "I recognize that it's hard to feel safe making mistakes, but I am committed to supporting you to take risks, experiment, and grow."

- Affirm, affirm, affirm. Consciously shut off the brain's negativity bias long enough to see something positive in every person's practice. Name it, lift it up, and celebrate it. Remember that happy neurotransmitters grease the wheels of new learning.

Question: The teachers at my school seem so discouraged by all the daunting problems they face. How do I convince them that it's worth making progress in small steps?

My thoughts: Remember that people need time for emotional release before they can consider even small steps. In meetings, use Constructivist Listening and other affective routines from Chapter 10 to allow colleagues to "empty the cup" and get distracting feelings and events off their chest. Then use the Strategic Listening stances to help teachers reflect on their values (reflective inquiry), consider new possibilities (orientation to vision), and choose a small action (bias toward action). Also be sure to build in time for practical routines that support people to try out the step they select: Remember, ideas + practice + repetition carves new neural pathways!

NOTES

1. Wheatley, M. J., & Frieze, D. (2011, January-February). Leadership in the age of complexity: From hero to host. *Resurgence*, no. 264. Retrieved from http://margaretwheatley.com/wp-content/uploads/2014/12/Leadership-in-Age-of-Complexity.pdf

2. Hattie, J. (2014). An interpretation of the visible learning story [PowerPoint presentation]. Retrieved from http://learningforward.org/docs/default-source/pdf/johnhattiepresentation.pdf

3. Lewin, K. (1944). The dynamics of group action. *Educational Leadership, 1*, 195–200.

4. Heifetz, R. A., & Linsky, M. (2002). A survival guide for leaders. *Harvard Business Review, 80*(6), 65–74.

5. Ganz, M. (2013). Making social movements matter [Interview]. Retrieved from http://billmoyers.com/segment/marshall-ganz-on-making-social-movements-matter/

6. Heron, J. (1999). *The complete facilitator's handbook*. Philadelphia, PA: Kogan Page (pp. 51–52).

7. Wheatley, M. (2009). *Turning to one another: Simple conversations to restore hope to the future*. San Francisco, CA: Berrett-Koehler.

8. Wheatley, M. (1999). Bringing schools back to life: Schools as living systems. Norwood, MA: Christopher-Gordon, p. 6. Retrieved from http://margaretwheatley.com/wp-content/uploads/2014/12/Bringing-Schools-Back-to-Life.pdf

Chapter 12

Listening for Liberation

The future comes from where we are now. The future won't change until we look thoughtfully at our present. We have sufficient human capacity to think and reflect together, to care about one another, to act courageously, to reclaim the future.

—MARGARET WHEATLEY[1]

CONVERSATION BY CONVERSATION

Matin Abdel-Qawi is transforming a large urban high school, conversation by conversation. When he became the principal of Oakland High School 3 years ago, he inherited a "two-school narrative. There was the Asian school with kids in class on time, focused, and graduating with a plan. Then there was the Black and Brown school: the kids who struggle academically, are caught in tardy sweeps, or get suspended." His equity imperative was stark.

Abdel-Qawi's first aim was to create a more visibly equitable school. In 3 years, he and his team have decreased suspension rates from 20% to 4%, but he has his sights set on zero. When he took up the mantle, Oakland High had two personalized "pathway" programs with mostly Asian students and a 20% higher graduation rate than the school at large. Today, it boasts six pathways in which students are equitably distributed by GPA, gender, and ethnicity. Despite these impressive accomplishments, for Abdel-Qawi, the work has just begun. Having changed the visual landscape, he and his team are now focused on ensuring that every student graduates and is college and career ready.

I ask Abdel-Qawi where his commitment to equity comes from, and he points first to his faith as a Muslim, citing a verse from the Quran: "We've divided you into tribes and nations not so you despise each other, but so you can get to know each other." Abdel-Qawi grew up in a New Jersey town that was 90% African American; he raised his own children with a "Black consciousness" and embedded in the multiracial Bay Area Islamic community. In the mosque, they "meet people from all over the world—Palestinians, Yemenis, Sudanese—and have a natural inclination to connect across difference."

He also reflects on his first principalship at a school in which he worked with equity-minded colleagues who pushed his thinking and "checked me in ways I didn't even know I needed to be checked."

"What made it possible for people to push you and one another?" I ask. His response rolls off the tongue: vulnerability, trust, engaging in difficult conversations, and still having trust and love afterwards.

Abdel-Qawi is a Listening Leader by disposition. He doesn't believe he has all the answers. He enters the work "humbly and authentically wanting and needing to hear what other folks have to say." He believes that society overvalues technical skills and underestimates the social-emotional skills that make a community thrive: "If you can't listen with your heart to adults and to young people, you're not going to develop the relationships you need to move the system forward."

As a parting gift, Abdel-Qawi offers me a few simple rules for leaders:

- Remain quiet for as long as possible. "In most settings, even when I'm facilitating, I'm listening. I intentionally don't chime in until the second or third time I want to. Once you engage, you have the potential to limit voice and input."
- When you hear a good idea, acknowledge it. "I heard So-and-So say this, and I really appreciate it. Let's unpack that some more."
- Embrace humility. Respect that you don't have to lead as the expert all the time.
- Slow the trip. Instead of going 60 miles per hour, go 30. If you can get there with more people at your side, it's worth it.
- Be truthful always—100% authentic. Don't make anything up, and if you drop the ball, own it.

BUILDING A MOVEMENT

Matin Abdel-Qawi is using the power of listening to orchestrate a movement for change at Oakland High School. Instead of racing to the top, he is building from the bottom up—a beloved community in which every child and every adult is seen, heard, and valued. I ask you this: What if instead of leading institutions, we thought of ourselves as creating movements? What if "stakeholders" were constituents whose power and passion we need to harness? What if instead of looking for answers outside of our communities, we started looking within?

Public schools are the last remaining hope of a democratic society. In a country characterized by increasing income inequality, structural racism, and the highest incarceration rate on the globe, schools are the one institution that holds the potential to level the playing field. But it's going to require more than good soldiers to transform our schools. We need movement-builders. We need creative thinkers. We need people of humility, integrity, and moral purpose—people like Abdel-Qawi.

Movements, says Harvard University professor and former United Farm Workers organizer Marshall Ganz, "tell stories. . . They rearrange meaning. They're not just about redistributing the goods, they're about figuring out what *is* good."[2] To figure out what is good for our schools, we have to listen deeply to ourselves, our colleagues, and our students and families. External measures of success will come and go, but you have the capacity to define success and hold yourself and your community accountable to that vision. What do you hope every student will know and be able to do when he or she leaves your school or system? Name those outcomes and pursue them doggedly.

Envision the story that you and your team will author together. Think about the characters you can further develop through listening. Think about the tensions you'll encounter, the inevitable plot twists on the path to transformation. Imagine yourself shifting the discourse, question by question, until a more just and inclusive narrative emerges. And imagine the small scenes—the words, gestures, and nonverbal cues—in which you see yourself becoming the leader you want and need to be.

THE COURAGE TO LISTEN

To transform our schools and systems will require courage. We must unapologetically name the current reality. We must change the conversation about our most underserved students and families, interrupting unconscious biases and recognizing the brilliance of every child and the powerful assets of every family. We must value the voices of the unheard. Finally, we need to step back and reflect critically on our own practice, asking ourselves each day, *What can I celebrate?* and *What will I do differently tomorrow?* This takes courage, and it builds resilience.

If nothing else, I hope this book has persuaded you that listening is a complex and comprehensive strategy for equitable school transformation. More than a receptive act, listening fundamentally changes our way of being as leaders. It teaches us to pick up important data in the smallest everyday moment, to invest in cultivating a deep reserve of relational capital, and to distribute leadership and capacity across our teams and organizations. Listening Leadership isn't a playbook or a scripted curriculum; it's an opportunity to change the game entirely.

June Jordan was a writer and professor at UC Berkeley who created a program called Poetry for the People (P4P), which was really a movement to liberate the voices of young people and cultivate a generation of warrior-poets. As a young teacher, I won a fellowship that allowed me to take Jordan's final P4P class before she lost a battle with cancer. When we opened June Jordan School for Equity in 2003, the school had no name, but through a democratic process of debate and voting, the first graduating class chose to honor this visionary leader.

We need a generation of Listening Leaders at every level of the school system. Together we can transform our schools into spaces of humanity and critical consciousness. We need not look beyond ourselves. In the prescient words of June Jordan, "We are the ones we've been waiting for."

NOTES

1. Wheatley, M. J. (2009). *Turning to one another: Simple conversations to restore hope to the future.* San Francisco, CA: Berrett-Koehler, p. 73.
2. Ganz, M. (2013). Making social movements matter [Interview]. Retrieved from http://billmoyers.com/segment/marshall-ganz-on-making-social-movements-matter/

LISTENING LEADERSHIP RUBRIC

Beginning	The leader *is aware of* these ideas and approaches and occasionally tries them out.
Emerging	The leader *begins to use* these ideas and approaches, but without consistency or effectiveness.
Developing	The leader *consistently applies* these ideas and approaches and can point to early indicators of impact on trust, adult learning, and/or school culture and climate.
Refining	The leader *has internalized* these ideas and approaches and can point to clear, observable, sustained results in the areas of trust, adult learning, and/or school culture and climate.
Modeling	The leader's practice *is exemplary*; he or she innovates, shares new knowledge and strategies with colleagues, and helps shape structures and systems that sustain progress.

1. Listening for Transformation — Leader recognizes and leverages the transformative power of listening for equitable school transformation.	Beginning	Emerging	Developing	Refining	Modeling	Evidence
Element						
a. Leader understands the difference between Discourse I and Discourse II.	○	○	○	○	○	
b. Leader recognizes and shifts the dominant narratives (Discourse I) in his or her school, team, or organization.	○	○	○	○	○	
c. Leader listens with emotional intelligence in the face of student trauma and educator "secondary trauma."	○	○	○	○	○	
d. Leader can articulate his or her core values and holds strong to those values in the face of external pressures.	○	○	○	○	○	
e. Leader understands the three levels of data: satellite, map, and street.	○	○	○	○	○	
f. Leader collects data at all three levels to set school or team goals and to monitor progress.	○	○	○	○	○	
g. Leader defines local measures of success, including essential student knowledge, skills, and values.	○	○	○	○	○	

2. Awareness
Leader applies critical concepts to lead a process of equitable school transformation.

Element	Beginning	Emerging	Developing	Refining	Modeling	Evidence
a. Leader applies knowledge of the brain's structures and functions to interactions with staff, students, and families.	○	○	○	○	○	
b. Leader uses the brain mandates of a Listening Leader to inform his or her moves and decisions.	○	○	○	○	○	
c. Leader builds staff literacy around the equity channels: structural racism, unconscious bias, and cultural difference.	○	○	○	○	○	
d. Leader names and addresses microaggressions and other manifestations of bias.	○	○	○	○	○	
e. Leader actively monitors his or her own biases.	○	○	○	○	○	
f. Leader models humility, self-awareness, and a learning stance with respect to cultural difference.	○	○	○	○	○	
g. Leader recognizes and responds positively to cultural difference.	○	○	○	○	○	
h. Leader builds trust with staff, students, and parents by consciously responding to "bids" for attention.	○	○	○	○	○	
i. Leader demonstrates systems awareness, paying equal attention to technical and relational change elements.	○	○	○	○	○	
j. Leader takes time to slow down, cultivate mindful awareness, and prepare to listen.	○	○	○	○	○	

	Beginning	Emerging	Developing	Refining	Modeling	Evidence
3. Relational Capital Leader cultivates relational capital, a key resource in school transformation, to move an equity agenda.						
Element						
a. Leader uses Deep Listening to build trust and decrease emotional distress among staff, students, and parents.	○	○	○	○	○	
b. Leader pays attention to nonverbal cues, his or her own as well as those coming from staff, students, and parents.	○	○	○	○	○	
c. Leader uses verbal and nonverbal signals to demonstrate mature empathy toward staff, students, and parents.	○	○	○	○	○	
d. Leader uses verbal and nonverbal signals to model affirmation toward colleagues, priming the brain to learn.	○	○	○	○	○	
e. Leader uses Strategic Listening to positively influence the beliefs, mindsets, and behaviors of teachers and staff.	○	○	○	○	○	

f. Leader models an orientation to vision in formal and informal interactions and communications.	○	○	○	○	○
g. Leader models reflective inquiry with colleagues by framing questions that inspire new insight and action.	○	○	○	○	○
h. Leader models the use of data, especially Level 3 street data, to inform thoughtful instructional decisions.	○	○	○	○	○
i. Leader models a bias toward action, prompting colleagues to innovate, experiment, and take risks.	○	○	○	○	○
j. Leader incorporates the Six Stances into instructional conversations with teachers and one-on-ones with parents, students, and staff.	○	○	○	○	○
k. Leader models ways to listen to parents that break down traditional school-family barriers.	○	○	○	○	○
l. Leader models ways to listen to students that break down educator-student scripts and promote student voice.	○	○	○	○	○

4. Complex Change

Leader harnesses the power of the group to create a focused strategy for moving complex change.

Element	Beginning	Emerging	Developing	Refining	Modeling	Evidence
a. Leader applies the properties of complex change to influence, rather than control, the change process.	○	○	○	○	○	
b. Leader recognizes the difference between complex adaptive challenges and complicated, technical problems.	○	○	○	○	○	
c. Leader applies knowledge of different problem types to adjust his or her leadership moves and approach.	○	○	○	○	○	
d. Leader gathers all three levels of data, with a focus on Level 3 micronarratives, to construct a current-state story.	○	○	○	○	○	
e. Leader facilitates his or her team to identify a clear and compelling equity imperative, rooted in the current-state story.	○	○	○	○	○	
f. Leader supports his or her team to identify a few simple rules and principles to guide decision making and behavior.	○	○	○	○	○	

		1	2	3	4	5
g.	Leader works with his or her team to craft a skinny plan that hones a focused vision and "must-dos" for the work.	○	○	○	○	○
h.	Leader creates a structure for distributed leadership by recruiting and empowering a diverse group of stakeholders.	○	○	○	○	○
i.	Leader meets regularly with teachers and staff leaders and uses the Six Stances to build people's capacity.	○	○	○	○	○
j.	Leader takes the temperature of his or her team, actively monitoring the group dynamic.	○	○	○	○	○
k.	Leader uses the Six Stances and strategic facilitation moves to shift the group dynamic when necessary.	○	○	○	○	○
l.	Leader designs technical (above-the-green-line), and relational (below-the-green-line), outcomes for meetings.	○	○	○	○	○
m.	Leader uses the experiential learning cycle to design meetings that address both affective and cognitive needs.	○	○	○	○	○
n.	Leader becomes a host of public spaces, intentionally creating and managing a positive group dynamic.	○	○	○	○	○

o.	Leader facilitates extended team time (e.g., annual retreats) to set the tone, revisit the vision, and foster collaboration.	○	○	○	○
p.	Leader grows a listening culture with routines that keep his or her finger on the pulse and promote information flow.	○	○	○	○
q.	Leader engages in regular one-on-one meetings with key team members to build capacity and trust.	○	○	○	○
r.	Leader uses safe-to-learn inquiry that fosters a developmental climate of experimentation and innovation.	○	○	○	○

APPENDIX B

THE SIX STANCES OF A LISTENING LEADER

DEEP LISTENING STANCES

The Deep Listening stances help you listen without an agenda to support healing, release emotions, and build relational capital.

Stance	How To Use This Stance	What It Looks Or Sounds Like
Attention to nonverbal cues	Tune in to nonverbal cues. Question your interpretation of nonverbal cues through the lenses of culture, gender, and power. Don't make snap judgments. Pay attention to your own nonverbal cues. To convey mature empathy, select cues that mirror the speaker's disposition.	Pay close attention to • Facial expressions • Body language • Eye contact (frequency of glances, patterns of gaze, pupil dilation, and blink rate) • Breathing patterns • Mediation of personal space (distance vs. proximity) • Voice and tone • Use of safe, appropriate touch • Perception of time • Vocalizations like "uh-huh," "ohhh," or "hmmm"
Mature empathy	Form a mental picture of the other person's experience. Demonstrate compassion through mirroring cues. Notice and manage your own anxiety; if you feel triggered, take a deep breath and refocus on listening. Use active listening stems—for example, • What I hear you saying is . . . • Am I missing anything? • In other words . . . • Is there anything else you feel I should know?	• How are you doing, really? • How are you feeling about . . .? • What's going on for you right now? • Tell me a little bit about why this is challenging for you. • It seems like this is bringing up a lot of emotion for you. Can you share what is coming up? • I have a hunch there's something you want to say, but are not saying. Do you want to put it out there?

Stance	How To Use This Stance	What It Looks Or Sounds Like
Affirmation	Set your brain to notice the positive—from the small to the significant. Pick out *specific* behaviors and actions to reinforce with verbal affirmation. Use nonverbal affirmations like smiling, nodding, a warm handshake, or a gentle pat on the back. Model affirmation consistently over time, with a 5:1 ratio of positive to critical feedback, to build trust and flood the brain with positive neurochemicals.	• I really appreciate how you . . . • I'm impressed by how you . . . • Here is the direct impact that I witnessed . . . • I want to share a strength I've noticed in your [teaching, leadership, etc.] . . . • What is one specific piece of that lesson that you want to lift up and celebrate?

STRATEGIC LISTENING STANCES

The Strategic Listening stances help you leverage data, probing questions, and vision to generate new insight and action.

Stance	How To Use This Stance	What It Looks Or Sounds Like
Orientation to vision	Listen for opportunities to connect what people care about with a vision of equity and transformation. Reference vision in your messages and questions—from district and schoolwide visions to the teacher's own goals and values. Embrace storientation to build a cohesive narrative of where your school or team is headed and why it matters.	• What would success look like at the end of this year? • What most excites you about where we're headed as a school, and what concerns you? • What do you want to be a part of creating for our [team, school, community]?
Reflective inquiry	Engage the speaker's brain with questions that provoke new ways of thinking or viewing a situation. Use street-level data to challenge single stories (Discourse I) and problematic beliefs and mindsets. Leverage reflective questions to water the brain for deep roots, helping it grow new neural pathways.	• What are your hopes and fears about . . .? • What might be getting in the way of . . .? • What evidence supports that interpretation? • If you step back for a moment, what's a different way of seeing this challenge? • What does this data (e.g., student interview transcript, piece of student work, video clip of students interacting with a task) reveal?

Stance	How To Use This Stance	What It Looks Or Sounds Like
Bias toward action	Tap into the adult learner's need for autonomy and agency with questions that prompt thoughtful action. Invite your team to experiment with and "try on" new ideas, with an expectation that they'll reflect on what they learn in the process. Every chance you get, ask people "What did you notice?" and "What did you learn?"	• As a result of this conversation, what specific action steps will you take, and when can we debrief? • I want to encourage you to try out this practice, even if it doesn't go perfectly at first. • Let's take a few minutes for you to practice the instructional move you've identified . . . How did that feel? • Now that we've debriefed the lesson, let's take a few minutes to improve it together. What are one or two concrete changes you could make?

THE INSTRUCTIONAL CONVERSATION PLANNING TOOL

FOCAL TEACHER: _____

I. Goal setting: What's my goal for this conversation?

II. Mindful intention: How do I need to show up with this person?

III. Formative assessment: How will I know that the teacher and I have made progress toward the goal?

IV. Plan: What will I say or ask to push the teacher's thinking and practice?

Steps	Key Stance	I'll Say or Ask . . .
1. Open	Mature empathy	
2. Frame	Orientation to vision	
3. Prime	Affirmation	
4. Probe	Reflective inquiry	
5. Focus.	Reflective inquiry	
6. Prepare.	Bias toward action	
7. Close	Mature empathy and affirmation	
Postconversation reflection (This is for you as the leader and could be done in writing, with a discussion partner, or as a silent reflection.)	How did it go? What worked and didn't work? What did you learn?	

ADDITIONAL RESOURCES FOR LISTENING TO PARENTS

RESOURCES FOR CONDUCTING HOME VISITS

For more information about home visits, check out these resources:

Website: The Parent Teacher Home Visit Project
http://www.pthvp.org

Video: "Teacher Home Visits Can Lead to School Transformation"
https://www.youtube.com/watch?v=G72S3dgtJ2E

Articles: "Teacher Home Visits Transform Learning"
http://chicago.suntimes.com/other-views/7/71/184751/teacher-home-visits-transform-learning

"How Teacher Home Visits Can Lead to School Transformation"

http://neatoday.org/2014/10/28/all-in-the-family-how-teacher-home-visits-can-lead-to-school-transformation/

"These Teachers Visit Every Student Before School Starts"

http://blogs.edweek.org/teachers/teaching_now/2014/08/teachers_visit_every_student_at_home_in_henderson_county_ky.html

TIPS FOR IMPLEMENTING FOCUS GROUPS

1. Determine when it makes sense to host focus groups, given what you know about parents' schedules and availability.
2. Create a written plan of action around the following:

   - What type of data do we need from parents to better understand our challenges? Therefore, whom/which parent groups are we trying to engage?
   - How will we use this data with care and respect for what is shared?
   - What open-ended questions will we pose in the meeting? (Limit to five.)
   - How we will establish clear norms for the conversation (e.g., confidentiality, equity of voice)?
   - When will the focus groups happen, and who will facilitate them? (Develop a time line.)

3. Drum up interest.

   - Inform participants about the meeting in advance (at least 2 weeks).
   - Consider one-on-one outreach to parents who are less likely to show up.

4. Facilitate the group.

   - Be comfortable and familiar with group dynamics (see Chapter 10).
   - Practice the Six Stances (see Appendix B).
   - Keep the group on task while staying open to what participants want to discuss.
   - Communicate clearly and precisely. Use everyday language that is understandable. Provide dual-language assistance if needed.
   - Provide refreshments and snacks to feed the lizard.
   - Arrange for child-care support and supplies (coloring books, crayons, books).

A PRIMER ON COMMUNITY WALKS

Steps	Checkpoint
1. Set a clear purpose.	Can you thoughtfully answer these questions: "Why has [our school or team] chosen to do community walks? Which community do we hope to learn more about?"
2. Craft a learning question.	Have you and your staff or team articulated a question to guide your learning? Can you clearly state what you wonder or hope to learn from this experience?
3. Create norms to promote respect.	Have you and your staff discussed how to model respect as you enter the community? Have you created norms to guide faculty behavior during walks?
4. Invite your families to participate.	Have you organized a meeting with people from the community you will visit?
	Have you asked parents and students to identify the most important places for teachers to visit and learn about?
5. Structure the experience.	Have you created time during the workday for staff to participate? Have you built in time for a thorough debrief of the experience (at least 1 hour)? Have you planned a reflection process for staff to share key learnings?

ADDITIONAL RESOURCES FOR LISTENING TO STUDENTS

STUDENT FEEDBACK INTERVIEW TOOL

Note: This is a fantastic way to collect Level 3 street data directly from students.

Step	Rationale
Step 1. The teacher identifies 4–6 students who he or she believes represent a range of experiences and viewpoints.	We want the teacher to drive the self-reflection process and to get feedback from a range of students, including those who are succeeding and those who are not.
Step 2. The interviewer (administrator or teacher colleague) prepares questions based on the school's definition of quality teaching.	We want to focus the feedback on objective criteria of good teaching. We use our school's "Art of Social Justice Teaching" pedagogy, which is aligned with the California Standards for the Teaching Profession.
Step 3. The interviewer conducts a "focus group" style interview with the students and takes notes on their feedback, including the teacher's strengths and areas where the students believe improvement is needed.	We have found that group interviews allow students to express themselves more freely and bounce ideas off one another. Disagreements among students become areas for exploration: For example, why might one student view a teacher's class as "boring" while another says it is "challenging"?
Step 4. The interviewer compiles the notes from the focus group into a written summary of the student's comments and recommendations, keeping individual students' views confidential while quoting students anonymously to describe their experiences.	Raw notes from the focus group can be misleading without context. The process of organizing the notes into narrative feedback allows the interviewer to identify patterns and share the important themes. Although the teacher selected the group of students, a level of anonymity is maintained so that students can give critical feedback as well as positive.

Step	Rationale
Step 5. The interviewer shares the written summary with the teacher and meets with the teacher for a coaching session to discuss potential next steps.	The follow-up meeting provides a space for the teacher to ask clarifying questions and to strategize around how to use the feedback. We encourage teachers to use a bias toward action to think creatively and pilot new ideas without fear of failure.

Adapted from the June Jordan School for Equity Staff Handbook, 2015

ESSENTIAL ELEMENTS OF A TALKING CIRCLE

Room arrangement	Chairs are placed in a circle, with no furniture blocking any participants. Do not neglect this step: It sets an important tone.
Opening	A poem, quote, guided meditation, or breathing exercise is used to create a special space where everyone will come together to share.
Guidelines/values	Set the expectation of the circle to reflect the core values on which it is based, every time a circle forms. Common guidelines include "Respect the talking piece," "Listen from the heart," "Speak your truth," and "Bring your best self to the circle."
Talking piece	The talking piece is a physical object, usually with some meaning to the circle keeper or the group. It is passed around the circle in a single direction. The only person authorized to speak is the person holding the talking piece, which creates an equitable environment for sharing.
Discussion rounds	Discussion questions vary depending on the purpose of the circle.
Closing	It is important to close the circle with intention and acknowledge the sharing and the emotional work done in the circle.

Adapted from the June Jordan School for Equity Staff Handbook, 2015

TALKING CIRCLE PLANNING TOOL

1. What is the main purpose of this talking circle?	Which of the three main categories will this circle fall into? ☐ Community building ☐ Academic ☐ Restorative What is the specific purpose, given this group of students and my objectives as the circle keeper?
2. What do I know about the group of students in the circle today?	How well do they know one another? Who are the strong leaders? Are there conflicts or tensions among particular students? How comfortable are they with the planned topic and purpose? Is anyone likely to feel unsafe or be unwilling to speak?
3. What are the low-stakes questions I will begin with?	All circles, even serious restorative circles, should begin with some low-stakes questions to make participants feel safe. These could be simple questions ("What is one word to describe how you are feeling today?"); open-ended academic questions ("What is one question or idea you have about the topic we are studying?"); or, when appropriate, light-hearted and fun questions ("What's your favorite breakfast cereal?").
4. What are the higher stakes questions I will ask in subsequent circle rounds?	These questions will vary depending on the purpose of the circle. Good circle keepers have a list of questions and an initial plan for how to sequence them, but are flexible and adjust questions based on listening deeply to the group in the early circle rounds. Remember that unexpected information or viewpoints may emerge, which is part of the circle's power. Your job is to guide the circle, not control it.
5. Do I need to prepare any participants in advance?	Given what you know about the group and your planned questions, do you need to meet individually with any students before the circle? This can be important when the topic is more sensitive or there are tensions in the group. You may want to ask particular students to speak up in response to specific questions.
6. How will I set the tone?	Given the topic and the group, how will you open the circle? (In a restorative circle, sometimes this includes stating the facts of a particular incident or conflict.) Are you ready to review our circle guidelines and set the right tone? Do you have your talking piece ready? How do you anticipate closing the circle?

TELLING THE CURRENT-STATE STORY TOOL

	What data do we need to study?	What do we see? What patterns exist? What are our equity challenges?
Level 1 satellite data		
Level 2 map data		
Level 3 street data		
Deeper inquiry	Possible guiding questions: • Which student captures what most concerns us about student learning? • What does this student's average day of learning look and feel like? Can we interview the student to gain more insight? • How prevalent are the patterns we are uncovering? • What Level 1 and 2 data substantiate our concerns? • What Level 3 data do we need to collect? • Given all of this evidence, what aspect(s) of student learning do we need to change? What is the core problem of learning? • Why are we prioritizing this facet of student learning? What's our rationale?	

Story summary: (Synthesize your current-state story into two or three sentences.)

TOOLS AND FACILITATION STEPS FOR LISTENING ROUTINES

QUICK DESIGN TIPS FOR MEETINGS

As you prepare to design any meeting or PD session, keep the following tips in mind. Note that the examples following each tip are illustrative, but not exhaustive. You'll find more sample activities in Chapter 10.

Always begin by identifying both *relational* and *technical* outcomes.
Because people remember the experience of a meeting most of all and because the learner's brain seeks clarity of purpose.
Consider these questions:

- How do I hope people will feel during and after the meeting? (relational)
- What do I want participants to learn, do, or produce? (technical)

Address the affective (feeling) and cognitive (thinking) needs of adult learners.
Because people need to feel safe and connected in order to learn, stretch, and grow their practice.

- Open and close every gathering with some sort of affective routine to calm the amygdala and reimagine rewards (Chapter 2 brain mandates).
- Use mindfulness, Constructivist Listening, or an active listening exercise with prompts such as the following:
    - Share a recent success in your classroom (or) share a recent struggle.
    - What do you need from the team to bring your best thinking forward today?
    - What's the best thing that's happened to you lately?
    - What's it like to be you lately?

Prioritize dialogue and reflection to water the brain for deep roots.

Because people are meaning-making machines whose brains develop through the social processes of dialogue and collaborative inquiry.

- Have people discuss a compelling TED Talk.
- Give team members a collection of quotes from a relevant article or author—one quote per paper and one paper per person—and have them stand up to meet, greet, and discuss the ideas with a rotating cast of partners. (This is sometimes called a tea party and can be used with equal impact in the classroom.)
- Play a song that your students are listening to, and invite people to interpret the lyrics from the perspective of a student, using the 4 R's of information processing—react, reflect, reason, and relate:
  - What words, phrases, or ideas stood out to (or resonated with) you? (React)
  - What surprised you? What thoughts or feelings came up for you? (Reflect)
  - What does this mean to you? Why are these ideas important? (Reason)
  - What have you/we learned? What are the implications for our work? (Relate)

Infuse choice.

Because adults need to engage in learning of their own volition.

- The Kiva Process opens up dialogue on an issue of importance to the community. Structured as a panel discussion interspersed with small-group conversations, this routine allows you to bring new voices and perspectives into the public domain and capture the collective wisdom of the group. The panel should represent different but equally strong positions on a topic. For example, regarding school discipline, the prompts might be as follows:
  - Share your experience and feelings around how the school approached discipline last year.
  - How could the school promote a restorative justice approach that balances a high level of order with a high level of support for students?
  - What other ideas do you have to strengthen our school culture?

Infuse movement.

Because movement is liberating, releases pent-up stress, and primes the brain with positive neurochemicals.

- Four Corners is a movement-based activity that can crack open dialogue and new ways of perceiving an issue. Think of a topic about which you want to push people's thinking, and craft four related scenarios, or statements. Post large number signs around the room (1, 2, 3, 4) to represent each scenario. Then, during the meeting, invite people to choose one scenario that resonates with them, move to the corresponding corner, and discuss their thoughts with whoever else landed there. The following are some examples for these scenarios from a leadership angle:

- Think about a time when you missed or avoided an opportunity to have a courageous conversation.
- Think about a time when you set a compelling vision for the work, but realized later that your team wasn't on board.
- Think about a time when you complied with a mandate that went against your core beliefs and values.
- Think about a time when your sense of urgency prevented you from taking time to listen to others and address their emotions.

Build in application and work time.
Because adults need to see the immediate relevance of new learning and apply it into practice.

- Be mindful to frame the work as low-stakes and experimental in an effort to calm the amygdala and avert performance anxiety.
- The Helping Trios protocol is a simple and efficient format for consultancy in which every team member can get feedback within a 30- to 45-minute window. The protocol begins with the presenter providing the context for his or her dilemma and a question for discussion; after this, listeners typically have time to ask clarifying and probing questions before the group enters into a conversation while the presenter listens and takes notes. Ideally, a well-guided consultancy provides the presenter with fresh insight into his or her dilemma, and perhaps even a new way to approach it. (See Helping Trios Protocol later in this appendix.)
- "I Like, I Wonder" is a routine that offers quick feedback to teams who present a proposal. It works best if people are divided into working groups in which they tackle different issues or different angles on a single issue. When the groups arrive at a natural pause in their thinking, have each present to another group, explaining their current thinking and any questions or roadblocks they've bumped into. Then time the listening for 5 minutes of "I Like" statements and 5 minutes of "I Wonder" statements. Urge people to offer concrete, specific feedback—both "warm," or affirming, and "cool," or constructive. This routine normalizes feedback as a low-stakes and supportive practice.

WAYS TO FACILITATE CONSTRUCTIVIST LISTENING

There are several ways to practice Constructivist Listening (CL): in pairs (called dyads), small groups (called support groups), or a panel (called a personal experience panel, or PEP). A dyad is a simple listening exchange between two people, typically 2 to 3 minutes per participant. A support group is a group of five or six people in which a trained facilitator ensures equal reflection time for everyone. Finally, PEPs provide a whole-group forum for CL in which three to five panelists reflect on a prompt in front of a group of listeners.

Guidelines. If you incorporate CL into your adult learning spaces, be sure to introduce these four guidelines and their accompanying rationale (in italics) each time.

- Each person is given equal time to talk. *Because everyone deserves attention.*
- The listener(s) do not interpret, paraphrase, analyze, give advice, or break in with a personal story. *Because people are capable of solving their own problems.*
- Double confidentiality is maintained. (The listener doesn't talk about what the speaker has shared to anyone else, nor does he or she bring it up to the speaker again.) *Because a person needs confidentiality in order to be authentic. Also, one's feelings at any moment are not representative of one's thinking, or perhaps even one's feelings, 5 minutes later.*
- The talker(s) do not criticize or complain about the listener(s) or about mutual colleagues during their time to talk. *Because a person cannot listen well if he or she is feeling attacked or defensive.*

The guidelines help ensure a safe emotional climate for participants to reflect, and distinguish a CL exchange from a standard turn-and-talk conversation.

Dyads. From start to finish, a dyad can take 10 minutes—a small but high-leverage investment. When inviting people into a dyad, ask them to sit "knee to knee, eye to eye, with nothing in between you" to foster attentive listening. After the dyad, open the floor for participants to comment, but remind people to speak only for themselves in light of the confidentiality guideline.

A good dyad prompt calls for personal narrative and/or self-reflection; for example:

- "As you think about…, what thoughts and feelings come up for you?"
- "What's it been like to be you lately?"
- "What are your hopes and fears about…?"

Support groups. The facilitator sets the tone by reviewing the guidelines, reminding the group of the purpose of CL, and perhaps sharing a quote to introduce a theme or focus. While the facilitator typically offers a prompt, the speaker has the option to speak about anything that is weighing on them. After each participant has shared, the facilitator can open up the circle to a few minutes of additional reflection. When led with care and consistency, support groups build community and shared understanding among colleagues.

Personal experience panels (PEPs). Like a support group, a PEP requires a skilled facilitator. PEP prompts can address equity issues, leadership challenges, or any sensitive topic for which a structured process feels necessary. A good PEP prompt models storientation by providing an opportunity for panelists to reflect on a pivotal and emotional experience:

- "Share an early experience of racial bias that pained and confused you. How did the experience affect you later on?"
- "Share a time where you struggled mightily to connect with a student across difference. What were you left feeling and wondering?"

WAYS TO FACILITATE AGREEMENTS

Facilitation Tips

- Be clear and explicit about the purpose of agreements.
- Ask participants to think about a thriving and a dysfunctional team they've been a part of.
- Use this graphic organizer to activate participants' prior team experiences.

	A thriving team I've been a part of	A dysfunctional team I've been a part of
Brief description of your experience		
Conditions What conditions led to the dynamic and experience you described?		
Impact What did (or didn't) this team accomplish?		

- Invite people to self-organize into small groups to share their experiences.
- Bring the whole group back together and ask people to reflect on this question: "What conditions led to the thriving or dysfunctional team?" Chart responses on a poster in two columns.
- Next, have the group brainstorm agreements on sticky notes, asking, "How do we need to be and work together to accomplish our vision?"
- Invite small groups to reconvene, share, and cluster possible agreements.
- In a large group, have people circulate around the room looking at other small-group posters. Cue them to look for what similarities emerge from the discussions.
- Finally, engage the group in a process of elimination, voting, and formal adoption.
- To make agreements come alive, include them on your agendas. Blow them up on a poster. Revisit them at the start of each meeting, inviting people to focus on one.

WAYS TO FACILITATE A KIVA PROCESS

Use these steps to prepare for and facilitate a Kiva Process:

1. First decide on your theme or focus. As a rule of thumb, identify a challenging issue on which the team does not have consensus. For example: Why are we struggling to engage the families of our second-language learners? or What's getting in the way of creating a safe, strong school culture?

2. Next, construct two to three questions that will guide each "round" of the process.

3. Recruit three to five panelists; aim for a range of perspectives on the issue.

4. Facilitate the Kiva rounds. Invite the panelists to speak to each prompt twice—first for 2 minutes, then for 1 minute. Ask the audience to jot down a word or phrase.

5. Invite small groups of three to four listeners to discuss what they've heard, after you have made clear that "Each person gets to speak once before anybody speaks twice."

6. Ask small groups to begin by sharing a word or phrase they heard. They can do this in a circle, one person at a time, and they may repeat it two or three times.

7. Have each small group designate a recorder to capture big themes on chart paper.

8. For subsequent rounds, repeat the cycle.

9. After the final round, have small groups circulate around the room to observe other groups' notes.

10. At the end, facilitate a whole-group dialogue to draw out the collective knowledge of the group. Ask, What is our emerging understanding of the issue? What new insights did we gain today? What are possible implications for how we organize ourselves?

TOP TEN TED TALKS AND CORRESPONDING PROMPTS

Go to ted.com/talks.

1. "Changing Education Paradigms," Sir Ken Robinson
2. "Do Schools Kill Creativity?" Sir Ken Robinson
3. "Why Leaders Eat Last," Simon Sinek
4. "How to Overcome Our Biases: Walk Boldly Toward Them," Verna Myers
5. "Every Kid Needs a Champion," Rita Pierson
6. "The Power of Vulnerability," Brené Brown
7. "We Need to TALK About an Injustice," Bryan Stevenson
8. "Teach Girls Bravery, Not Perfection," Reshma Saujani
9. "The Danger of a Single Story," Chimamanda Ngozie Adichie
10. "Teaching With the World Peace Game," John Hunter
11. "What Really Matters at the End of Life," BJ Miller

Here are four questions you can adapt to spark dialogue, using the four R's of information processing: react, reflect, reason, and relate.

- What words, phrases, or ideas stood out to (or resonated with) you? (React)
- What surprised you? What thoughts or feelings came up for you? (Reflect)
- What does this mean to you? Why are these ideas important? (Reason)
- What have you/we learned? What are the implications for our work? (Relate)

GUIDELINES FOR DATA-BASED INQUIRY

Before engaging a team in data-based inquiry, I would recommend that you provide a set of guidelines for looking at data. Here are five that I've adapted over time:

- Only describe what you see. Don't leap to interpretations or describe what's not plainly on the page.
- Capture questions on what you don't see. Notice what's not in the data, and chart questions to drive further study.
- Fight the temptation to "solve" the problem before studying the data in depth. Probe for root causes; what does the data reveal?
- Open to multiple perspectives on the data. Listen deeply to colleagues and ask clarifying questions. Ask the team, "How might one of our parents view this data?" "How might our students view this data?"
- Challenge your assumptions. If the data doesn't match your predictions, discuss the gap.

HELPING TRIOS PROTOCOL

Initial Instructions:

- Form trios. (Either assign people to trios or allow them to self-organize.)
- Have trios decide the order of presentations and label themselves A, B, and C.
- Follow the steps below.

Time	Step
5 minutes	A shares the context and essential issues or questions while B and C listen and take notes.
5–7 minutes	B and C ask clarifying questions, followed by probing questions. A responds
8–10 minutes	B and C converse about what they heard, similar situations they have resolved, and ideas of what they might do, while A listens and takes notes.
5–7 minutes	A responds to what he or she heard as desired, addressing what was helpful to hear, questions that have surfaced, and so on. The trio has an open conversation.

Round 2 Partner B (rinse and repeat).
Round 3 Partner C (rinse and repeat).

AGENDA TEMPLATE (ALIGNED WITH THE EXPERIENTIAL LEARNING CYCLE)

| Insert Team |
| Agreements here. |

NAME OF TEAM

NAME OF MEETING

DATE

Outcomes: Today we will...

- •
- •
- •

    (Note: Relational outcomes tend to align with affective and imaginal routines, whereas technical outcomes tend to align with conceptual and practical routines. You may or may not choose to share your relational outcomes, depending on the level of group trust and whether it seems helpful to be transparent around the experience you want people to have.)

Cycle	Activity
Affective	Opening moves
	How will you frame the purpose and "story" of the meeting—the "why"?
	How will you help participants reflect and connect—with each other and with their own sense of purpose and intention (mindfulness practice, setting an intention, turn and talk prompt, check-in, community circle, Constructivist Listening dyad, move and mix around the room with different partners, etc.)?
Imaginal	High-engagement activity
	What inspiring or provocative text could you use to capture the brain's attention (an image, a song, a metaphor, quote, a video, a TED Talk, etc.)?
	How will you give participants time to make meaning *individually* (think-pair-share, quick write, etc.) AND *collectively* (Four Corners, Kiva Process, fishbowl discussion, etc.)?
Conceptual	Core learning
	What concept, framework, or data do people need to grapple with to push their thinking and/or practice?
	How will you give participants time to process the information and make meaning together (text protocols, data-based inquiry, sorting activity, study groups, etc.)?

Cycle	Activity
Practical	Core work
	What is the core "work" of your meeting? What do team members need to produce or prototype?
	How will they practice a new skill and/or get feedback on a piece of work?
Affective	Closing moves
	How can you provide clarity, and model a bias toward action, by formalizing next steps and summarizing relevant decisions?
	How will this information be collected and shared? (Remember the Six Circle model from Chapter 4 and the need for healthy information flow.)
	How will you close the meeting to bind the affective energy in the room (appreciations, dyads, seashells, etc.)?

APPLYING THE SIX STANCES IN A CHALLENGING MEETING

Here are tips for managing meeting flashpoints with the Six Stances of a Listening Leader.

Stance	The Move	Sounds Like . . .
Attention to nonverbal cues	Name the nonverbal cues in the room.	"I'm seeing a lot of crossed arms and furrowed brows. Let's pause and talk about what's coming up for people."
Mature empathy	Mirror the group's affective state with mature empathy stems.	"I'm noticing that people are [quiet, upset, etc.] right now. I know this is a challenging topic to discuss." Or, "It seems like this data brings up feelings of frustration and vulnerability. That's normal, and I want to assure you that we are here to support each other to make progress, not to judge each other for struggling."
Affirmation	Affirm people's willingness to take risks and stay at the table.	"I really appreciate the effort you are putting into learning the new content standards. Thank you for staying the course." Or, "Equity conversations are bound to surface emotion. I applaud you for being willing to sit with the discomfort and stay at the table."
Orientation to vision	Take the group to the balcony by modeling an orientation to vision.	"How can our equity imperative guide us here?" Or, "Which of our guiding principles do we need to call on right now?"
Reflective inquiry	Pose a reflective inquiry question to foster dialogue.	"Turn and talk with a partner: What would help us move through this moment of tension to take productive action together?"
Bias toward action	Model a bias toward action.	"Okay, let's attack this problem together. Self-organize into groups of four or five, and take 15 minutes to brainstorm on chart paper how we can address this problem. Think creatively! Every idea is legitimate as we brainstorm." Next, have people do a "gallery walk" around the room, leaving sticky note comments on what they like and questions they have about other groups' ideas. To get consensus, facilitate a "dot vote," giving members colored sticky dots to place on their preferred approach.

TOOLS FOR GROWING A LISTENING CULTURE

SEASONAL RUBRIC OF GROUP BEHAVIORS

Winter	Spring	Summer	Fall
The Season of Defensiveness	**Working Through defensiveness**	**Authentic Behavior**	**Closure**
• Expressing differences of ideas, opinions, etc. • Forming subgroups • "One-upsmanship" • Vying for position and power • Frustration about individual vs. team responsibilities • Confusion about roles • Lack of unity • Resisting structure • Minimal cooperation or collaboration • Lack of decision making • Gripes and complaints • Minimal trust, high suspicion • Little or no measurable accomplishment	• Early signs of listening to each other • More open body language • Hesitant participation • Tentative trust and commitment to group mission • Looking for sense of belonging • Emerging clarity about group goals • Early, small wins and accomplishments	• Visible cooperation and collaboration • Commitment to group mission and goals • Information readily shared • Roles and responsibilities understood • Effective decision making • Increased appreciation and trust • Average to good performance	• Sense of identity and cohesiveness • Pride in accomplishments and team • Efficient team operations • "We" vs. "I" orientation • High trust and openness • High appreciation and support • Creative problem solving • High confidence • Increase in innovation • Superior performance

Note. Inspired by group behaviors chart in Steve Zuieback's *Leadership Practices for Challenging Times,* 2010, Ukiah, CA: Synectics, pp. 16–17.

TIPS FOR CREATING SIMPLE RULES

- Your rules, or principles, should flow directly from the equity imperative.
- Write them in simple, accessible language.
- Less is more: Discuss, debate, and eliminate until you have no more than five or six.
- Use a consensus process like Thumbs Up, Side, Down to ensure agreement among all present stakeholders. (Anyone who uses a downward-pointing thumb must offer an alternative. A sideways thumb signifies a concern, which the person should have an opportunity to speak to. Thumbs up is, well, thumbs up!)
- Create a plan for engaging other stakeholders in dialogue about the principles.
- Once the principles are agreed on, post them—in your office, in meeting spaces, in classrooms, and on walls—as visible reminders of what you stand for as a team or organization.

LISTENING CAMPAIGN TOOL

Here are the essential steps and sample questions for a Listening Campaign.

Steps	Stems
1. Identify your **purpose** (What am I trying to learn or achieve?). 2. Identify the **people** (Whom will I engage? Whose voices haven't been heard historically?). 3. Identity the necessary **conditions** (Where and how will I hold these meetings so that participants are able to share their experiences honestly and openly?). Consider everything from location and privacy to confidentiality norms to translation if necessary. When possible, hold the listening sessions in person to have access to nonverbal data. 4. Identify the **calendar**. I generally allot 30 minutes per meeting, with a 15-minute transition period in between. 5. Identify the **information system**. (How will I record responses? Will people's comments be confidential? Who will have access to the Listening Campaign report?)	• What's working here, and who is being served well? • What's not working, and who is not being well served? (e.g., Which students don't tend to do well here?) • What changes would you suggest in the future? • Whose voices tend to be heard when decisions are made, and whose voices do not? • What is the quality of relationships among staff? Among staff, families, and students? Between leadership and staff? • How would you characterize teaching and learning here? • How often do teachers and staff collaborate? What is the quality of the collaboration? • What feedback do you have for me as a leader to improve the culture and conditions?

FACILITATION AND DESIGN TIPS FOR SAFE-TO-LEARN INQUIRY

As you customize this routine, keep a few tips in mind:

- View the whole year as a big, spiraling inquiry cycle. Schedule at least two points in the year where all staff members engaged in inquiry come together to share and reflect. (See the Listening Leader Year at a Glance sample calendar following this section.)
- Push teachers to come up with an inquiry question that is rooted in data and has no easy answer.
- Begin the cycle by reminding teachers of the overarching instructional focus and by sharing relevant data.
- Provide meeting times for teachers to develop an approach, or prototype, for the puzzle they identify. You might say, "I want everyone to experiment with a couple of different strategies over the next couple of weeks, and then we'll come back to share and reflect in teams."
- Bring the inquiry team together on a biweekly or monthly basis to share data, reflect, and adjust the question and approach. Note that you can engage in this process schoolwide in departments or grade levels, or you might begin with a pilot group of teacher volunteers.
- Give everyone a journal. At each team meeting, ask people to write on this topic: "What did I notice about my question this week or month?"
- At the end of a short cycle, build in team time to discuss and chart emerging learning, new ideas, and questions to inform the next cycle.
- "Hold space" for people's discomfort. Reassure them that discomfort and failure are essential pieces of the puzzle. Insert Constructivist Listening dyads when you sense emotional distress in the room.

THE LISTENING LEADER YEAR AT A GLANCE (SAMPLE CALENDAR)

Month	Key Routines	Reflective Inquiry Questions and Chapter Links
		Note: Use the core tenets and brain mandates from Chapter 2, and the Six Stances from Chapters 5 and 6, as guideposts across all of these activities. For challenging or high-stakes conversations, prepare with the Instructional Conversation Planning Tool in Appendix C.
June/July	• Take time to reflect in writing on the past year. • Consider attending professional learning around leadership, facilitation, instructional coaching, and/or equity.	*What have I learned this year? What are my leadership goals for next year? Which of the Six Stances do I want to strengthen?* See Chapter 4 for additional self-reflection questions.
August	• Host a staff or team retreat. (Build community below the green line, look at all three levels of data, revisit the equity imperative and guiding principles, develop shared language around equity, establish or unpack the instructional focus, etc.) • Facilitate a Listening Campaign with teacher and staff leaders; survey leaders on the supports they need to effectively facilitate their teams. • (Advanced/optional) Train teacher and staff leaders to conduct a Listening Campaign with their team members.	*Who will be on the retreat facilitation team? How can I begin to model distributed leadership through distributed facilitation?* *How will we use the experiential learning cycle to create a humanizing experience at the retreat? (See Chapter 10.)* *How will we build the staff's common language and "literacy" around equity? (See Chapter 3: consider using a jigsaw structure to discuss the three channels.)* *What is the current capacity of teacher and staff leaders? What training and development will people need to be effective?* See Chapter 11 for a description of retreats and Listening Campaigns. To build background knowledge around culturally responsive teaching and information processing in the classroom, consider reading Zaretta Hammond's wonderful book *Culturally Responsive Teaching and the Brain* with your leadership team, staff, or a voluntary study group.

Month	Key Routines	Reflective Inquiry Questions and Chapter Links
September	• First 6 weeks' PD: Support teachers in getting to know their students (see Chapter 8). At the end of 6 weeks, invite teachers to develop an inquiry question that they are genuinely curious about pursuing. • Do home visits and/or focus groups with parents and caregivers. • Do first round of team member one-on-ones at end of the month.	*What resources will I draw on to help teachers and staff think differently about listening to students?* (I love Chris Emdin's *For White Folks Who Teach in the Hood . . . and the Rest of Y'all Too* and Kathleen Cushman's *Fires in the Bathroom: Advice for Teachers from High School Students.*) *What am I [or are we] trying to learn from home visits or focus groups with parents?* *Is the leadership team ready to lead safe-to-learn inquiry?* (If not, consider scaffolding the process at first in a whole-group setting.) See Chapters 7 and 8 for ways to listen and to build relationship with parents and students; consider sharing excerpts with staff. See Chapter 11 for support around one-on-ones.
October	• Launch Safe-to-Learn Inquiry Cycle 1. • Support team leaders to facilitate a monthly inquiry check-in within teams. • Begin biweekly cycles of leadership team member one-on-ones.	*Does every teacher have an inquiry question he or she feels excited about?* (Use a quick survey to gather Level 2 map data on this question. Simple Lichert scale statements will do the trick, e.g., "Rate the following on a 1 to 5 scale: I have an inquiry question that I am excited to pursue" or ". . . that I believe could significantly impact my practice") *What stumbling blocks are team leaders bumping up against?* (Incorporate the consultancy or Helping Trios protocols from Chapter 10 into leadership team meetings.)

(Continued)

Month	Key Routines	Reflective Inquiry Questions and Chapter Links
November	• Launch Safe-to-Learn Inquiry Cycle 2 to keep the momentum going. • Hold midyear Learning Leader Chats with key teams or sites. • Continue biweekly one-on-ones.	Before launching cycle 2, debrief with the leadership team: *What did we learn from cycle 1, and what adjustments should we make?* *Are there specific questions for which I want to gather Level 3 street data through the Learning Leader Chats?* *How and with whom will I share the themes I hear in the chats?* (Possibilities include a PowerPoint presentation or a gallery walk of anonymous quotes) See Chapter 11 for support around the chats.
December	• Reflect on learning from safe-to-learn inquiry cycles; set goals for Spring. • Convene a planning committee to design the midyear retreat. • Break from biweekly one-on-ones. • Administer a midyear parent/caregiver survey; examine results with the leadership team. • Invite staff members to do a midyear written reflection on what they are learning and how they are growing through inquiry.	*What have we learned through our inquiry cycles? How will we use this learning to set Spring growth goals?* *What data patterns are revealed by the midyear parent survey? How will we respond so that parents feel heard?* See Chapters 7 (parent surveys) and 11 (retreats).
January	• Host midyear retreat (bring data, reflect on progress, adjust skinny plan). • Facilitate midyear Listening Campaign. • Launch Safe-to-Learn Inquiry Cycle 3 at the end of the month. • Resume biweekly one-on-ones.	*How will we incorporate the experiential learning cycle into the midyear retreat?* (See Chapter 10, and don't forget to build in affective and imaginal learning!) *Which stakeholders do I most need to listen to at this point in the year?* *What data patterns emerged from the Listening Campaign? What adjustments do we need to make?*
Feb/March	• Reflect on learning from cycle 3. • Hold second round of Learning Leader Chats. • Continue biweekly one-on-ones. • Launch Safe-to-Learn Inquiry Cycle 4.	*Again, how will I share the themes from Learning Leader Chats?* *What street-level evidence of growth do I see in team members? How can I explicitly affirm and amplify those changes into new systems or practices?*

Month	Key Routines	Reflective Inquiry Questions and Chapter Links
March/April	• Hold a leadership team retreat (focus: monitor progress, revisit guiding principles/simple rules, begin planning for next school year).	*How can I model distributed leadership (DL) by having different team members lead different pieces of the retreat?* See Chapter 9 for a review of DL.
April	• Continue biweekly one-on-ones. • Reflect on learning from Safe-to-Learn Inquiry Cycle 4; set goals for next year. • Begin to discuss the instructional focus for the following year. • Finalize leadership team membership.	*What adjustments should we make to the inquiry process next year?* *Based on our inquiry findings, what should be our instructional focus for next year?* *Will the leadership team remain the same, or will there be a rotation? Whom do we need to recruit to ensure that the team represents a diverse cross-section of the community on multiple measures (gender, race, culture, years in profession, viewpoints, position, etc.)?* See Chapter 8 for innovative instructional approaches that promote listening to students.
May/June	• Administer end-of-year parent/caregiver survey. • Hold leadership team retreat or paid planning days. • Engage in cross-team or cross-department curriculum sharing. • Conduct training for teacher and staff leaders in leadership, adult learning, and/or facilitation.	*What have we learned this year as a leadership team?* *What further capacity do teacher and staff leaders need to build?* See protocols in Chapter 10 to design cross-team sharing opportunities.

GLOSSARY

90/10 principle   A community organizing approach wherein the organizer or leader devotes 90% of a one-on-one meeting to listening and 10% to talking.

Active listening   A way of listening and responding to another person that improves mutual understanding. Indicators of active listening include paraphrasing, summarizing, and validating what the speaker has said.

Adaptive challenges   See *complex challenges*.

Adult learning   The full range of formal and informal learning activities that are undertaken by adults after initial training and education, resulting in the acquisition of new knowledge and skills. Adult learning theory posits that grown-ups have learning needs that are different from those of children and warrant a particular set of effective leadership practices. The optimal adult learning environment is self-directed, collaborative, and inquiry based, meaning that educators design and dig into meaty problems of practice together.

Affective filter   A term coined by Dulay and Burt to describe the interplay of negative social and emotional factors that can interfere with our ability to process information. These factors include anxiety, insecurity, boredom, and irritation, among others.

Affirmation   A Listening Leader stance that uses positive verbal and nonverbal communication, which stimulates the release of positive neurotransmitters in adult learners' brains and primes them for further learning.

Agreements   Explicit ways of being and working together that a team adopts through consensus.

Amygdala   A limbic system structure that is involved in many of our emotions and motivations, particularly those that are related to survival. The amygdala is involved in the processing of emotions such as fear, anger, and pleasure. The amygdala is also one of the structures responsible for determining what memories are stored and where the memories are stored in the brain.

Amygdala hijack   An immediate and overwhelming emotional response out of proportion to the stimulus; it is often due to the perception of a significant social threat.

Appreciations   A few minutes at the end of a meeting during which anyone can express gratitude for a colleague's ideas or actions.

Audio interviews   Interviews with individuals or a small group, recorded and edited for reflection afterward.

Automaticity   The ability to do things without occupying the conscious mind with the low-level details required; it is usually the result of learning, repetition, and practice.

Bias toward action   A Listening Leader stance that derives from the principle that adults must see the immediate application of their learning into practice.

Cognitive dissonance   The state of having inconsistent thoughts, beliefs, or attitudes, typically related to behavioral decisions or attitudinal change.

Complex adaptive system (CAS), or living system   A system consisting of many diverse, dynamic components or parts, which are interrelated and interdependent. The "parts" behave as a unified whole, influenced by feedback loops and adjustments to environmental changes.

Complex challenges   Challenges that have no known solution and can only be addressed through changes in priorities, beliefs, habits, and loyalties.

Complicated problems   Important and often multifaceted problems that have known solutions and can be addressed with a standard toolkit, which often includes goals, benchmarks, and work plans with discrete steps.

Constructivist Listening   A listening structure promoting equity of voice. In this structure, participants listen to and give quality attention to one another.

Consultancy   A structured process designed to help a person think deeply about a professional dilemma; the purpose is for the presenter to look at his or her dilemma from multiple angles and perspectives by listening to and engaging with his or her colleagues.

Contractual trust   Trust based on a binding agreement that explicitly defines the actions to be taken by the involved parties in order to ensure an outcome.

Core memory maps   An activity where participants put together a collection of critical memories demonstrating key components of each participant's identity.

Cortisol   Cortisol belongs to a group of hormones called glucocorticoids. As a group, these hormones are involved in the regulation of cellular metabolism, and they play a central role in the body's response to stress.

Cultural proficiency continuum   A spectrum identifying the range of values and behaviors of an individual or the policies and practices of an organization in relation to cultural competency.

Cultural synchronicity   The ability to connect across difference so that one can avoid cultural miscommunication cues that can trigger an amygdala hijack.

Culturally proficient leader   A leader who has the ability to recognize and respond positively to differences, to anticipate triggers and adjust his or her moves, and to embrace humility and a learning orientation around culture.

Data-based inquiry   The process of carefully and critically analyzing key data related to an important problem or question.

Deep culture   The feelings, attitudes, and worldviews that we learn by being a member of a particular cultural group. It includes thoughts and beliefs, personal values, and the subtle dynamics of interpersonal relationships as expressed in actions, words, and nonverbal cues.

Deep Listening   A type of listening that aims to relieve the suffering of the other person; also called compassionate listening. Deep Listening supports personal healing and the development of relational trust through the stances of attention to nonverbal cues, mature empathy, and affirmation.

Dendrites Short branched extensions of a nerve cell, which receive impulses from other cells and transmit them to the cell body.

Discourse Verbal expression, exchange, or conversation in speech or writing.

Discourse I The dominant discourse, or way of talking and thinking about school improvement, that serves to reproduce inequitable practices and results.

Discourse II Discourse that promotes conversations about uncomfortable, unequal, ineffective, and/or prejudicial conditions and relationships. Participants are continually learning, and ambiguity and change become part of a purposeful process of inquiry.

Disproportionality The over- or underrepresentation of a given population group, often according to racial and ethnic backgrounds, but also defined by socioeconomic status, national origin, English proficiency, gender, and sexual orientation.

Distress-free authority The ability to manage one's own judgments and anxieties without displacing them onto one's interactions.

Dominant culture in schooling A way of understanding schools as more than merely institutions where teachers impart skills and lessons; they are places where teachers transmit cultural knowledge. Students are introduced to the ways of the "culture of power," based on the European American values of individualism and independence, self-direction, initiative, and competitiveness (among others), using traditionally European American methods of teaching.

Dopamine Often associated with positive feelings when released, dopamine is one of the chemical signals that pass information from one neuron to the next in the tiny spaces between them. When it is released from the first neuron, it floats into the space (the synapse) between the two neurons, and it bumps against receptors for it on the other side that then send a signal down the receiving neuron.

Driver (archetype) These leaders are seen as change agents: decisive, authoritative, and moving quickly to promote a results-driven agenda. They may view adult concerns and dynamics as a distraction from student needs. Although these leaders are respected as visionaries, they may create a dysfunctional culture.

Dyads A simple, uninterrupted listening exchange between two people, ranging from 2 to 5 minutes per participant.

Emotional intelligence The ability to identify one's own emotions and those of others and to harness the understanding of these emotions to accomplish such tasks as thinking and problem solving.

Equity Providing every student with the resources he or she needs to learn and thrive; requires a willingness to redistribute resources *unequally* in order to close entrenched opportunity gaps.

Equity imperative A moral standard toward which a school or system will strive, based in principles of equity.

Essential questions Questions that probe for deeper meaning and set the stage for further questioning, ones that foster the development of critical thinking skills and higher order capabilities, such as problem solving and understanding complex systems.

Executive function A set of mental skills that help you get things done. These skills are controlled by an area of the brain called the frontal lobe.

Experiential learning cycle   A process of learning that focuses on the whole experience of an individual, taking into account the learner's affective and cognitive needs; based on the work of John Heron.

Feedback interviews   Focus groups focused on gathering the input of and insight from stakeholders.

Fight-or-flight   Also known as the acute stress response, it refers to a physiological reaction that occurs in the presence of something that is terrifying, either mentally or physically. The response is triggered by the release of hormones that prepare one's body either to stay and respond to a threat, or to run away to safety.

Fishbowl discussion   An activity in which two or more group members sit in an inner circle and engage in discussion while the other members of the group sit in an outer circle and listen and observe.

Four Corners   A learning activity in which participants respond to a prompt by walking to one of four corners, each of which represents a different perspective. Participants discuss their reflections with others who have chosen the same corner, as well as with those in the other corners.

Fractal   A never-ending pattern that self-replicates across different scales.

Group dynamics   The positive and negative forces and dispositions that arise within a group.

Helping Trios   A simple form of the Consultancy protocol in which each member of the trio presents a question or challenge and gets supportive feedback through three 15–20 minute rotations.

Holding space   An approach to active facilitation, holding space involves creating structure within groups so that stakeholders can safely engage around and address problems.

"I Like, I Wonder"   A protocol that offers immediate feedback to teams who present an emerging idea or proposal.

Implicit bias   See *unconscious bias*.

Inquiry-based teaching   An approach that involves posing questions, problems, or scenarios—rather than simply presenting established facts or portraying a smooth path to knowledge. This process positions the teacher as a facilitator of learning, not a sage on stage.

Instructional core   The factors that directly influence student learning; the intersection of content, teacher facilitation, and student interests and abilities.

Kiva Process   A learning activity aimed at capturing the collective wisdom and experience of a group through structured public dialogue.

Leader   Anyone willing to take responsibility for what matters to him or her in the work of school improvement (attributed to Julian Weissglass, founder of the National Coalition for Equity in Education).

Leader-as-Host   A leader who creates the conditions for people to come together positively and productively to uncover local solutions.

Learning Leader Chats   A listening strategy typically used in larger organizations in which a leader holds a series of listening sessions to gain insights into the concerns and priorities of stakeholders; similar to a town hall meeting, but with a listening emphasis.

Levels of Data framework   A framework that supports deep thinking around the types of data needed in a given context.

Limbic system   A complex system of nerves in the brain, involving several areas near the edge of the cortex, which is concerned with instinct and mood. It controls the basic emotions (fear, pleasure, anger) and drives (hunger, sex, dominance, care of offspring).

Listening Campaign   A focused effort to identify concerns and priorities through a series of structured one-on-one meetings with key stakeholders.

Listening mindset   Close kin to a growth mindset, a listening mindset is an orientation that reminds leaders to slow down, solicit multiple perspectives, and harness the wisdom of the group to drive change.

Lizard brain/reptilian region   The most primitive part of the brain, in charge of fight, flight, feeding, and fear. This part of the brain identifies danger; is where primal thoughts, instincts, and gut feelings originate; and is the seat of most subconscious or involuntary processes.

Looking at student work   A deliberate process of examining student assignments, which informs teachers' instructional decisions while building capacity for meaningful reflection.

Manager (archetype)   These leaders gets things done within the parameters of the status quo. They follow the rules of the system to keep their school running smoothly and are widely viewed as competent and reliable. This type of leader typically focuses on compliance over relationships and may be unable to perceive and respond to subtle messages from stakeholders.

Mature empathy   The ability to form a mental picture of another person's experience by drawing on one's own schemas.

Microaggressions (also called microassaults, microinvalidations, or microattacks)   Routine, everyday slights and insults toward those from nondominant groups; these create an experience of social threat.

Micronarratives   Collections of fragmented stories or anecdotes; in schools, they are often referred to as "water cooler conversations."

Mirror neuron   A neuron that fires both when a person performs a particular action and when he or she observes another person perform the same action. Thus the neuron "mirrors" the behavior of the other, as though the observer himself or herself were acting.

Negative self-talk   The expression of thoughts or feelings that are counterproductive and have the effect of devaluing and/or demotivating oneself.

Negativity bias   The phenomenon by which humans give more psychological weight to bad experiences than to good ones, even when the intensity of the events is equal.

Neocortex   The newer portion of the cerebral cortex that serves as the center of higher mental functions for humans. Containing some 100 billion cells, each with 1,000 to 10,000 synapses (connections), the regions and cells in the neocortex control vision, hearing, touch, the sense of balance, movement, emotional responses, and most other feats of cognition.

Neural coupling   The neural processes by which one individual's brain is connected to the neural processes in another's brain via the transmission of a signal through the environment. Brain-to-brain coupling constrains and simplifies the actions of each individual in a social network, leading to complex joint behaviors that could not have emerged in isolation.

Neural pathway   A series of neurons that connect different areas of the brain or nervous system.

Neuron   A specialized cell that transmits nerve impulses; a nerve cell.

Neuroplasticity   The brain's ability to reorganize itself by forming new neural connections throughout life. Neuroplasticity allows the neurons in the brain to compensate for injury and disease and to adjust their activities in response to changes in their environment.

Nondiscussables   Topics that are important enough to be merit frequent conversations, but so burdened with anxiety and fear that they are discussed only in private spaces—for example, in the parking lot, near the water cooler, or at happy hour.

Nonlinearity   A property of complex change which holds that changes occurs in a nonlinear fashion and rarely according to predictable lines of cause and effect.

One-on-one   A regular, nonevaluative meeting between a leader and a team member, geared toward the team member's growth and development. This listening routine fosters crucial conditions like open communication, feedback, and relational trust. (See also *90/10 principle*.)

One-word check-in   A check-in used during a group activity to get a pulse on the current mood and experience of participants.

Opportunity structures   Nonneutral arrangements among organizations and government agencies that help create and distribute society's benefits, burdens, and interests.

Orientation to vision   A Listening Leader stance with which the leader listens for ideas in reference to a clear picture of success.

Oxytocin   A hormone made in the brain that plays a role in relational bonding, mateguarding, and social memory; often called the "cuddle hormone."

Peacekeeper (archetype)   These leaders place a high value on relationships, but may lack a strong change agenda. Under the leadership of an Peacekeeper, people feel good and enjoy their work, but little improves with respect to student learning.

Personal Experience Panels   A Constructivist Listening structure in which a small number of panelists (typically three to five) sit before an audience and share their thoughts in response to a prompt.

Pobrecito **("poor little one" in Spanish) syndrome**   A pattern in which an educator feels sorry for students (or colleagues) and consequently lowers standards or makes excuses for poor behavior and/or performance; a common occurrence in high-poverty schools that operates as a barrier to equity.

Praxis   The continuous process of action, reflection, and experimentation.

Protocol   A step-by-step framework for discussion that advances the goal of equitable participation and can make it safer for participants to engage in meaningful conversation and pose probing questions to each other.

Prototyping, or piloting   A test or trial of an approach, an activity, or a project before introducing it more widely.

Reflective inquiry   The process of asking purposeful and probing questions in order to build understanding and capacity for change.

Relational capital The aggregate value of internal and external social relationships within a given team or organization; relational capital is accrued largely through listening.

Relational outcomes Explicit results related to the experiences a meeting designer wants participants to have.

Relational trust A form of trust that is grounded in beliefs and agreements about how people need to work together. Relational trust can only be informally monitored.

Restorative circle A structured dialogue that allows participants to listen, express themselves, and repair harm that has occurred.

Safe-to-learn inquiry cycles Small-scale experiments that promote a bias toward action and elevate failure as an essential component of learning. This routine engages teachers in rapid cycles of piloting or prototyping around complex instructional issues.

SCARF Five areas of social interaction, coined by author David Rock, that arouse threat and reward signals in the brain. SCARF stands for status, certainty, autonomy, relatedness, and fairness.

Seasons of cultural development The four seasons that a team or organizational culture tends to move through as it moves from low trust to authentic collaboration (inspired by the work of John Heron, 1999).

Secondary trauma An emotional, physical, and/or behavioral response resulting from helping or wanting to help a traumatized or suffering person. This is often experienced by professionals working in communities impacted by poverty, violence, and other forms of trauma.

Self-authorship Telling one's own story on one's own terms.

Self-organization Human beings' natural efforts to organize and cluster around issues that matter to them.

Serotonin A neurotransmitter involved in processes related to well-being and happiness.

Shadowing a student Following a selected student for a specific period of time (typically a day) to understand his or her personal experience.

Situatedness Understanding the social location of a person, specifically how a person became or becomes a member of a given sociocultural community and his or her access to opportunity structures.

Situational awareness A leader's ability to discern between complicated, technical problems and complex, adaptive challenges.

Six Circle Model A framework based on the work of Margaret Wheatley that describes the multiple dimensions of work involved in creating successful, sustainable organizational change. The six areas of focus include three "technical" areas that relate to the systemic infrastructure (referred to as "above the green line") and three "relational" areas that have to do with the human infrastructure, or culture ("below the green line").

Skinny plan A planning tool that is nimble, flexible, and responsive to the dynamic reality of school life; includes a "good enough" vision of progress and "must-do" actions.

Sort The process of sorting objects, text, ideas, or practices into categories based on importance and then discussing the rationale for the categorization with a group.

Storientation   The Listening Leader's careful attention to stories told as a vehicle for social and organizational change.

Strategic Listening   A form of listening that focuses not on emotional release but on influencing other people's mindsets and behaviors through the stances of orientation to vision, reflective inquiry, and a bias toward action.

Structural racism   The interaction between individual and institutional arrangements within social structures—including education, employment, health care, transportation, and the criminal justice system—that promotes the racially inequitable distribution of social, political, and economic goods and services.

Student feedback surveys   Surveys that allow students to give feedback on their experiences in school.

Support groups   A small-group version of a Constructivist Listening dyad in which six or seven individuals are accorded equal time to reflect on a prompt.

Synapse   The junction between two nerve cells where nerve impulses are transmitted via diffusion of a neurotransmitter.

Talking circle   A traditional methodology based on Native American traditions for creating a humanizing space that lifts barriers between people and allows all participants to speak and listen on an equal footing.

Technical outcomes   Meeting outcomes that are primarily technical in nature and point toward concrete deliverables, practices, or content.

Technical problems   See *complicated problems*.

Tend-and-befriend   A hypothesized stress response pattern that prompts humans—often women—to protect their own children, other children, and people who are hurt or vulnerable, and to join collaborative social groups that are intended to reduce human suffering.

Text-based discussions   A form of discussion anchored by text. Example protocols include having participants build knowledge around one piece of a text in preparation to discuss the entire text, building collective knowledge within a group.

Tone policing   A pattern of behavior whereby marginalized people speak up about their struggles, and people from more dominant groups focus not on what is said, but on how it is said—in particular, the level of legitimate emotion expressed.

Trauma   An emotional response to a difficult or unpleasant event such as an accident or violence, or even an ongoing "event" like relentless poverty. Trauma victims typically experience shock and denial or delayed reactions, such as volatile emotions, flashbacks, strained relationships, and physical symptoms like headaches or nausea.

Unconscious bias   The attitudes or stereotypes that affect our understanding, actions, and decisions in an unconscious manner. These biases, which encompass both favorable and unfavorable perspectives, are activated involuntarily and without an individual's awareness or intentional control.

Zone of proximal development (ZPD)   The gap between what a learner can do alone and what he or she can do with support and guidance.

ACKNOWLEDGMENTS

I think it's fair to say that it takes a village to write a book, and I am grateful for the personal and professional support I have received in the last year and a half or so. This book wouldn't exist without my beloved community of friends, family, and colleagues.

To the founding staff of June Jordan School for Equity—Matt Alexander, Kate Goka, Cuca Holsen, Danfeng Koon, Dickson Lam, Celia Monge Mana, and Lance Powell—I am humbled by the opportunity to have led and served alongside you while we poured blood, sweat, and tears into the dream of a new, equitable school. Each of you helped me grow as a leader, especially in the moments when you held up a mirror that reflected back my weaknesses. I draw much inspiration from those years and the mighty little team we built. A special shout-out goes to Matt Alexander for 20 years of collegial partnership and the beautiful chapter he contributed to this book.

I want to honor some of the leaders I have had the good fortune to coach over the last 10 years: from Life Academy, my humanities A-team Suneal Kolluri, Yumi Matsui, Jill Thomas, and Kimberly Young; teacher leaders Jennifer Caldwell, Danielle Casimiro, Kelsey Chandler, Jennifer Comeans, Ariana Contreras, Lindsay Hatfield, Maggie Knutson, Nikki Street, Dom Tucker, and Barbara Vogel, among others; the instructional coaches and subject area coordinators of the East Side Union High School District; site leaders Audrey Amos, Martha Brazil, Kristin Collins, Silvia Cordero, Josue Diaz, Teresa Marquez, Alcine Mumby, Eric Rice, Staci Ross-Morrison, and Preston Thomas, among others; and fearless central-office leaders like Dee Dee Desmond, Chris Funk, Dongshil Kim, and Norma Martinez-Palmer. Each of you has helped me see what's possible when courageous people commit to transforming outcomes for students.

Both informal conversations and formal interviews shaped the thinking behind this book. Although many of those happened with leaders I've already named, I also acknowledge Matin Abdel-Qawi, Laureen Adams,

Amy Carozza, Noelle Apostol Colin, Kelli Evans, Joe Feldman, Tanya Friedman, Eve Gordon, Dr. Tyrone Howard, Jessica Huang, Jackie Jenkins, Stephan Jost, Michele Reinhart, Carmelita Reyes, Bill Scott, Dr. Darrick Smith, Dr. Dianne Smith, Tuyen Tran, and John Watkins.

I offer my appreciation to my colleagues at the National Equity Project (NEP), with a special shout-out to Victor Cary, Colm Davis, LaShawn Routé-Chatmon, and Mark Salinas, who have all inspired me deeply over the years. Victor, I am grateful beyond measure for our ongoing thought partnership and the brainstorming sessions we did together as I wrote the book. My 5 years on staff at NEP exposed me to many of the ideas that show up in this manuscript.

For impeccable research support—even as she ran a school, completed a dissertation, and raised two small children—I am forever grateful to Jamila Dugan. She is a star, and I look forward to continued collaboration. Thanks, too, to Emily Lewellen for bringing several of my napkin sketches to life in compelling visual designs.

Michael Fullan's work has long inspired me. For his beautiful foreword and his willingness to back an emerging writer, I am indebted. I also thank my longtime mentor and friend Deborah Meier for her steadfast support and for connecting me with another writer and friend who has helped me along this journey, the brilliant Kathleen Cushman.

At Jossey-Bass, I am grateful to Marjorie McAneny for taking a chance on a fledgling author and to Kate Gagnon for her incredible support in this last leg of the journey. You are both models of grace under pressure.

Two dear friends and sister-authors helped me stay the course when I was ready to abandon this project: Zaretta Hammond and Elena Aguilar. Watching each of you bring your wisdom to life in the form of a book gave me courage, and I carried dog-eared copies of *Culturally Responsive Teaching and the Brain* and *The Art of Coaching* around with me to many writing sessions. Thank you for fielding my questions and doula-ing me through this process.

For over two decades of dialogue around social and political issues that have deeply shaped me as an educator and a human being, I thank my dear friend Andrea Dehlendorf. The work you are leading to bring justice to Walmart workers inspires me daily. I again thank my friend Dongshil Kim for modeling spiritual grace and mindfulness, and for her partnership in developing a women's leadership retreat. I hold that experience close to my heart and look forward to the next.

My parents have contributed to this book in subtle ways. Dad, you are a wonderful listener and have always carved out time to support me. Mom, your career as a public health nurse was incredible to witness. The love and humanity you brought into every interaction with the homeless, the dying, the mentally ill, and the recently incarcerated hatched in my young self a belief that caring for others is just what we do as human beings. I am grateful to you both.

I can't form the right words to express my gratitude to my precious family: Manny, my partner and best friend, and my two children, Mona and Maximo. Manny, the passion and compassion you bring to teaching recent immigrants is a daily reminder that transformation emerges from small acts, not grand proclamations. You have listened, given feedback, and done parenting double duty countless times as I wrote this book, and I appreciate you.

And to my babies, Mona and Maximo, you remind me daily to improve my listening. Your joy and curiosity are infectious, your smiles are my everything.

ABOUT THE AUTHOR

Shane Safir has spent more than 20 years working toward educational equity as a teacher, principal, school coach, and facilitator. She began her career at San Francisco's Balboa High School, where her students' project investigating the gap between public and private education was featured in a widely viewed KQED documentary titled "Making the Grade" (1999). In 2003, she became the founding coprincipal of June Jordan School for Equity (JJSE) in San Francisco, an innovative national model identified by scholar Linda Darling-Hammond as having "beaten the odds in supporting the success of low-income students of color." In 2010–11, Shane spent a sabbatical year with her family teaching high school English outside of Amman, Jordan.

Shane provides coaching and professional development for schools, districts, and organizations across the country, hosting workshops on Listening Leadership, facilitating adult learning, creating brave spaces for addressing inequity, and engaging in instructional conversations with teachers, among other topics. She is also a frequent contributor to *Edutopia*. Shane has a BA in history from Brown University and an MA in education from Stanford University. She received her administrative credential through Cal State East Bay. Shane is the proud mother of Mona and Maximo and is married to an Oakland math teacher. You can learn more about Shane and her work, as well as access her articles, at www.shanesafir.com.

INDEX

Page references followed by *fig* indicate an illustrated figure; followed by *t* indicate a table; followed by *e* indicate an exhibit.

A

Abby's story: applying bias toward action to, 141; applying orientation to vision in, 134; applying reflective inquiry to, 137, 140; practicing Strategic Listening with ELL student in, 127–128; seeds of transformation in, 142, 144

Abdel-Qawi, M., 259–260

Above the green line: measuring success through, 207*t*; operational meeting agreements, 225*t*; Six Circle Model on, 87*fig*–88; technical outcomes of meetings live, 223. *See also* Patterns; Processes; Structures

Accountability: benchmark assessment data and local, 18; Driver leadership archetype of, 4, 5, 6*fig*; fear of trying out new practices due to climate of, 141; Manager leadership archetype of, 4, 6*fig*

Active listening: as component of Deep Listening and Strategic Listening, 110; mature empathy bolstered by, 117–118, 119

Activities. *See* Listening culture routines; Staff meeting routines

Adaptive challenges, 195

Administration. *See* Principals

Affective filter, 50

Affective routines: agreements as, 225*t*–226; appreciations as, 226, 234; Constructivist Listening (CL) as, 225; description of, 224; experiential learning cycle of, 223*t*; premise from moving to practical from, 232–233

Affirmation stance: applying to conversation with Sandra, 123–124; classroom handshakes as, 121; Deep Listening using the, 110*t*, 120–124, 129*t*, 170*t*; 5:1 feedback ratio for, 121–122; how it rewards the brain by, 120; micro-affirmation strategies, 120–121; stems for practicing, 122*e*; tips for using, 122

African American students: fears of mothers of young male, 153; JJSE staff meeting on serving, 176*e*; stories of racism gathered from, 175–176. *See also* Students of color

African Americans: PRRI study on unconscious bias in schools against, 66; young Black men killed by police officers, 153. *See also* People of color

Age differences bias, 64–65

"Age minus two" rule for teacher talk, 137*e*

Agreements: establishing meeting, 225–226; interpersonal, 225*t*; operational, 225*t*; Ways to Facilitate Agreements tool for, 226

Alexander, M., 59, 166, 215, 216, 226

39; becoming aware of cultural difference, 69; conceptual routines, 229; on creating a listening culture, 240; cultivate integrity with, 13; detect social threats at work using the SCARF model, 44; four seasons of a listening culture, 244; look in the mirror for mindful listening, 91; noticing nonverbal cues, 113; practice conscious attention to listening, 35; stepping into the other person's shoes, 92; stepping up to the balcony, 93–94; thinking about a challenging meeting your facilitated, 222. *See also* Mindfulness

Manager leadership archetype, 4, 6*fig*

Map data (Level 2): description of, 16, 17*fig*; Learning Leader Chats to gather, 251*e*; Patrick's story on reflecting on school's, 239; reflective inquiry to leverage, 135; on student learning and teacher effectiveness evidence, 19*t*

The Mask We Live (film), 229

Matt on listening to students story: on failing undocumented immigrant students, 166–167; listening to Brenda, 168

Mature empathy stance: active listening to bolster, 117–118, 119; applying to conversation with Sandra, 119–120; based on understanding mirror neurons, 116; cartoon on, 118*fig*; Deep Listening and, 110*t*, 116–120, 129*t*, 170*t*; how Jessica Huang models, 233; importance for navigating differences, 116–117; stems for using, 120*e*; tips for using, 119

McTighe, J., 181

Meetings: one-on-one with parents, 154–156; one-on-ones between leader and team members, 95, 252–253*e*; parent conferences, 151*t*–152*t*, 159*e*. *See also* Staff meetings

Meier, D., 49

Meister, D., 90

Metrics. *See* Complex change metrics

Metropolitan Life Insurance Company survey (2013), 3

Microaggressions: description of, 63; examples of recognizing implicit messages of, 64*t*; unconscious biases behind, 35–36, 58*t*, 63–65

Micronarratives, 198–199

Mindful listening: Bianca's protocol for early one-on-ones for, 95*e*; how the rumination problem is a barrier to, 94–96; Mindful Listening Tool for, 96*e*–97*e*; steps in, 89*t*–94

Mindful listening steps: step 1: look in the mirror, 89*t*, 90–91; step 2: step into the other person's shoes, 89*t*, 92–93; step 3: step up to the balcony, 89*t*, 93–94

Mindful Listening Tool, 96*e*–97*e*

Mindfulness: description of, 22; listening acceptance practice of, 23; listening awareness practice of, 22–23. *See also* Make It Mindful

Mindfulness-based stress reduction (MBSR), 22

Mintrop, R., 11

Miss Representation (film), 229

Mission High School (San Francisco), 170

Motivation, 131

N

National Coalition on Equity in Education, 75

National Equity Project (NEP), 111, 192–193, 196, 241

National School Reform Faculty website, 229

Negative self-talk, 120

Negativity bias: affirmation 5:1 feedback ratio to overcome, 121–122; Estella and Jason's story example of, 48–49; organizational core memories and, 34*t*, 48–49; overcoming the brain's, 50*e*

Neocortex (or prefrontal cortex): description of, 36*fig*–37; purpose and functions of, 37*t*

Neural coupling, 41–42

Neural pathway, 46

Neurons, 45*fig*–46

Neuroplasticity, 46

The New Jim Crow: Mass Incarceration in the Age of Colorblindness (Alexander), 59, 77

Newsome, B., 12*e*–13

96 degrees (emotional repression), 218, 219*fig*, 235*fig*

98 degrees (cool compliance), 219*fig*, 220, 235*fig*

Nondiscussables, 192

Nonverbal communication: body language, 115*t*; breathing patterns, 115*t*; eye contact, 113, 115*t*; facial expression, 115*t*; physical space, 115*t*; practice observation of, 113; voice and tone, 115*t*

Nonverbal cues: accounting for two thirds of meaning in communication, 112*fig*; Deep Listening by paying attention to, 110*t*, 112–114, 129*t*, 170*t*; gender differences in, 113; interpreting, 115*t*; paying attention to a student's, 169; transmitted to lizard brain ("read the lizard"), 112; video-recording a one-on-one meeting to observe, 114. *See also* Body language; Communication

Nuri-Robinsm, K., 73

O

Oakland High School (Oakland, CA), 259–261

Oakland International High School (OIHS), 158*e*, 161, 162

101 degrees (rising anxiety), 219*fig*, 220, 235*fig*

104 degrees (amygdala hijack!), 219*fig*, 220–221, 235*fig*

One-on-one meetings: Bianca's protocol for early, 95; between leader and team members, 245*t*,

Processes: Six Circles Model on system level of, 87*fig*, 88; step up to the balcony to assess, 94. *See also* Above the green line

Proctor, C., 181

Professional development (PD): as attempts for change, 192; build home visits into your PD schedule, 157; investing in community walks for, 162; JJSE (and Sandra) story on Deep Listening on, 105–106, 114, 119–120, 123–124. *See also* Teachers

Professional learning communities (PLCs): Abby's story on Strategic Listening in, 130; equity conversations taking place in, 77; JJSE's proposal for cross-disciplinary, 106

Protocols: consultancy, 231–232; practical routines using, 231

Prototyping (or piloting), 254

PRRI developmental experiences study, 66

PTSD (posttraumatic stress disorder), 14–15

Purpose, 131

Q

Quran, 259–260

R

Race: Estella and Jason's communication miscues and factor of, 31–33, 34; Implicit Association Test to assess unconscious bias against, 64–65; look in the mirror consideration of, 91; step into other person's shoes to understand, 92; "water for deep roots" with respect to awareness of, 57. *See also* Structural racism

Racial violence: post-racial tension stress disorder due to, 15; young Black men killed by police officers, 153

Reflective inquiry stance: creating cognitive dissonance through, 134; data collection using, 135, 136*e*–137*e*; description of, 134; stems for practicing, 140*e*; Strategic Listening and, 110*t*, 129*t*, 134–140*e*; structuring meetings around, 217*t*; when it triggers a defensive reaction, 134–135

Relatedness domain (SCARF model): applied to Estella and Jason's story, 44; on threats and rewards in schools, 43*t*

Relational capital: Deep and Strategic Listening for building with families, 154; description of, 107; Listening Leadership ARC on, 20, 21*fig*; listening to build, 107–108*fig*

Relational outcomes: leadership retreat, 241, 242*t*; of meetings, 223

Relational trust: characteristics of, 83*t*; early indicators of, 85*e*–86*e*

Relationship management: emotional intelligence component of, 13; tend-and-befriend response, 34*t*, 40, 195

Relationships: Peacemaker leadership archetype as being about, 4–5; Six Circle Model level of, 87*fig*, 88; step up to the balcony to assess, 93; story patterns around, 199. *See also* Below the green line

Restorative circles, 162, 179–180

Rewards: affirmation used as, 110*t*, 120–124; meeting appreciations as, 226, 234; reimaging, 44–45; SCARF model on examples of school social threats and, 43*t*, 44

Reyes, C., 158*e*, 161, 162

Reyes, D., 41–42

Rigotti, E., 252

Rizga, K., 170

Rock, D., 42, 43

Roles/position: facilitating meetings, 218–233; leaders-as-host, 240–243; step into other person's shoes to understand, 92

Ross-Morrison, S., 137*e*

Roth, R., 170

Routines. *See* Listening culture routines; Staff meeting routines

Rowe, M., 120–121

Rules. *See* A few simple rules

Rumination problem, 94–96

S

Safe-to-learn inquiry: bias toward action stance foundation of, 110*t*, 129*t*, 141, 141–142, 143*t*; listening culture promoted through, 245*t*, 254–255; traditional planning vs., 255*t*

Sameerah (student), 201–202

San Diego Unified School District, 11

San Francisco Organizing Project, 111

San Francisco State University, 106

San Francisco Unified School District, 11

Sandra's story: applying affirmation to conversation with Sandra, 123–124; applying nonverbal cues to conversation at, 114; failing to listen at, 105–106; mature empathy applied to conversation with Sandra, 119–120

Satellite data level (Level 1): description of, 16, 17*fig*; Patrick's story on reflecting on school's, 239; reflective inquiry to leverage, 135; on student learning and teacher effectiveness evidence, 19*t*

Save the Last Word for Me, 229

SCARF model: applied to the Estella and Jason story, 44; description and purpose of, 43; detect social threats at work using the, 44; examples of threats and rewards in schools under the, 43*t*, 44

Schneider, B., 82, 83

Scholastic magazine, 55

School district CCSS implementation, 204*e*